GIANTS

A history of the American Conservative Movement

Table Of Contents

CHAPTER ONE - Pre Revolutionary Roots of Conservatism

A thoughtful discussion of the men who contributed the most to what is now the dominant political pattern of conservatism in America. It has been long suggested by the left that conservatives are racist relics of a time gone by when in fact it is the liberals who are doomed to the dust pan of history. This book will lay out the case for a new revolution of political thought by remembering the past we can predict the future. As the saying goes, those that forget history are doomed to repeat it.

We will look at the conservative movement in America from pre revolutionary days, through our young development as a nation through the civil war and on to the present and into our future in what I hope will be a well reasoned argument. As such proving that indeed America and its conservative roots and thrust has and will make America that shining city on the hill.

Any discussion of conservatism must begin with Edmund Burke. Burke's view of society was one that was class based and authoritarian, yet one of his noblest characteristics was his repeated defense of those who were too weak to defend themselves. Outstanding in 18th-century British politics for intellect, oratory, and drive, he lacked the ability either to lead or to conciliate men and never exerted an influence to go along with his capabilities. His career as a practical politician was a failure; his political theories found favor only with posterity.

He was born on Jan. 12, 1729, in Dublin of middleclass parents.

His mother suffered from what Burke called "a cruel nervous disorder," and his relations with his demanding father, a Dublin attorney, were unhappy.

After attending Trinity College, Dublin, Burke in 1750 crossed to England to study law at the Middle Temple. But he unconsciously resisted his father's plans for him and made little progress in the law. Indecision marked his life at this time: he described himself as "a runaway son" and his "manner of life" as "chequered with various designs."

In 1755 he considered applying for a post in the Colonies but dropped the idea when his father objected.

In 1756 Burke published two philosophical treatises, *A Vindication of Natural Society and A Philosophical Enquiry into the Origin of Our Ideas of the Sublime and Beautiful.* In the *Vindication* Burke exposed the futility of demanding a reason for moral and social institutions and, with the foresight which was one of the most remarkable of his gifts, distinguished the coming attack of rationalistic criticism on the established order. The *Enquiry,* which he had begun when only 19, was considered by Samuel Johnson to be "an example of true criticism." These works were followed in 1757 by *An Account of the European Settlement in America,* to which Burke, although he denied authorship, clearly contributed a great deal. The early sheets of *The Abridgement of the History of England* were also printed in 1757, although the book itself was not published until after Burke's death. These works introduced Burke's name into London literary circles and seemed to open up a reputable career.

Family unity, which he had never known as a boy, became an article of Burke's adult philosophy.

In 1757 he married the daughter of his physician and settled into family life with his father-in-law, his brother Richard, and his so called cousin William. With them he found a domestic harmony he had never known in his father's home.

Financial security, however, was elusive, and Burke was forced to take a minor secretarial post in the government establishment in Ireland. But contact with the depressed and persecuted Irish Catholics unsettled him, and early in 1765 he resigned his position. Necessity now led Burke into politics. In July 1765, when the Whig administration of Lord Rockingham was being formed, he was recommended to Rockingham, who took him on as his private secretary. In December 1765, Burke entered Parliament as member of the House of Commons.

Burke's subsequent political career was bound to the fortunes of the Rockingham group. Emotional and hysterical by nature, without a profession or a secure income, he found stability and independence through his attachment to the Whig aristocrats. When Rockingham lost the premiership in 1766, Burke, though offered employment under the new administration, followed him into opposition. "I believe in any body of men in England I should have been in the minority," he later said. "I have always been in the minority." Certainly the dominant characteristic of his political career was an overwhelming impulse to argue and oppose; to that was added enormous persistence, courage, concentration, and energy. Endowed with many of the qualities of leadership, he lacked the sensitivity to gauge and respect the feelings and opinions of others.

Hence his political life was a series of negative crusades - against the American war, Warren Hastings, and the French Revolution - and his reputation as a statesman rests on his wisdom in opposition, not on his achievements in office.

Edmund Burke is usually regarded as the founder of modern conservative thought. He championed the cause of the American colonies both before and during the Revolutionary War, and launched a seven year long prosecution of the former Governor General of India, Warren Hastings, for abuses committed by the East India Company against its Indian subjects.
His reasons for defending the cause of the American colonies, however, were of a certain kind. That emerged in Burke's most famous work, Reflections on the Revolution in France (1790), where Burke turned against the tendencies of the French Revolution, even before the Reign of Terror had begun.

The difference, as it happened, between the two revolutions was that the American Revolution was based on the demand for rights that had been already recognized in English law, while the French revolution had turned into an exercise in rationalistic and a priority legislation of rights that had never existed in France.

Burke is thus identified as a conservative because he distrusted the rationalistic project of the French and believed that history had accomplished what human speculation could not: history is a kind of discovery process, a learning process, which mostly transcends the ability of individual persons at one time and place to comprehend.

The products of history have proven themselves, while rational attempts to abruptly institute a new order are perilous experiments that can easily cause immense damage, indeed slaughter, as the French Revolution, and later the Russian Revolution, certainly did.

The conservative aspect of Burke's thought is the dignity it gives to history and to existing institutions, yet it is also essentially about change, since history cannot prove anything unless it actually does encompass change, as the hallowed rights of the English were slowly evolved over the centuries, from the Magna Carta to the Glorious Revolution of 1688. Burke himself said, "A state without the means of change is without the means of its conservation."

He believed that the revolution represented a move away from a form of government in which those most apt to rule, the aristocracy, held power, to a form of government in which the emerging class of economists, lawyers and doctors preponderated - and this, for him, was undesirable. He believed that the aristocracy, by virtue of their experience and the fact that they had no profession, could best rule in the general interest. The emergent bourgeoisie, on the other hand, had neither the experience nor the impartiality, so were considered ill prepared for the business of government.

Burke was also weary about the violation of tradition that came with the French revolution. To a large extent Burke concurred in the principle: 'what is, is good', meaning that he was of the opinion that if something had existed for a long time it had proved its functionality.

For this reason, Burke believed that it was better to preserve established institutions rather than create new ones, which could potentially work poorly. From his viewpoint, established institutions acted as a reservoir of accumulated wisdom, slowly built up over time. It was only by adding to this stored wisdom, not by destroying it and starting afresh, that human society could hope to develop.

The most disturbing interference with tradition, as far as Burke was concerned, was the desecration of the established church. Burke was a true believer, and this is part of the reason for his opposition, but there was another, perhaps more important reason.

That is, that religion functioned as an instrument of social control. Unlike the aristocracy, poor people did not have the time to educate themselves about the world and learn the most appropriate ways of living, but through religion, the aristocracy could prescribe how poor people should live their life. In addition, religion, preaching salvation in the afterlife, helped to quell social unrest and demands for change.

Burke was a commoner, a lawyer and a supporter of representative democracy. There are some passages in which he praises the elegance of the old aristocratic order in France, but his purpose is to contrast it to the what he saw as the depredation by the moneyed classes that were then being justified by the "Rights of Man" exemplified by the leading role of rich speculators, who held government bonds, in promoting the policy of expropriating Church lands. To characterize his views as support for government by the aristocracy is, I think, highly misleading.

Similarly, passages in which he argues that those who enjoy leisure to become educated on political and philosophical matters are more qualified for government is not an argument for government by the aristocracy, but rather for representative instead of direct democracy. Few Egyptian Pharaohs came to the throne without undertaking to restore things "as they were in the beginning." That is, of course, the hallmark of the conservatism of traditional cultures. All traditional human societies justify their practices either by saying, "that is the way things have always been," or, if origins are in issue, by saying that the gods established things that way. Mythic accounts may or may not have been offered, briefly or elaborately, to explain how or why the gods did establish things in the proper way. Eventually the explanation becomes the thing itself, and the historical dimension is simply eliminated, as religions like Judaism, Christianity, and Islam directly present the founding commands of God in revelatory literature.

This is reasonable enough, but it does raise serious questions, including an important moral issue. "Innovations" can mean anything, and it could easily include the French Reign of Terror or the police state and mass murders of Lenin, Stalin, or Hitler. Even if we conclude that much of importance has been definitely learned from these experiments, the very idea that they would merely be experiments is rather appalling. Oops, sorry, made a mistake, or such interesting results! is not what we would like to hear after the massive poverty, terror, and death of the Soviet Union or Hitler's horrific war and genocide. But we are still left with the original question. Just because something is, does not mean that it is good.

Traditional societies may have thought just such a thing, but Burke certainly does not, yet he does not explain how innovations originate and how history can be relied upon to produce valuable results. "All that is necessary for the triumph of evil is that good men do nothing." Attempting to answer the questions about origins and justification, however, can easily produce a more conservative take on things than Burke has.

For the last 5 years of his life Burke occupied a unique position. "He is," remarked a contemporary, "a sort of power in Europe, though totally without any of those means ... which give or maintain power in other men." He corresponded with Louis XVIII and the French royalists and counseled Stanislaus of Poland to pursue a liberal policy. The Irish Catholics regarded him as their champion. As each succeeding act of revolution became more bloody, his foresight was praised more widely. He urged the necessity of war with France, and the declaration of hostilities further increased his prestige. On the last day of his life he spoke of his hatred for the revolutionary spirit in France and of his belief that the war was for the good of humanity. He died on July 9, 1797, and in accordance with his wishes was buried in the parish church of Beaconsfield in Buckinghamshire.

he hallmark of our conservative mood is an intense devotion to tradition. This devotion is not new or unusual for America; in fact it is the heartbeat of Americans. Because of our youth as a nation, or more probably because of it, our people have always been fond of symbolism and slogans that bind us to a glorious past, and our present problems and issues that face our people serve only to stiffen the conviction that the American dream still exists.

One of the most interesting signs of an increased devotion to tradition is the way in which Americans of all kinds and political shadings are searching the past avidly for heroes who can teach, inspire, and comfort. Whether we look to our founding fathers, Andrew Jackson or Lincoln or even if we look to Babe Ruth or Roy Rogers for heroes to inspire us as a people we do seek. But who is there for the millions of solid Americans who, standing confidently on the ancient ways and avoiding political extremism, are setting the tone for politics and culture in America today?

They, like all Americans, cherish Washington, Jefferson, Franklin and Lincoln; but who are their heroes? What valiant Americans should they look to before all others for support of their common-sense, middle-of-the-road approach to the issues of our time? Who, in a word, are the giants of American conservatism? This is a question that demands an answer. In the hope of answering it satisfactorily, let us survey American history with an eye for great men who did conservative deeds, thought conservative thoughts, practiced conservative virtues, and stood for conservative principles.

The search for the giants of American philosophy begins at the Constitutional Convention of 1787. There were, to be sure, outstanding men of conservative principle in the colonial period. George Washington, James Madison, Alexander Hamilton, John Adams and others to name a few whose lives and works have much to teach but their purposes and arguments are too unfamiliar to modern Americans to attract the attention of any large number of conservatives.

The American Revolution has been interpreted as an essentially liberal event to gain liberty. In fact the revolution was a conservative event that led a large scale rebellion to preserve rather than gain liberty, but it was an event that appeals as much to liberals and radicals as to conservatives. The history of American conservatism may be said to date from the decision of a group of Revolutionary leaders mostly conservatives or at least right leaning all to end the uncertainties of the post Revolutionary years by establishing a national government that would secure peace and order, protect the legitimate rights of property, and place political power in the hands of citizens like themselves. Having filled with distinction the roles of rebels against royal and ancient authority, these able conservatives now undertook to play the roles of framers of a new government of, by and for the people.

The monument to their success is the Constitution, a triumph of conservative statesmanship. The framers of the Constitution, who were reluctant toward democracy, deserve all the credit for the success of our democracy. Lacking faith in the people, they none the less rested their new Constitution on the broad base of popular sovereignty. Placing faith in government by the gentry, they none the less raised a structure that could be converted without bloodshed into government by the people. The framers insisted in 1787, and their document insists today, that law is the price of liberty, duty of happiness, deliberation of wise decision, and constitutionalism of democracy.

It has been perhaps the most successful conservative device in the history of mankind, and Americans, a primarily conservative people for all their restlessness, have adored it with good reason.

American conservatives, for whom the Constitution has special meaning, may also take special pride in the men who framed it, in James Madison, Roger Sherman, John Dickinson, Governor Morris, the Pinckney's of South Carolina, and the rest.

They may take even greater pride in four men two of whom were at Philadelphia in 1787, two who were not but might just as well have been who loom above all other men of their age as models of conservative statesmanship and wellsprings of conservative thought.

The first of these, as he is the first of Americans, is George Washington. He is, to be sure, the property of the whole nation, yet it is impossible to deny that he will always have a peculiar appeal for Americans anxious to preserve their unique way of life, just as Jefferson always will for Americans anxious to improve it. In him all the virtues of gentility, integrity, and duty met to form the archetype of the conservative statesman. In his career those great abstractions service, loyalty, patriotism, morality came nobly to life.

For four months he presided over the convention, breaking his silence only once upon a minor question of congressional apportionment. Although he said little in debate, no one did more outside the hall to insist on stern measures. "My wish is," he wrote, "that the convention may adopt no temporizing expedients, but probe the defects of the Constitution to the bottom, and provide a radical cure." His weight of character did more than any other single force to bring the convention to an agreement and obtain ratification of the instrument afterward. He did not believe it perfect, though his precise criticisms of it are unknown.

But his support gave it victory in Virginia, where he sent copies to Patrick Henry and other leaders with a hint that the alternative to adoption was anarchy, declaring that "it or dis-union is before us to choose from." He received and personally circulated copies of *The Federalist*. When ratification was obtained, he wrote to leaders in the various states urging that men staunchly favorable to it be elected to Congress. For a time he sincerely believed that, the new framework completed, he would be allowed to retire again to privacy. But all eyes immediately turned to him for the first president.

The electors chosen in the first days of 1789 cast a unanimous vote for him, and reluctantly for his love of peace, his distrust of his own abilities, and his fear that his motives in advocating the new government might be misconstrued all made him unwilling he accepted. On April 16, after receiving congressional notification of the honor, he set out from Mount Vernon, reaching New York City in time to be inaugurated on April 30 primary source document: First Inaugural Address.

His journey northward was a celebratory procession as people in every town and village through which he passed turned out to greet him, often with banners and speeches, and in some places with triumphal arches. He came across the Hudson River in a specially built barge decorated in red, white, and blue. The inaugural ceremony was performed on Wall Street, near the spot now marked by John Quincy Adams Ward's statue of Washington. A great crowd broke into cheers as, standing on the balcony of Federal Hall, he took the oath administered by Chancellor Robert Livingston and retired indoors to read Congress his inaugural address.

Washington was clad in a brown suit of American manufacture, but he wore white stockings and a sword after the fashion of European courts.

And from him the nation heard, in his Farewell Address, the earnest plea of the true conservative for that firm support of ordered liberty:

Extolled the benefits of the federal government. "The unity of government...is a main pillar in the edifice of your real independence...of your tranquility at home, your peace abroad; of your safety; of your prosperity; of that very liberty which you so highly prize."

Warns against the party system. "It serves to distract the Public Councils, and enfeeble the Public Administration....agitates the Community with ill-founded jealousies and false alarms; kindles the animosity of one....against another....it opens the door to foreign influence and corruption...thus the policy and the will of one country are subjected to the policy and will of another."

Stresses the importance of religion and morality. "Where is the security for property, for reputation, for life, if the sense of religious obligation deserts the oaths, which are the instruments of investigation in Courts of Justice?"

Warns against permanent foreign alliances. "It is our true policy to steer clear of permanent alliances with any portion of the foreign world..."

On an over-powerful military establishment. "...avoid the necessity of those overgrown military establishments, which, under any form of government, are inauspicious to liberty, and which are to be regarded as particularly hostile to Republican Liberty."

In saying farewell to the new nation he helped create Washington pointed out that ".......the name of American, which belongs to you, in your national capacity, must always exalt the just pride of Patriotism..."
To the great soldier, statesman and leader of his country...no tribute could be more fitting.

John Adams was another breed. His roots were in the American land, his home was the New England town, his vision of the Republic was much the same as Jefferson's. His whole approach to life was different from that of Hamilton. Virtue, loyalty, reverence, moderation, and traditionalism these qualities were made real in the person of Honest John Adams. He was, moreover, a conscious political thinker, and his beliefs in the corruptibility of men, the persistence of inequality, the need for aristocracy, the potential tyranny of the majority, the beauties of balanced government, and the sanctity of private property have proved at least as relevant to the American experience as those of his early and late friend Thomas Jefferson. If we add to this tough-minded political theory Adams' Puritan sense of sin, his reverence for history and its teachings, his veneration of "the little platoons" of New England's way of life, his intense constitutionalism and spotless patriotism, and his supreme devotion to public duty, we must grant him the first rank among American conservatives. Here was no lover of government by plutocracy, here no rootless dreamer of an America filled with factories and hard-packed cities. Here was a man who loved America as it was and had been one whose life was a doughty testament to the trials and glories of ordered liberty.

Here, in John Adams of Quincy, was the very model of an American conservative. In his own words "Because power corrupts society's demands for moral authority and character increase as the importance of the position increases."

"Democracy... while it lasts is more bloody than either aristocracy or monarchy. Remember, democracy never lasts long. It soon wastes, exhausts, and murders itself. There is never a democracy that did not commit suicide. "

"Facts are stubborn things; and whatever may be our wishes, our inclinations, or the dictates of our passions, they cannot alter the state of facts and evidence. "

"Fear is the foundation of most governments."

Learned and thoughtful, John Adams was more remarkable as a political philosopher than as a politician. "People and nations are forged in the fires of adversity," he said, doubtless thinking of his own as well as the American experience.
Adams was admitted to the Massachusetts bar in 1758. He steadily built his law practice, and his most celebrated case was his successful defense of the British soldiers accused of carrying out the Boston Massacre. Of the eight accused of murder, six were acquitted and two were convicted only of manslaughter.

In 1770, Adams was elected to the General Court (Lower House) of the Massachusetts legislature. Three years later, he was elected to the Governor's Council, but his election was vetoed by the Royal Governor, most likely due to Adams' support for the Boston Tea Party.

Adams served from 1774 to 1777 as a member of the Continental Congress. It was he who nominated Washington to be commander of the armed forces. From 1778 to 1788, Adams served abroad as a diplomat. In France, with Benjamin Franklin, then in the Netherlands, where he succeeded in gaining Dutch recognition, and loans, for the United States, he earned a reputation as a skillful negotiator and spokesman for his fledgling country.

Alexander Hamilton presents a hard problem. That he was a "man on the Right" is beyond dispute. No prominent American was ever so unashamedly committed to government by "the wise and good and rich," so opposed to political radicalism, so distrustful of the bright promises of democracy. If he was conservative in practical politics and in his concern for property, he was reactionary in his devotion to monarchy and hereditary aristocracy, visionary in his schemes for an industrial America, and who-knows-what radical, reactionary, or just plain opportunistic? In his eagerness to reduce the states to an inferior position. His basic ideas, which he voiced on the floor of the Convention, were irrelevant in the American environment and were certainly not those of a man who knew and cherished the American tradition.

His reports and speeches as secretary of the treasury expressed a high-toned, mercantilist, opportunistic brand of Federalism that can only be regarded as conservatism run wild.

Hamilton was a great man and, despite what Woodrow Wilson may have once said, a great American. He was, it will be remembered, one of the two chief authors of The Federalist, and The Federalist is conservatism at its finest and most constructive.

It is a book that voices in all its pages the conditional hope that men who are properly educated, informed, and restrained can govern themselves wisely and well, a book whose grim confidence in the feasibility of liberty makes it one of the three or four basic texts of American conservatism. More important still is the well-documented fact that in one area of immense concern for Americans today, the formulation of foreign policy and conduct of diplomacy, Hamilton acted consistently and wrote eloquently in the spirit of genuine conservatism.

The solid reputation of Alexander Hamilton places him among but a handful of figures in the history of America. No single figure was ever a stronger advocate of our Constitution; and only a few people have made a comparable contribution to the substance of American government.

Because of his fame, few Americans have been as widely controversial as Hamilton. To this day, his importance remains unsurpassed in the areas of sharp finance, principled politics, romantic scandal, hard work, intellectual acuteness, and bravery. Hamilton's visage on the $10 bill is the only non-presidential face besides Benjamin Franklin to appear on our common currency. Alexander Hamilton was born as a British subject on the island of Nevis in the West Indies on the 11th of January 1755. His father was James Hamilton, a Scottish merchant of St. Christopher. His grandfather was Alexander Hamilton, of Grange, Lanarkshire. One of his great grandfathers was Sir R. Pollock, the Laird of Cambuskeith. Hamilton's mother was Rachael Fawcette Levine, of French Huguenot descent. When she was very young, she married a Danish proprietor of St. Croix named John Michael Levine.

Ms. Levine left her husband and was later divorced from him on June 25, 1759. Under Danish law, the court ordering the divorce Ms. Levine was forbidden from remarrying. Thus, Hamilton's birth was illegitimate. Alexander Hamilton had one brother, James Hamilton. Heavy burdens fell upon Hamilton's shoulders during childhood. Business failures caused Hamilton's father to become bankrupt. Soon thereafter, his mother died in 1768. At twelve, Alexander entered the counting house of Nicholas Cruger and David Beekman. There, young Alexander served as a clerk and apprentice. At the age of fifteen, Mr. Cruger left Alexander in charge of the business. Early on, Hamilton wished to increase his opportunities in life. This is evidenced by a letter written to his friend Edward Stevens at the age of fourteen on Nov. 11, 1769 where he stated, "my ambition is prevalent, so that I contemn the groveling condition of a clerk or the like … and would willingly risk my life, though not my character, to exalt my station."

During adolescence, Hamilton had few opportunities for regular schooling. However, he possessed a commanding knowledge of French, due to the teaching of his late mother. This was a very rare trait in the English continental colonies.

Hamilton was first published in the Royal Danish-American Gazette with his description of the terrible hurricane of August 30th, 1772 that gutted Christiandend. Impressed by this, an opportunity to gain his education was provided by family friends. Seizing this, Hamilton arrived the grammar school in Elizabethtown, New Jersey in the autumn of 1772. One year later, in 1774, Hamilton graduated and entered King's College in New York City.

There, Hamilton obtained a bachelor's of arts degree in just one year.

John Marshall of Virginia drew on both Hamilton and Adams. For the former, whose constitutional writings he must have known by heart, he carried on the great work of nationalism and centralization with Gibbons v. Ogden and McCulloch v. Maryland; for the latter, who placed him at the head of the Supreme Court, he carried on the great work of protecting property against headstrong democracy with Fletcher v. Peck and Dartmouth College v. Woodward. For both, he made the judiciary the darling instrument of conservatism when he conjured up judicial review in Marbury v. Madison. By asserting the power of the Court to ignore and thus invalidate laws judged unconstitutional, Marshall put the last and most essential stone in place in the wall of conservative constitutionalism.

He was born at Germantown (now Midland) in *Fauquier County, Virginia* and attended the *College of William and Mary*. In 1780, while at William & Mary, he studied under the tutelage of jurist *George Wythe* the nation's first Law Professor. A member of the *Culpeper Minutemen* early in the *American Revolutionary War*, he entered the Third *Virginia* Continental Regiment on *July 30, 1776* and served ably in a number of important campaigns, rising to Captain.

President James Monroe also served in this regiment as a lieutenant. After the war Marshall became a lawyer, serving his state as a leader in the Assembly and in the new *Federalist Party*. He attracted attention from national leaders, and was offered several diplomatic posts, but preferred to remain in *Virginia*.

In *1797*, however, he accepted an appointment on a three-man commission to negotiate with *France*. After French leaders demanded personal bribes (see *XYZ Affair*) in return for engaging in the negotiations, Marshall answered for his colleagues in a brilliant memorial which rejected this extortion and upheld the honor and dignity of the new country.

The achievements of these eminent men, the Federalists, were of such huge consequence to the founding of the Republic that we may salute them not only as the first but the greatest of American conservatives.

These achievements were essentially three in number: the Revolution, for which they provided much of the political, diplomatic, and military leadership; the Constitution, which they planned for at Annapolis, hammered out at Philadelphia, and pushed through enough state conventions to secure ratification; and the Administrations of Washington and Adams, which won respect for the new Republic abroad, placed the government on a firm financial footing, and set standards of morality and efficiency in the public service that have never been surpassed.

I think it's important to understand that the American colonies and their populace were for the overwhelming majority happy to be subjects of England. In deed most Americans were proud to be thusly thought. Our language and traditions were similar we truly were Englishmen and proud to be so. That is why our revolution is without doubt a struggle to return to life, liberty and the pursuit of happiness that existed in the colonies before the tyranny of King George.

We fought with the crown against the French and Indians. We spilled blood for our common good and protected our freedom and liberty. In turn England spent their treasure in money and lives in this defense. In that struggle we were united with England as subjects to win our lives and our happiness as a people.

The French and Indian War is the common U.S. name for the war between Great Britain and France in North America from 1754 to 1763. In 1756 the war erupted into the world-wide conflict known as the Seven Years' War and thus came to be regarded as the North American theater of that war. In Canada, it is usually just referred to as the Seven Years' War, although many Canadians refer to it as The War of the Conquest. In Europe, there is no specific name for the North American part of the war. The name refers to the two main enemies of the British: the royal French forces and the various Native American forces allied with them.

The war was fought primarily along the frontiers between the British colonies from Virginia to Nova Scotia, and began with a dispute over the confluence of the Allegheny and Monongahela Rivers, the site of present-day Pittsburgh, Pennsylvania. The dispute resulted in the Battle of Jumonville Glen in May 1754. British attempts at expeditions in 1755, 1756, and 1757 in the frontier areas of Pennsylvania and New York all failed, due to a combination of poor management, internal divisions, and effective French and Indian offense. The 1755 capture of Fort Beauséjour on the border separating Nova Scotia from Acadia was followed by a British policy of deportation of its French inhabitants, to which there was some resistance.

After the disastrous 1757 British campaigns resulting in a failed expedition against Louisbourg and the Siege of Fort William Henry, which was followed by significant Indian atrocities, the British government fell, and William Pitt came to power, while France was unwilling to risk large convoys to aid the limited forces it had in New France. Pitt significantly increased British military resources in the colonies, and between 1758 and 1760 the British military successfully penetrated the heartland of New France, with Montreal finally falling in September 1760.

The outcome was one of the most significant developments in a century of Anglo-French conflict. To compensate its ally, Spain, for its loss of Florida to the British, France ceded its control of French Louisiana west of the Mississippi.

France's colonial presence north of the Caribbean was reduced to the tiny islands of Saint Pierre and Miquelon, confirming Britain's position as the dominant colonial power in the eastern half of North America.

The tide of conservatism runs in confusing patterns, but no one will now deny that it runs deep and strong.

CHAPTER TWO - The Federalists

The U.S. Constitution establishes a government based on "federalism," or the sharing of power between the national, state and local governments. Our power sharing form of government is the opposite of "centralized" governments, such as those in England and France, under which national government maintains total power. This was done purposefully to give regional rights to states understanding that there would exist regional concerns.

While each of the 50 states has its own constitution, all provisions of state constitutions must comply with the U.S. Constitution. For example, a state constitution cannot deny accused criminals the right to a trial by jury, as assured by the U.S. Constitution's 6th Amendment. Under the U.S. Constitution, both the national and state governments are granted certain exclusive powers and share other powers.

The Federalist Papers are a series of 85 articles or essays advocating the ratification of the United States Constitution. Seventy seven of the essays were published serially in The Independent Journal and The New York Packet between October 1787 and August 1788. A compilation of these and eight others, called The Federalist; or, The New Constitution, was published in two volumes in 1788. The series' correct title is The Federalist; the title The Federalist Papers did not emerge until the twentieth century.

The Federalist remains a primary source for interpretation of the U.S. Constitution, as the essays outline a lucid and compelling version of the philosophy and motivation of the proposed system of government.

The authors of The Federalist wanted both to influence the vote in favor of ratification and to shape future interpretations of the Constitution. According to historian Richard B. Morris, they are an "incomparable exposition of the Constitution, a classic in political science unsurpassed in both breadth and depth by the product of any later American writer."

At the time of publication, the authorship of the articles was a closely guarded secret, though astute observers guessed that Hamilton, Madison, and Jay were the likely authors. Following Hamilton's death in 1804, a list that he drew up became public; it claimed fully two thirds of the essays for Hamilton, including some that seemed more likely the work of Madison (Nos. 49-58, 62, and 63). The scholarly detective work of Douglass Adair in 1944 postulated the following assignments of authorship, corroborated in 1964 by a computer analysis of the text:

- Alexander Hamilton (51 articles: nos. 1, 6–9, 11–13, 15–17, 21–36, 59–61, and 65–85)
- James Madison (29 articles: nos. 10, 14, 37–58 and 62–63)
- John Jay (5 articles: 2–5 and 64).
- Nos. 18–20 was the result of collaboration between Madison and Hamilton. The author. s used the pseudonym "Publius," in honor of Roman consul Publius Valerius Publicola Madison, whom posterity generally credits as the father of the Constitution despite his repeated rejection of the honor during his lifetime, became a leading member of the U.S.

House of Representatives from Virginia (1789-1797), Secretary of State (1801-1809), and ultimately the fourth President of the United States. Hamilton, who had been a leading advocate of national constitutional reform throughout the 1780s and represented New York at the Constitutional Convention, in 1789 became the first Secretary of the Treasury, a post he held until his resignation in 1795. John Jay, who had been secretary for foreign affairs under the Articles of Confederation from 1784 through their expiration in 1789, became the first Chief Justice of the United States in 1789, stepping down in 1795 to accept election as governor of New York, a post he held for two terms, retiring in 1801.

There are many highlights among the essays comprising The Federalist. Federalist No. 10, in which Madison discusses the means of preventing rule by majority faction and advocates an extended republic, is generally regarded as the most important of the 85 articles from a philosophical perspective; it is complemented by Federalist No. 14, in which Madison takes the measure of the United States, declares it appropriate for an extended republic, and concludes with a memorable defense of the constitutional and political creativity of the Federal Convention. In Federalist No. 84, Hamilton makes the case that there is no need to amend the Constitution by adding a Bill of Rights, insisting that the various provisions in the proposed Constitution protecting liberty amount to a bill of rights. Federalist No. 78, also written by Hamilton, lays the groundwork for the doctrine of judicial review by federal courts of federal legislation or executive acts. Federalist No. 70 presents Hamilton's case for a one-man chief executive.

In Federalist No. 39, Madison presents the clearest exposition of what has come to be called "Federalism." In Federalist No. 51, Madison distills arguments for checks and balances in a memorable essay often quoted for its justification of government as "the greatest of all reflections on human nature."

The Federalist was written to support the ratification of the Constitution, specifically in New York. Whether they succeeded in this mission is questionable. Separate ratification proceedings took place in each state, and the essays were not reliably reprinted outside of New York; furthermore, by the time the series was well underway, a number of important states had already ratified it, for instance Pennsylvania on December 12. New York held out until July 26; certainly The Federalist was more important there than anywhere else, but many argue that it could hardly rival other major forces in the ratification contests specifically, these forces included the personal influence of well-known Federalists, for instance Hamilton and Jay, and Anti-Federalists, including Governor George Dewitt Clinton. Further, by the time New York came to a vote, ten states had already ratified the Constitution and it had thus already passed only nine states had to ratify it for the new government to be established among them; the ratification by Virginia, the tenth state, placed pressure on New York to ratify.

As for Virginia, which only ratified the Constitution at its convention on June 25, Hamilton writes in a letter to Madison that the collected edition of The Federalist had been sent to Virginia; it was presumed that it was to act as a debater's handbook for the convention there, though claims that this indirect influence would be a dubious distinction.

Probably of greater importance to the Virginia debate, in any case, was George Washington's support for the proposed Constitution and the presence of Madison and Edmund Randolph, the governor, at the convention arguing for ratification.

Another purpose that The Federalist was supposed to serve was as a debater's handbook during the ratification controversy, and indeed advocates for the Constitution in the conventions in New York and Virginia used the essays for precisely that purpose.

Federal judges, when interpreting the Constitution, frequently use the Federalist Papers as a contemporary account of the intentions of the framers and ratifiers. They have been applied on issues ranging from the power of the federal government in foreign affairs in Hines v. Davidowitz to the validity of laws in the 1798 decision Calder v. Bull, apparently the first decision to mention The Federalist. By 2000[update], The Federalist had been quoted 291 times in Supreme Court decisions.

The amount of deference that should be given to the Federalist Papers in constitutional interpretation has always been somewhat controversial. As early as 1819, Chief Justice John Marshall noted in the famous case McCulloch v. Maryland that "the opinions expressed by the authors of that work have been justly supposed to be entitled to great respect in expounding the Constitution. No tribute can be paid to them which exceed their merit; but in applying their opinions to the cases which may arise in the progress of our government, a right to judge of their correctness must be retained."

Madison himself believed not only that The Federalist Papers were not a direct expression of the ideas of the Founders, but that those ideas themselves, and the "debates and incidental decisions of the Convention," should not be viewed as having any "authoritative character."

In short, "the legitimate meaning of the Instrument must be derived from the text itself; or if a key is to be sought elsewhere, it must be not in the opinions or intentions of the Body which planned & proposed the Constitution, but in the sense attached to it by the people in their respective State Conventions where it recd. all the Authority which it possesses." Its too bad that Madison drifted as he did from some elements of both federalism and the constitution as he did.

The United States presidential election of 1789 was the first presidential election in the United States of America. The election took place following the ratification of the United States Constitution in 1788. In this election, George Washington was elected for the first of his two terms as President of the United States, and John Adams became the first Vice President of the United States. Before this election, the United States had no chief executive. Under the previous system the Articles of Confederation the national government was headed by the Confederation Congress, which had a ceremonial presiding officer and several executive departments, but no independent executive branch.

In this election, the enormously popular Washington essentially ran unopposed. The only real issue to be decided was who would be chosen as vice president.

Under the system then in place, each elector cast two votes; if a person received a vote from a majority of the electors, that person became president, and the runner-up became vice president. All 69 electors cast one vote each for Washington. Their other votes were divided among eleven other candidates; John Adams received the most, becoming vice president. The Twelfth Amendment, ratified in 1804, would change this procedure, requiring each elector to cast distinct votes for president and vice president.

In the absence of conventions, there was no formal nomination process. The framers of the Constitution had presumed that Washington would be the first president, and once he agreed to come out of retirement to accept the office, there was no opposition to him. Individual states chose their electors, who voted all together for Washington when they met.

Electors used their second vote to cast a scattering of votes, many voting for someone besides Adams a carefully organized scheme originating with Alexander Hamilton less out of opposition to him than to prevent Adams from matching Washington's total.

Only ten states out of the original thirteen cast electoral votes in this election. North Carolina and Rhode Island were ineligible to participate as they had not yet ratified the United States Constitution. New York failed to appoint its allotment of eight electors because of a deadlock in the state legislature.
I
In this first of all Presidential elections the Federalists emerged as the preeminent power in American politics.

A strong centralized government with three distinct branches and rights regionally recognized as States Rights. Thus the experiment begins with a strong but limited central power and life, liberty and the pursuit of happiness. Not a constitutional monarchy that some had seen but one that a man like Washington and those close to him could only accept.

Most people wouldn't know or realize that Washington was all but installed as the overwhelmingly popular first President of the United States of America. They wouldn't know that North Carolina, Rhode Island and New York actually had no say in this first election for our highest office.

George Washington as our first president helped to orchestrate a series of treaties that assured the american people of prosperity and security. The Treaty of Greenville was signed at Fort Greenville now Greenville, Ohio, on August 2, 1795, between a coalition of Native Americans known as the Western Confederacy and the United States following the Native American loss at the Battle of Fallen Timbers. It put an end to the Northwest Indian War. The United States was represented by General "Mad Anthony" Wayne, who led the victory at Fallen Timbers. In exchange for goods to the value of $20,000 such as blankets, utensils, and domestic animals, the Native Americans turned over to the United States large parts of modern day Ohio, the future site of downtown Chicago and the Fort Detroit area.

The treaty established what became known as the "Greenville Treaty Line," which was for several years a boundary between Native American territory and lands open to white settlers, although the treaty line was frequently disregarded by settlers as they continued to encroach on native lands guaranteed by the treaty.

Jay Treaty, also known as Jay's Treaty, The British Treaty and the Treaty of London of 1794, was a treaty between the United States and Great Britain which averted war , solved many issues left over from the American Revolution , and opened ten years of largely peaceful trade in the midst of the French Revolutionary Wars. It was hotly contested by Jeffersonians but was ratified by Congress and became a central issue in the formation of the First Party System. The treaty was signed in November 1794, but was not proclaimed to be in effect until February 29, 1796. Treaties that extended and expanded trade and left us at peace is a lost art of the days of federalism.

The terms were designed primarily by Secretary of the Treasury Alexander Hamilton with strong support from President George Washington and chief negotiator John Jay. The treaty increased trade and averted war, which pleased both sides. Jay obtained the primary American requirements: British withdrawal from the posts that they occupied in the Northwest Territory of the United States, which they had promised to abandon in 1783. Wartime debts and the US Canada boundary were sent to arbitration one of the first major uses of arbitration in diplomatic history. The Americans were also granted some rights to trade with British possessions in India and the Caribbean in exchange for American limits on the export of cotton.

The treaty averted possible war but immediately became one of the central issues in domestic American politics, with Thomas Jefferson and James Madison leading the opposition. They feared that closer economic ties with Britain would strengthen the Federalists.

Particularly on Jefferson's part a tactic more motivated by politics than by righteousness. The treaty encouraged trade between the two nations for a decade, but it broke down after 1803. The main parts of the treaty expired after 10 years. Efforts to agree on a replacement treaty failed in 1806; the U.S. rejected the Monroe - Pinckney Treaty as tensions escalated to the War of 1812.

From the British perspective, the war with France made it imperative to improve relations with the U.S. to keep the U.S. from falling into the French orbit. From the American viewpoint, the most pressing foreign policy issues were normalizing trade relations with Britain, America's leading trading partner, and resolving issues left over from the American Revolution.

As one observer explained, the British government was "well disposed to America… They have made their arrangements upon a plan that comprehends the neutrality of the United States, and are anxious that it should be preserved."

In 1793–94, the British Navy captured hundreds of American neutral ships and the British in Canada were supporting Indian tribes fighting the U.S. in Ohio territory the British gave the U.S. in 1783. Congress voted an embargo for two months. Hamilton and the Federalists favored Britain over France and sought to normalize relations. Hamilton designed the plan and Washington sent Chief Justice Jay to London to negotiate a comprehensive treaty.

Pinckney's Treaty, also known as the Treaty of San Lorenzo or the Treaty of Madrid, was signed in San Lorenzo de El Escorial on October 27, 1795 and established intentions of friendship between the United States and Spain. It also defined the boundaries of the United States with the Spanish colonies and guaranteed the United States navigation rights on the Mississippi River. The treaty's full title is Treaty of Friendship, Limits, and Navigation between Spain and the United States. Thomas Pinckney negotiated the treaty for the United States. The treaty was proclaimed on August 3, 1796.

By terms of the treaty, Spain and the United States agreed that the southern boundary of the United States with the Spanish Colonies of East Florida and West Florida was a line beginning on the Mississippi River. This describes the current boundary between the present states of Florida and Georgia and the line from the northern boundary of the Florida panhandle to the northern boundary of that portion of Louisiana east of the Mississippi.

This boundary had been in dispute since the British had expanded the territory of the Florida colonies while it was in their possession. After the American Revolutionary War, Spain claimed the British border at the day of the Treaty of Paris while the United States insisted on the old boundary.

The Treaty of Tripoli usually refers to the first treaty concluded between the United States of America and Tripoli, otherwise known in English as the Treaty of Peace and Friendship between the United States of America and the Bey and Subjects of Tripoli of Barbary.

The treaty was signed at Tripoli on November 4, 1796 and at Algiers for a third party witness on January 3, 1797, finally receiving ratification from the U.S. Senate on June 7, 1797 and signed by President John Adams on June 10, 1797.

Soon after the formation of the United States, privateering in the Mediterranean Sea and Atlantic Ocean from the nations of the Barbary Coast prompted the U.S. to form a series of so-called "peace treaties", collectively known as the Barbary Treaties. Individual treaties were negotiated with Morocco (1786), Algeria (1795), Tripoli (1797) and Tunis (1797), all of them more than once.

John Jay was another great stalwart of the conservative and Federalist movements. John Jay's long and eventful life, from 1745 to 1829, encompassed the movement for American independence and the creation of a new nation both processes in which he played a full part. His achievements were many, varied and of key importance in the birth and early years of the fledgling nation. Although he did not initially favor separation from Britain, he was nonetheless among the American commissioners who negotiated the peace with Great Britain that secured independence for the former colonies. Serving the new republic he was Secretary for Foreign Affairs under the Articles of Confederation, a contributor to the Federalist, the first Chief Justice of the United States, negotiator of the 1794 Jay Treaty with Great Britain, and a two-term Governor of the State of New York. In his personal life, Jay embraced a wide range of social and cultural concerns.

In 1787 and 1788 Jay collaborated with Alexander Hamilton and James Madison on the Federalist, authoring essays numbers two, three, four, five and, following an illness, sixty-four, thus contributing to the political arguments and intellectual discourse that led to Constitution's ratification.

Jay also played a key role in shepherding the Constitution through the New York State Ratification Convention in the face of vigorous opposition. In this battle Jay relied not only on skillful political maneuvering, he also produced a pamphlet, "An Address to the People of New York," that powerfully restated the Federalist case for the new Constitution.

In 1789, Washington appointed John Jay Chief Justice of the new Supreme Court. Though none too pleased with the rigors of riding circuit, Jay used his position to expound upon the inviolability of contracts whether in the supportive climate of New England or the hostile environment of Virginia. He was always a committed nationalist, and indeed the opinion he rendered in Chisholm v. Georgia provoked the adoption of the states rights oriented Eleventh Amendment. Throughout his time on the bench, Jay was an outspoken presence in national politics, actively interceding, for example, in the Genet affair of 1793.

In April of 1794 Washington selected John Jay to negotiate a treaty with Great Britain aimed at resolving outstanding issues between the two nations. The resulting Treaty of Amity, Commerce and Navigation, commonly referred to as the Jay Treaty, was extremely controversial.

Critics charged that it failed to address British impressments of American sailors or provide compensation for
those slaves that the British had taken with them during
the Revolutionary war. The Treaty's unpopularity played
a significant role in the development of an organized opposition to the Federalists.

On his return from London in 1795, Jay discovered that,
in his absence, he had been elected the new Governor
of New York, a position that he had sought three years
earlier only to be frustrated, in controversial circumstances, by the incumbent, George Clinton.   During his
two terms as governor, Jay confronted issues ranging
from Indian affairs, to the fortification of the city's harbor
in advance of a suspected French attack, to the construction of a new state prison.

On his retirement from public life in 1801, Jay maintained
a close interest in state and national affairs, evidenced in
his correspondence with his sons, Peter Augustus, who
was active in local Federalist political circles, and William, who, among other things, became an outspoken
abolitionist.
In his retirement Jay also pursued a number of intellectual and benevolent interests, becoming President of the
American Bible Society, maintaining an interest in the
anti-slavery movement and keeping up a correspondence with agricultural reformers about latest developments in that field.

Jay died on May 17, 1829, at the age of 83. His longev-
ity enabled biographers and early historians of the founding era to draw directly upon his personal recollections of
the people and events of the early years of the nation.

In his later years, Jay's own correspondence with various members of the founding generation revealed a keen interest in ensuring an accurate appraisal of his own role in the momentous events of that time.

The United States presidential election of 1796 was the first contested American presidential election and the only one to elect a President and Vice President from opposing tickets.

With incumbent President George Washington having refused a third term in office, incumbent Vice President John Adams of Massachusetts was a candidate for the presidency on the Federalist Party ticket with former Governor Thomas Pinckney of South Carolina as the next most popular Federalist. Their opponents were former Secretary of State Thomas Jefferson of Virginia along with Senator Aaron Burr of New York on the Democratic-Republican ticket. At this point, each man from any party ran alone, as the formal position of "running mate" had not yet been established.
Unlike the previous election where the outcome had been a foregone conclusion, Democratic-Republicans campaigned heavily for Jefferson, and Federalists campaigned heavily for Adams.

The debate was a hotley contested one, with Federalists tying the Democratic-Republicans to the violence of the French Revolution and the Democratic-Republicans accusing the Federalists of favoring monarchism and aristocracy.

In foreign policy, the Democratic-Republicans denounced the Federalists over Jay's Treaty, perceived as too favorable to Britain, while the French ambassador embarrassed the Democratic-Republicans by publicly backing them and attacking the Federalists right before the election. Although Adams won, Thomas Jefferson received more electoral votes than Pinckney and was elected Vice-President.

The relations among the United States, Great Britain and France became the key issue of the Adams Presidency. Adams started his administration with a conciliatory posture.

The United States was just 20 years old, and the Constitution eight, when Adams began his presidency. Foreign issues would command the young nation's attention during the next four years. Europe was embroiled in war and revolution. Despite peace treaties with both Great Britain and France, both countries were attacking U.S. ships on the high seas and impressing U.S. sailors into foreign naval service. Adams immediately faced questions concerning development of the U.S. Navy and the military. The country debated how to maintain its independence. Federalists, largely comprising Americans in growing urban areas, favored a strong national government to support the development of commerce.
Despite rising passion against France, he sent three representatives to France to try to work out differences between the French and the US government. His emissaries were met by three French representatives demanding a bribe.

When word of this outrage reached Adams, he decided that this was tantamount to war. He requested that the US make preparations for a war with France. The republican opposition demanded that Adams release the contents of the correspondence with France. They believed he had exaggerated the affair.

Adams at first refused, citing executive privilege. This is the doctrine that activities of the executive branch need not be released to Congress. Eventually, after he was convinced by his Federalist supporters, Adams released the documents, but withheld the names of the Frenchmen involved.

The release of the documents brought the cry for war against the French to a fever pitch. The United States armed its merchantmen and preceded to successful combat the French in repeated naval encounters. Adams never asked for a Declaration of War. Soon the French came to realize that they had nothing to gain by pursuing a war with the United States. They soon expressed their willingness to receive a new envoy from the United States to work out their differences.

Adams' pursuit of peace was roundly condemned by the popular opinion. Adams lost his bid for re-election to Jefferson, due largely to the disarray of the Federalist Party. The Alien and Sedition Acts marked an attempt by Federalists to suppress opposition at home. The acts gave the President power to arrest and deport any alien suspected of having treasonable or secret leanings. There existed in our nation's infancy a huge amount of foreign influences and the Federalists who were more conservative by nature realized this problem.

This threatened many of the Jeffersonian who were not naturalized citizens.

The most controversial part of the acts was the section which established heavy fines, or even imprisonment; for saying anything false, scandalous or malicious against the government. Opponents claimed that this law abridged rights granted by the First Amendment.
The Federalists responded that the First Amendment did not cover acts of sedition. All together, 25 people were arrested under Alien and Sedition Acts; 10 were convicted and imprisoned.

The United States signed the Convention of Paris with France. Under this treaty, France accepted US neutrality rights at sea. The French also discharged the US from its obligations established under the alliance formed by the two nations during the American Revolution. In return, the United States granted France most favored trading status. Ultimately Adams kept us out of war and very prosperous as a nation. Even though he served only one term John Adams truly was a Giant of a little man.
The Federalists had their full share of failures, from both their point of view and mine, but their successes outweigh them by far in the balance of history.
When we consider that they, like all men and movements, were devoted primarily to their own interests, we must marvel at the services they rendered to the whole Republic. These were American conservatism's finest years, and all Americans, conservatives and liberals alike, may be grateful that the Federalists wrought their prudent deeds.

As our fledgling democracy takes shape and political divisions become more inevitable and deeper than ever the old Federalists go by the wayside. As America begins to expand west and become more homogenous back east liberal ideas creep into the political landscape that begins with the Jeffersonian Democrats and the National Republicans wait for a great leader. In the meantime a series of founding fathers some that've gone astray come to power. Much good will is done in these coming years as conservatism takes a back seat to history and liberalism moves forward. In my opinion to some cost in treasury both from a monetary and humane standpoint.

John Marshall was asked by *Adams* to be an *Associate Justice of the Supreme Court*, but instead Marshall opted to run for a position in *Congress*. He was elected in *1799*, but Adams appointed Marshall as *Secretary of State* on *June 6, 1800*. Here he strongly opposed violations of American rights on the high seas and adopted a policy which necessitated a strong Navy to give force to American diplomatic protests.

Appointed *Chief Justice* on *January 20, 1801*, Marshall continued to serve as *Secretary of State* until the end of Adams' administration *March 4, 1801*. At 45 years of age at the time of his appointment, Marshall was the youngest *Chief Justice* in U.S. history. In the *United States Supreme Court*, Marshall made his greatest contributions to the development of American government. In a series of historic decisions, he established the judiciary as an independent and influential branch of the government equal to Congress and the Presidency.

Perhaps the most significant of these cases was that of *Marbury v. Madison*, in which the principle of *judicial review* was simply stated by Marshall: "A legislative act contrary to the *Constitution* is not law." Then, as the young nation was endangered by regional and local interests who often threatened to tear it to shreds, Marshall again and again interpreted the *Constitution* broadly so that the Federal Government had the power to become a respected and creative force guiding and encouraging the nation's growth. For practical purposes, the *Constitution* in its most important aspects today is the *Constitution* as John Marshall interpreted it. As *Chief Justice* he embodied the majesty of the *Judicial Branch* of the government as fully as the President stood for the power of the *Executive Branch*.

Marshall served as Chief Justice through five presidential administrations, a stalwart proponent of *Federalism* and nemesis of the Jeffersonian school of government throughout its heyday. While Chief Justice, Marshall wrote a five-volume biography of *George Washington*, *The Life of George Washington* (published *1804–1807*). The work reflected Marshall's Federalist principles, and consequently was not well received by President Jefferson.

Marshall died *July 6, 1835* at the age of 79, having served as Chief Justice for over 34 years. This makes Marshall the longest-serving Chief Justice of the United States in history. His mark championing the Conservative cause of Federalism is still felt today.
Many arguments for federalism have traditionally been put in terms of promoting various forms of liberty in the form of non domination, immunity or enhanced opportunity sets.

When considering reasons offered in the literature for federal political orders, many appear to be in favor of decentralization without requiring constitutional entrenchment of split authority. Two sets of arguments can be distinguished: Arguments favoring federal orders compared with secession and completely independent sovereign states; and arguments supporting federal arrangements rather than a centralized unitary state. They occur in different forms and from different starting points, in defense of 'coming together' federalism, and in favor of 'holding together' federalism.

As political orders go, federal political arrangements pose peculiar problems concerning stability and trust. Federations tend to drift toward disintegration in the form of secession, or toward centralization in the direction of a unitary state.

Such instability should come as no surprise given the tensions typically giving rise to federal political orders in the first place, such as tensions between majority and minority national communities in multinational federations. Federal political orders are therefore often marked by a high level of 'constitutional politics'.

The details of their constitutions and other institutions may affect these conflicts and their outcomes in drastic ways. Political parties often disagree on constitutional issues regarding the appropriate areas of member unit autonomy, the forms of cooperation and how to prevent fragmentation. Such sampling bias among states that federalize to hold together makes it difficult to assess claims that federal responses perpetuate cleavages and fuel rather than quell secessionist movements.

Regarding distributive justice, federal political orders must manage tensions between ensuring member unit autonomy and securing the requisite redistribution within and among the member units. Indeed, the Federalists regarded federal arrangements as an important safeguard against "the equal division of property".

The U.S. Constitution establishes a government based on "federalism," or the sharing of power between the national, and state and local governments. Our power sharing form of government is the opposite of centralized governments, such as those in England and France, under which national government maintains total power. While each of the 50 states has its own constitution, all provisions of state constitutions must comply with the U.S. Constitution. For example, a state constitution cannot deny accused criminals the right to a trial by jury, as assured by the U.S. Constitution's 6th Amendment.

The very basis of our government as originally laid out by our fore fathers is Federalism and a conservation of our basic inalienable rights to life, liberty and the pursuit of happiness.

CHAPTER THREE - Jeffersonian Democracy

Perhaps the most striking evidence of this triumph in conservative statesmanship is the fact that after twelve years of Federalist rule another group of men, many of whom had originally been opposed to the Constitution, could take over the machinery of government with hardly a hitch or break or a call for a new Constitution.

So rapid was the advance of the new nation toward political equality that many old Jeffersonian now found themselves in the ranks of conservatism side by side with long-time enemies from the Federalist camp. The drive of the plain people and their able leaders to democratize the limited Republic of the fathers was aimed at concrete political goals: removal of property restrictions for voting and office-holding; popular election of the executive; popular election, to short terms, of the judiciary; devices, like the convention, for popular control of parties; popular election of state constitutional conventions and ratification of their results; and the "spoils system." The counter drive of the conservatives, the men who feared Jacksonian democracy, was aimed at fighting off these innovations just as long as possible. The mission of American conservatism had shifted from construction to obstruction, and few conservatives were entirely happy about it.

In the Presidential election of 1800, sometimes referred to as the "Revolution of 1800," Vice President Thomas Jefferson defeated incumbent president John Adams.

The election was a realigning election that ushered in a generation of Democratic-Republican Party rule and the eventual demise of the Federalist Party in the First Party System. It was a lengthy, bitter rematch of the 1796 election between the pro-French and pro-decentralization Democratic-Republicans under Jefferson and Aaron Burr, against incumbent Adams and Charles Pinckney's pro-British and pro-centralization Federalists. The jockeying for electoral votes, regional divisions, and the propaganda smear campaigns created by both parties made the election recognizably modern.

The election exposed one of the flaws in the original Constitution. Members of the Electoral College could only vote for President; each elector could vote for two candidates, and the Vice President was the person who received the second largest number of votes during the election. The Democratic-Republicans had planned for one of the electors to abstain from casting his second vote for Aaron Burr, which would have led to Jefferson receiving one electoral vote more than Burr. The plan, however, was bungled, resulting in a tied electoral vote between Jefferson and Burr. The election was then put into the hands of the outgoing House of Representatives controlled by the Federalist Party. Many Federalists voted for Burr, and the result was a week of deadlock. Federalist Alexander Hamilton, who detested both but preferred Jefferson to Burr, was one of those who vigorously lobbied against Burr. Burr remained in New York during the debates and votes, as his only daughter was married there on February 1, 1801. No evidence exists to prove that he did anything to sway the vote his way. Hamilton's actions were one episode of the ill-fated relationship between Hamilton and Burr, which ended in Hamilton's fatal duel with Burr in 1804.

In the absence of efforts on Burr's behalf, lobbying by Jefferson's supporters and Hamilton allowed Jefferson to ascend to the Presidency.

The Twelfth Amendment, ratified in 1804, was added to the United States Constitution. The Twelfth Amendment stipulates that electors make a discrete choice between their selections for President and Vice President.
Thomas Jefferson was as one of our founding fathers a larger than life figure, but in my opinion he was bordering upon demagoguery. His ideas of active revolution every 19 years because he calculated that based upon life expectancy a new generation would raise to power is quite radical to say the least. His gift for writing and expression of ideas were second to none but much of what he wrote he also turned his own back on. He was driven by power and a self belief that he knew best for the masses and in his benevolence would lead the people in their best interest.

Jefferson had no love for the constitutional republic and he felt that the constitution itself was a fluid document. His liberal philosophy is not hard to see and his effect on Madison and Monroe who would also be categorized as Jeffersonian Democrats by me and most conservatives. They drifted from their conservative roots and became more interested in self than republic in my opinion.
The real shame of the Jeffersonian movement was James Madison's movement away from Federalism. A great author of the federalist movement was now being secured as a democrat under the influence of Jefferson. Madison was brilliant but weak in spirit to be drawn away in such a manner.

During Jefferson's presidency many federal taxes were repealed, and he sought to rely mainly on customs revenue. He pardoned people who had been imprisoned under the Alien and Sedition Acts, passed in John Adams' term, which Jefferson believed to be unconstitutional. He repealed the Judiciary Act of 1801 and removed many of Adams' judges from office, which led to the Supreme Court deciding the important case of *Marbury v. Madison*. Which he also opposed in fact he opposed the whole idea of judicial supremacy.

He began and won the First Barbary War (1801–1805), America's first significant overseas war, and established the United States Military Academy at West Point in 1802. His failure to reach compromise lead to the Barbary war and ultimately the policies of he and Madison led to the War of 1812. They forgot that the duty of the central government was first to keep its citizens secure and free.

In 1803, despite his misgivings about the constitutionality of Congress's power to buy land, Jefferson bought Louisiana from France, doubling the size of the United States. The land thus acquired amounts to 23 percent of the United States today.

In 1807, his former vice president, Aaron Burr, was tried for treason on Jefferson's order, but was acquitted. During the trial Chief Justice John Marshall subpoenaed Jefferson, who invoked executive privilege and claimed that as president he did not need to comply. As usual the rules didn't apply to him.

When Marshall held that the Constitution did not provide the president with any exception to the duty to obey a court order, Jefferson backed down. Jefferson's reputation was damaged by the Embargo Act of 1807, which was ineffective and was repealed at the end of his second term.

Charles Pinckney of South Carolina carried the Federalist and conservative flags during much of the Jeffersonian era. In the 1800 presidential election, Pinckney was the Federalist candidate for vice-president, running with the incumbent president, John Adams. They were defeated by the Democratic-Republicans Thomas Jefferson who became president and Aaron Burr who became vice president. In 1804, the Federalist Party nominated Pinckney to run for the presidency against Jefferson. Jefferson, who was very popular due to the acquisition of the Louisiana Purchase and booming trade defeated Pinckney in a landslide, winning only 27.2% of the popular vote and carrying only two states. In 1808 he was again the Federalist nominee for president, running against Jefferson's Secretary of State, James Madison. Pinckney did not fare much better against Madison, carrying only five states and winning 32.4% of the popular vote.

From 1805 until his death, Pinckney was president-general of the Society of the Cincinnati. Pinckney died on August 16, 1825 and was buried in St. Michael's Churchyard in Charleston, South Carolina. His tombstone reads, "One of the founders of the American Republic. In war he was a companion in arms and friend of Washington. In peace he enjoyed his unchanging confidence."

The War of 1812 was a war fought between the United States of America and the British Empire particularly Great Britain and the provinces of British North America, the antecedent of Canada. Lasting from 1812 to 1815, it was fought chiefly on the Atlantic Ocean and on the land, coasts and waterways of North America.

The United States took the initiative in declaring war for multiple reasons. In 1807, Britain introduced a series of trade restrictions to impede on-going American trade with France, with which Britain was at war.

The U.S. contested these restrictions as illegal under international law. Both the impressments of American citizens into the Royal Navy, and Britain's military support of American Indians who were attacking American settlers moving into the Northwest further aggravated tensions. Indian raids hindered the expansion of U.S. into potentially valuable farmlands in the Northwest Territory, comprising the modern states of Ohio, Indiana, Illinois, Michigan, and Wisconsin.‐ Some British officials and some dissident Americans charged that the goal was to annex part of Canada, but they did not specify which part.
The states nearest Canada strongly opposed the war.

President Madison didn't represent his country well in my opinion this war could have been avoided by better trade negotiation and we were not well served by an alliance with France. Remember what Washington said about permanent alliances, they are to be avoided. Meanwhile the British burn the White House and nearly capture our capitol. For what amounts to a failed attempt at trade negotiations.

Just as importantly, the United States sought to defend its national honor and sovereign rights against perceived British insults. Although the British made some concessions before the war on neutral trade, they insisted on the right to reclaim their deserting sailors. The American rallying cry of "free trade and sailors rights" reflected the dual economic and political aspects of the administration. The British also had the long-standing goal of creating a large "neutral" Indian state that would cover much of Ohio, Indiana and Michigan. They made the demand as late as the fall of 1814 at the peace conference, but lost control of western Ontario at key battles on Lake Erie, thus giving the Americans control of the proposed neutral zone.

The war was fought in four theatres. Warships and privateers of both sides attacked each other's merchant ships. The British blockaded the Atlantic coast of the U.S. and mounted large-scale raids in the later stages of the war. Battles were also fought on the frontier, which ran along the Great Lakes and Saint Lawrence River and separated the U.S. from Upper and Lower Canada, and along the coast of the Gulf of Mexico. During the war, the Americans and British invaded each other's territory. These invasions were unsuccessful or temporary.

At the end of the war, the British held parts of Maine and some outposts in the sparsely populated West, while the Americans held Canadian territory near Detroit, but these occupied territories were restored at the end of the war. It was a senseless loss of life and treasure. But little James Madison needed his war for while he was small in stature he was large in ego.

Madison wrote most of the US Constitution at the Constitutional Convention in 1787. Even though he would later write the Virginia Resolutions which were hailed by antifederalists, the Constitution created a strong federal government. Once the Convention ended, he along with John Jay and Alexander Hamilton wrote the *Federalist Papers*, essays that were intended to sway public opinion to ratifying the new Constitution. His contributions to Federalism were great and had he never been President all would have been well but he was president and carried on the Jeffersonian revolution against many of his own writings and philosophy.

In the U.S., battles such the Battle of New Orleans and the earlier successful defense of Baltimore which inspired the lyrics of the U.S. national anthem, The Star-Spangled Banner produced a sense of euphoria over a "second war of independence" against Britain. It ushered in an "Era of Good Feelings," in which the partisan animosity that had once verged on treason practically vanished. Canada also emerged from the war with a heightened sense of national feeling and solidarity. Britain, which had regarded the war as a sideshow to the Napoleonic Wars raging in Europe, was less affected by the fighting; its government and people subsequently welcomed an era of peaceful relations and trade with the U.S. which is exactly what a central government should be concerned with. Free and open trade so that we can allow our citizenry to flourish by creating jobs for the populace and profits for our companies.

During the War of 1812 James Monroe held the critical roles of Secretary of State and the Secretary of War under President James Madison.

Facing little opposition from the fractured Federalist Party, Monroe was easily elected president in 1816, winning over 80 percent of the electoral vote.

As president, he sought to ease partisan tensions and embarked on a tour of the country. He was well received everywhere, as nationalism surged, partisan fury subsided and the "Era of Good Feelings" persisted. The Panic of 1819 struck and the dispute over the admission of Missouri embroiled the country in 1820. Nonetheless, Monroe won near-unanimous reelection. In 1823, he announced the Monroe Doctrine, which became a landmark in American foreign policy. Of course as Jefferson, Monroe was good with words yet we had no naval force to speak of to back up what he was saying. He spoke loudly with a small stick. Had the right idea, but failed to build a naval supremacy needed for such a proclamation to hold weight. Following his retirement in 1825, Monroe was plagued by financial difficulties. He died in New York City on July 4, 1831.

The Federalists passed into oblivion as a party in the election of 1816. Since the opening phase of the Revolution, the inherited system of government by gentlemen chosen by a restricted electorate had been under severe assault from the disfranchised and disinherited. Now, in the first decades of the new century, the collapse of the federalism heralded the triumph of the Jeffersonian.

In three conventions that met to revise state constitutions in Massachusetts (1820-21), New York (1821), and Virginia (1829-30) the conservatives made their hardest fight to preserve the old ways.

John Adams, Daniel Webster, Joseph Story, and Josiah Quincy in Massachusetts; Chancellor James Kent in New York; John Marshall, and John Randolph in Virginia all these worthies, old Federalists together, threw themselves into the hopeless struggle against universal suffrage.

The conventions of the 1820's were the last and most outspoken stand of genuine, antidemocratic conservatism as a major force in the life of the whole nation. The blunt language of the old-fashioned republicans was not to be heard again in public debate. While Kent wailed and Randolph sputtered, Story held fast on a Court "gone mad" and Marshall was gathered still unyielding to his fathers, the "practical" men of the Right, even such as Daniel Webster, were already moving toward a new political faith.

There was little place for a hard-bitten, plain-spoken Federalist in a land where farms, factories, railroads, and states were sprouting all over the map, and where the new voters, all of them real or potential capitalists, were proving themselves something other than European animal organ meats. Democracy had become, thanks to its breath taking yet peaceful surge to victory, the national religion, and conservatism, except in the South, was in demoralized rout.

It was Webster who made perhaps the most honorable peace, at least intellectually, with the victorious democracy; it is Webster, therefore, and who stands out from other conservatives of his time as the most promising candidate for election to the conservative hall of fame.

His political philosophy, which he expressed most powerfully in the great speech at Plymouth, December 22, 1820, looked to a "property-owner's democracy," a formula for liberty that is still dear to conservative hearts. His political actions were aimed consistently at preserving the Republic inherited from the fathers: "I go for the Constitution as it is, and for the Union as it is." For his words and deeds Webster is well remembered by thoughtful conservatives.

His character, too, is worth remembering, not because it was replete with those virtues the conservative cherishes, which it certainly was not, but because it was such an astonishing mixture of strength and weakness. While we cherish Webster the matchless orator, brilliant lawyer, and fervent patriot, we must not ignore the other Webster, the man whose hunger for cash, thirst for whiskey, and all-around appetite for the White House could never be satisfied here on earth. Webster's life is a vivid reminder that a man may be heroic in his very faults and still be a hero.

The Presidential election of 1820 was the third and last presidential election in United States history in which a candidate ran effectively unopposed. The previous two were the presidential elections of 1789 and 1792, in which George Washington ran without serious opposition.

President James Monroe and Vice President Daniel D. Tompkins were re-elected without a serious campaign. Despite the continuation of single party politics known in this case as the Era of Good Feelings, serious issues emerged during the election in 1820.

The nation had endured a widespread depression following the Panic of 1819 and the momentous issue of the extension of slavery into the territories was taking center stage. Nevertheless, James Monroe faced no opposition party or candidate in his reelection bid, although he did not receive all the electoral votes. Massachusetts had been entitled to 22 electoral votes four years earlier, but cast only 15 in 1820. This diminishing of power was brought about by the Missouri Compromise of that year that had made the region of Maine long part of Massachusetts a free state to balance the pending admission of slave state Missouri.

Pennsylvania, Tennessee, and Mississippi each cast one fewer electoral vote than the state was entitled to, on account of one elector dying before the electoral meeting. This explains the anomaly of Mississippi casting only two votes, when any state is always entitled to a minimum of three. Mississippi, Illinois and Alabama also participated in their first presidential election in 1820, but it would be almost 15 years before another state was admitted to the Union.

As we head toward the election of 1824 the country is waking from the hangover of the Jeffersonian era of more than twenty years and trying to rediscover her conservative roots.

The election was a contest among:

General Andrew Jackson of Tennessee, a charismatic hero of the War of 1812, a former United States Representative, and a then current United States Senator from Tennessee.

John Quincy Adams of Massachusetts, son of former President John Adams, former member of the Federalist Party, former United States Minister to Russia, one of the drafters of the Treaty of Ghent, former United States Senator from Massachusetts, and the then current Secretary of State.

William H. Crawford of Georgia, former United States Minister to France, former United States Senator from Georgia, former Secretary of War, and the then current Secretary of the Treasury. Henry Clay of Kentucky, the "Great Compromiser," and the then current Speaker of the United States House of Representatives.

In 1822, Jackson was nominated for president by the legislature of Tennessee; a convention of Pennsylvanian Democratic-Republicans nominated Jackson in 1824. The traditional Congressional caucus nominated Crawford for president and Albert Gallatin for vice president, but it was sparsely attended and was widely attacked as undemocratic. Gallatin later withdrew from the contest for the vice presidency. In 1823, Crawford suffered a stroke. Even though he recovered in 1824, this crippled his bid for the presidency. Also, John Quincy Adams had more support than Henry Clay because of the huge popularity he had among the old Federalist voters in New England; by now, the Adams family too had united with the Democratic-Republican Party.

The election was as much a contest of favorite sons as it was a conflict over policy positions on tariffs and internal improvements was where some significant disagreement existed, as the candidates were backed by different sections of the country. Adams was strong in the Northeast, Jackson in the South, West and mid-Atlantic, Clay in parts of the West, and Crawford in parts of the East.

John C. Calhoun of South Carolina, current Secretary of War, was initially a fifth candidate in the early stages of consideration, but he opted instead to seek the vice presidency and backed Jackson after seeing the popularity of Crawford in the South. Both Adams' and Jackson's supporters backed Calhoun, giving him an easy majority of electoral votes to be elected vice president. Campaigning for this presidential election occurred in many forms. Well known songs and tunes which have been lyrically altered, were used to promote political agendas and presidential candidates. Contrafacta such as this one, which promoted Andrew Jackson as a national hero, have been a long standing tradition in presidential elections.

Another form of campaigning during this election was through newsprint. Political cartoons and partisan writings were best circulated amongst the voting public through newspapers.

Presidential candidate John C. Calhoun may have been one of the most directly involved candidates in this election through his participation in the newspaper *The Patriot* as a member of the editorial staff. This was a sure way to promote his own political agendas and campaign. Yet it was notably unusual in that most candidates involved in early 19th century elections did not run their own political campaigns. Instead it was left to volunteer citizens and partisans to speak on behalf of and promote the candidates.

John Quincy Adams was elected President on February 9, 1825, after the election was decided by the House of Representatives.

The previous few years had seen a one-party government in the United States, as the Federalist Party had
dissolved, leaving only the Democratic-Republican Party.
In this election, the Democratic-Republican Party splin-
tered as four separate candidates sought the presidency.
Such splintering had not yet led to formal party organization, but later the faction led by Andrew Jackson would
evolve into the Democratic Party, while the factions led
by John Quincy Adams and Henry Clay would become
the National Republican Party and later the Whig Party.

This election is notable for being the only time since the
passage of the Twelfth Amendment in which the presidential election was decided by the House of Representatives, as no candidate received a majority of the electoral vote.

This presidential election was also the only one in which
the candidate receiving the most electoral votes did not
become president because a majority, not just a plurality,
is required to win. It is also often said to be the first election in which the president did not win the popular vote,
although the popular vote was not measured nationwide.
At that time, several states did not conduct a popular
vote, allowing their state legislature to choose their electors.

Adams' victory shocked Jackson, who, as the winner of a
plurality of both the popular and electoral votes, expected to be elected president. Interestingly enough, not
too long before the results of the House election, an
anonymous statement appeared in a Philadelphia paper,
called the *Columbian Observer*.

The statement, said to be from a member of Congress, essentially accused Clay of selling Adams his support for the office of Secretary of State. No formal investigation was performed, so the matter was neither confirmed nor denied. When Clay was indeed offered the position after Adams was victorious, he opted to accept and continue to support the administration he voted for; knowing that declining the position would not have helped to dispel the rumors brought against him. By appointing Clay his Secretary of State, President Adams essentially declared him heir to the Presidency, as Adams and his three predecessors had all served as Secretary of State. Jackson and his followers accused Adams and Clay of striking a "corrupt bargain". The Jacksonians would campaign on this claim for the next four years, ultimately attaining Jackson's victory in the Adams-Jackson rematch in 1828.

As president, he proposed a program of modernization and educational advancement, but was stymied by Congress, controlled by his enemies. President, Adams presented a vision of national greatness resting on economic growth and a strong federal government, but his presidency was not a success as he lacked political adroitness, popularity or a network of supporters, and ran afoul of politicians eager to undercut him.

Adams is best known as a diplomat who shaped American's foreign policy in line with his deeply conservative and ardently nationalist commitment to America's republican values. More recently he has been portrayed as the exemplar and moral leader in an era of modernization when new technologies and networks of infrastructure and communication brought to the people messages of religious revival, social reform, and party politics, as well as moving goods, money and people ever more rapidly and efficiently.

Adams was elected a U.S. Representative from Massachusetts after leaving office, the only president ever to do so, serving for the last 17 years of his life with far greater success than he had achieved in the presidency. In the House he became a leading opponent of the Slave Power and argued that if a civil war ever broke out the president could abolish slavery by using his war powers, which Abraham Lincoln partially did during the American Civil War in the 1863 Emancipation Proclamation. Deeply troubled by slavery, Adams correctly predicted the dissolution of the Union on the issue, though the series of bloody slave insurrections he foresaw never came to pass.

Adams' singular intelligence, vast experience, unquestionable integrity, and devotion to his country should have made him a great chief executive. But, like his father, he lacked political sense and ability to command public support, and his contentious spirit spelled defeat for him personally and for many of his policies. He proposed a comprehensive program of internal improvements roads, ports and canals, the creation of a national university, and federal support for the arts and sciences. He favored a high tariff to encourage the building of factories, and restricted land sales to slow the movement west. Opposition from the states' rights faction quickly killed the proposals.

During his term, Adams worked on developing the American System, consisting of a high tariff to support internal improvements such as road-building, and a national bank to encourage productive enterprise and form a national currency. In his first annual message to Congress, Adams presented an ambitious program for modernization that included roads, canals, a national university, an astronomical observatory, and other initiatives. The support for his proposals was limited, even from his own party. His critics accused him of unseemly arrogance because of his narrow victory. Most of his initiatives were opposed in Congress by Jackson's supporters, who remained outraged over the 1824 election.

After defeated for re election to Jackson in a near landslide he returned to Massachusetts In 1831, was elected to the U.S. House of Representatives. Although no abolitionist, he battled single-handedly against a southern-dominated House for the right to present petitions from antislavery groups. Subjected to a gag rule and threatened with censure and even expulsion, Adams persisted in his efforts to defend a constitutional right. Finally, in 1844, Congress repealed its gag rule and the right of petition was restored. In many ways Adams's congressional record as a champion of civil rights was the crowning point of his long career in public service.

CHAPTER FOUR Jackson Democrats vs. The Whigs

Andrew Jackson was a south westerner who combined a sense of rough egalitarianism with the gentlemanly honor typical of his class. Born in the Carolina backwoods to an immigrant farming family from Ireland, he fought in the Revolution and was captured and imprisoned by the British as a young boy. By war's end, all but one member of his immediate family had died in connection with the conflict. Jackson eventually decided to study law and then to head farther west. Although immensely ambitious, he would never lose touch with his plebeian roots.

Jackson won national fame, however, in the military. During the War of 1812, he and his troops crushed the Creek Indians after a lengthy campaign in the Mississippi Territory. Rewarded with a U.S. Army commission, he led the American forces to victory at the Battle of New Orleans, emerging as the war's greatest hero. In 1818, he ruthlessly pursued the government's war with the Seminoles into Spanish Florida, and provoked controversy by summarily executing two British subjects suspected of aiding the Indians. His deep seeded hate of Britain would haunt him forever. In 1821, he was named military governor of the Florida Territory.

When the House of Representatives decided in favor of John Quincy Adams, Jackson thundered that he was the victim of a "corrupt bargain" between Adams and Henry Clay. But building a fresh coalition of southern strict constructionists, western expansionists, and anti administration forces in the Mid-Atlantic states, he defeated Adams in 1828, believing he had vindicated his principle that "the majority is to govern." thus becoming the 7th president of the U.S under his Democratic party.

It soon became clear that Jackson's ascent marked a change in the nation's political direction. Early on, he established the principle of rotation in office, on the premise that any plain and simple man could do the people's business. Even though he really in fact never consulted the people he led as if he knew what was best for them. Much in the Jeffersonian tradition only with much more ferocity.

He checked the program of federal internal improvements offered by Adams and Clay, believing it a dangerous expansion of federal power favorable to established wealth. On Indian affairs, he ran roughshod over his critics and proclaimed a policy of forced relocation of eastern tribes west of the Mississippi River, opening fresh lands for settlers. When John Marshall the Chief Justice of the Supreme court ruled that the Cherokee Indians remain in Georgia Jackson said "Let Marshall enforce it" and removed them in the famous trail of tears in which 1 of every 4 Cherokees died.

Yet this Imperial use of his presidency didn't get him impeached for this impeachable offense. He had his own view of the constitution and it was whatever he believed at that time.

As antislavery agitation mounted a danger, he thought, to national tranquility and his own democratic political project he condemned the abolitionists and backed efforts to curtail their activities.

At the same time, he angrily defeated those emerging southern nationalists led by his former ally, John C. Calhoun who defied federal authority in the name of states' rights.

But it was Jackson's war on the Second Bank of the United States that consolidated his reputation as a champion of the common man. A hard-money advocate, suspicious of personal debt, Jackson viewed the Bank as a monstrosity that gave power over the people's money to a few unelected private bankers. After vetoing the Bank's recharter in 1832 a move that helped secure his reelection he ordered the removal of U.S. funds, tried to put the nation's economy on a hard-money footing, and revived populist, anti capitalist sentiments latent since Thomas Jefferson's presidency.

By the close of his second term, Jackson and his supporters had transformed his following into an effective national party, fashioned more or less in his own image. After seeing his protégé Martin Van Buren elected as his successor, he returned to the Hermitage, where he lived out his final years as a country gentleman and elder statesman.

Jackson's career in many ways molded the contradictory forces at work in the democratization of the early Republic. In his appeals to the common man, his attacks on privileged wealth, and his help in building a new sort of mass political party, he advanced what he thought of as the causes of equal rights and majority democracy. He also typified the tyranny of the left. During Jackson's reign as President he went through four Secretaries of Treasury officers and five Secretaries of State.

No president before or since showed the disrespect for our constitutional democracy than Andrew Jackson.

His advances went hand in hand with the continued subjugation of Native Americans and a determination not to disturb the slavery issue. Jackson stood for a more citizen ruled America, but his vision of democracy stopped squarely at the color line.

Jackson's hand picked successor was elected president in 1836, Martin Van Buren of New York a Jackson loyalist through and through. After his election to the presidency, he was faced almost immediately with a financial panic and depression. Van Buren did what he could within the limits of his ability and philosophy to cope with the economic distress.

His major remedy was the creation of an independent treasury system that divorced the federal government from the banking system. But this measure split what was now the Democratic Party. Even in a political sense, he found it much easier to be elected president than to retain public confidence in his policies. Further depression, the political divisions, and a theatrical campaign put on by the newly created Whig party brought about his defeat in 1840. He sought the nomination again in 1844, but was unable to overcome southern and expansionist opposition because of his stand against the immediate annexation of Texas.

Daniel Webster was a leading American statesman during the nation's pre -Mexican war period. Those that rose to regional prominence through his defense of New England shipping interests.

His increasingly nationalistic views and the effectiveness with which he articulated them led Webster to become one of the most famous orators and influential Whig leaders of the Second Party System.

Daniel Webster was an attorney, and served as legal counsel in several cases that established important constitutional precedents that bolstered the authority of the Federal government. As Secretary of State, he negotiated the Webster- Ashburton Treaty that established the definitive eastern border between the United States and Canada. Primarily recognized for his Senate tenure, Webster was a key figure in the institution's Golden days. So well-known was his skill as a Senator throughout this period that Webster became the northern member of a trio known as the "Great Triumvirate", with his colleagues Henry Clay from the west and John C. Calhoun from the south. His Reply to Hayne in 1830 was generally regarded as the most eloquent speech ever delivered in Congress.

As with Henry Clay, Webster's desire to see the Union preserved and conflict averted led him to search out compromises designed to stave off the sectionalism that threatened war between the North and South. Webster tried three times to achieve the Presidency; all three bids failed the final one in part because of his compromises. Similarly, Webster's efforts to steer the nation away from civil war toward a definite peace ultimately proved futile. The swift passage of the Right from the old Federalism of 1824, when story talked about the rich helping the poor and the poor administering to the rich, to the new Whiggery of 1840, when birth in a log cabin was the test of political virtue, is evidence enough of the fullness and abruptness of the sweep of democracy across the American mind.

Any discussion of the Whigs in America must include the great comprising conservative Henry Clay. As Speaker of the House, Clay was a prominent War Hawk, pushing for expansion and war with Britain. He also served as a peace commissioner in Ghent in the negotiations ending the War of 1812.

Clay's efforts to forge the Missouri Compromise (1820) were the first of several such ventures dealing with expansion and the spread of slavery. Clay was himself a slave owner, but he favored the emancipation of slaves and their resettlement in Africa.

The Election of 1824 was decided in the House of Representatives. John Quincy Adams won the presidency and selected Clay as his secretary of state a move that encouraged critics to claim a "corrupt bargain." Clay gained widespread support in his home state and throughout the West for advocacy of the American System.

In 1831, Clay returned to the Senate and emerged as the leader of the National Republican party, which later became the Whig Party. He lost a bid for the presidency in 1832, but figured prominently in Jackson's and Biddle's Bank War and the Tariff of 1833. Clay's perhaps most notable achievement came in the Compromise of 1850, in which the "Great Compromiser" managed temporarily to tame sectional passions. The Whig Party lasted only a short while following Clay's death, but their ideas, particularly the American System, were taken over by the new Republican Party.

William Henry Harrison elected the ninth president of the United States, braved cold, wet March weather to deliver the longest inaugural address in American history. The speech was his only success and his biggest mistake.
As a brave General in the Jackson tradition "Tippecanoe" as he was known arose as the new Whig party candidate for president and trounced a failing Van Buren.
Always a supporter of Henry Clay, Harrison ran on the Whig ticket in 1836 and almost won the election. Largely through conservative influence the Whig party again nominated Harrison for the presidency in 1840.
Although scarcely a person of humble background, he was pictured as the epitome of the common man of the West, the adventurous individualist who had built his own log cabin and farmed his own acres in Ohio.
The Whigs outdid themselves in image building with coonskin caps, facsimile log cabins, popular tunes, slogans, and badges that added a theatrical dimension to the emerging two-party system. Their campaign also profited from economic depression. Harrison defeated Van Buren, the Democratic candidate, by a wide margin, but died of pneumonia after only one month in office. His nearly two hour inaugural address led him to a cold which turned to pneumonia and death.

John Tyler of Virginia was the first Vice President to ascend to the Presidency. In 1840, the Whig party, seeking a southern states' righter to balance William Henry Harrison's more nationalistic views, nominated Tyler as Harrison's running mate. Tyler swept into subordinate office in the famous "Tippecanoe and Tyler Too" campaign.

His Ascendancy's greatest problem was that Whig nationalists, in command of the party, would take no commands from a states' righter like Tyler. He was no conservative and in fact a choice the Whig's would regret. Twice Henry Clay drove nationalistic bank bills through Congress. Twice Tyler vetoed them. The second time, the Whig congressional caucus drummed the president out of the party. Almost the entire cabinet then resigned. But the seemingly powerless president still remained potent enough to take advantage of the emergence of the Texas annexation issue. In the early 1840s, both major parties' leaders opposed adding the Lone Star Republic as a slave state to the nation, fearing a possible war with Mexico and an escalation of North-South tension. But Tyler was afraid that Texas, if not annexed, would ally with England to secure protection against Mexico and would be forced to emancipate its relatively few slaves in order to seal the English bargain. Tyler, determined to protect the South and states' rights, secured an annexation treaty and demanded that southern states' righters come to his aid.

Southern Jacksonians answered the call. They forced the nomination of an annexationist, James K. Polk, at the Democratic convention and won the election of 1844. Although still lacking a two-thirds majority to ratify Tyler's treaty in the Senate, the Democrats admitted Texas to the Union by resolution which required only simple majorities in House and Senate in late February 1845. A few days later, Tyler retired to his Virginia plantation. Good bye and good riddens to Tyler but hello to a tyrant in the Jackson tradition in James Polk.

After graduating from the University of North Carolina, he took up the practice of law. In 1825 he won a seat in the U.S. House of Representatives, where as a Jacksonian Democrat he distinguished himself as an advocate of states' rights. He served as Speaker of the House and governor of Tennessee.

The Walker Tariff of 1846 lowered duties, and the Independent Treasury law restored a federal depository designed to keep public money out of private banks. But the Democrats lost control of the House in 1846, and his aggressive war policy provoked the Wilmot Proviso aimed at excluding slavery from the territories taken from Mexico.

Southern conservatism in the Nineteenth Century found its most able spokesman in John C Calhoun. Calhoun was a conservative, some insisting that he was committed more deeply than he realized to Jeffersonian democracy, others that he was the Karl Marx of the master class, still others that he was little better than a fabulous reactionary.

Actually, these people are saying only that he was an heir of the constitutional tradition, or that he was more realistic than most Americans about the facts of class warfare, or that he sought to prevent the agrarian South from going the way of the industrial North. None of these charges removes him unequivocally from the conservative ranks.

Zachary Taylor (1784-1850) had a long and successful military career before becoming the 12th president of the United States, winning major victories during the Mexican-American War. The issue of whether the western territories should be open to slavery became a central focus of his short presidency. Taylor angered many southerners by encouraging residents of California and New Mexico to apply for statehood even though he knew their constitutions would prohibit slavery.

Southern Whigs angrily denounced the president and threatened secession, while Henry Clay introduced a more extensive compromise plan early in 1850. Habitually suspicious of other men's motives, Taylor stubbornly clung to his plan, and his saber-rattling against Texas in its boundary dispute with New Mexico did nothing to defuse tensions. Matters were at a stalemate when the president died suddenly on July 9, 1850, from an attack of cholera.

Taylor was honest and well intentioned, but his blunt manner and unsophisticated mind handicapped him as president. An ardent nationalist, he did not appreciate southerners' fears, and his inflexible will, which had served him well in the military, was less useful in working with Congress. Under different circumstances, he might have been a successful president, but he lacked the intellectual subtlety or political tact necessary to handle the sectional crisis.

Vice-president under Zachary Taylor, Millard Fillmore (1800-1874) became the 13th U.S. president. As the question of slavery continued to divide the nation,

Fillmore supported a series of reconciliatory measures known as the Compromise of 1850 that briefly slowed the march toward secession and civil war.

Fillmore had little influence in the new administration, and in 1850, after much hesitancy, he backed Henry Clay's compromise proposals rather than the president's plan for settling the sectional conflict. When he became president following Taylor's death in July, Fillmore, displaying rare decisiveness, threw his influence behind the compromise movement in Congress.

By September, he had signed the various compromise measures into law, and in his annual message in December, he hailed them as a final settlement of the sectional controversy.

As part of his plan to purge the Whig party of its radicalism, Fillmore began removing opponents of the compromise from federal office. This ill considered policy deepened party divisions and precipitated a bruising struggle for the 1852 presidential nomination. Fillmore was at best a reluctant candidate: though eager for the popular endorsement that the nomination would convey, he believed that no Whig could win in 1852.

Despite Fillmore's strength in the South, the Whig convention eventually nominated General Winfield Scott, who suffered a crushing defeat. Although honest and hardworking, Fillmore manifested a habitual lack of self-confidence that significantly limited his political effectiveness. He was a pompous, colorless individual who rose far beyond his ability, and as such he left only a limited mark on his generation.

From John C. Calhoun to Abraham Lincoln is a long leap, but the leap should not be impossible for those who are careful to distinguish between Calhoun's purposes, which must now seem repellent to most Americans, and his principles, which have never seemed more relevant. Lincoln is even less the property of any one group than Washington; indeed, there was something about him, perhaps the quality of pure charity that transcends politics and political theory, which makes it almost an act of impiety to pin any sort of label upon him. Yet the modern conservative has much to learn from the ideals that guided Lincoln. If he cannot claim Lincoln for his own, surely he need yield to no American in his devotion to this giant among all men.

In U.S. history, the Whigs were the major political party active in the period 1834–54 that espoused a program of national development but foundered on the rising tide of sectional antagonism. The Whig Party was formally organized in 1834, bringing together a loose coalition of groups united in their opposition to what party members viewed as the executive tyranny of "King Andrew" Jackson. They borrowed the name Whig from the British party opposed to royal prerogatives.

In its two decades of existence, the Whig Party saw two of its candidates, William Henry Harrison and Zachary Taylor, elected president. Both, however, died in office. John Tyler became president after Harrison's death, but was expelled from the party. Millard Fillmore, who became president after Taylor's death, was the last Whig to hold the nation's highest office.

The party was ultimately destroyed by the question of whether to allow the expansion of slavery to the territories. With deep fissures in the party on this question, the anti-slavery faction successfully prevented the nomination of its own incumbent President Fillmore in the 1852 presidential election; instead, the party nominated General Winfield Scott. Its leaders quit politics as Lincoln did temporarily or changed parties. The voter base defected to the Republican Party, various coalition parties in some states, and to the Democratic Party.

By the 1856 presidential election, the party had lost its ability to maintain a national coalition of effective state parties and endorsed Millard Fillmore, now of the American or Know Nothing Party at its last national convention. Fillmore had adopted a following among anti immigration Americans which was popular but fairly short lived in the pre civil war era.

CHAPTER FIVE - The birth of the Republicans

Through most of his life a conservative in whose mind devotion to law and order, respect for property, and veneration for the men of old were entrenched, Lincoln was transformed in the crucible of war into a statesman with deeply conservative instincts. His awareness of the tragedy and mystery of human life, his feeling for the slow pace of history, his patience in the face of abuses he could not alter, his identification of freedom with the Union and the American Republic these were marks of a man who met Edmund Burke's standard of a statesman. He had a disposition to preserve, and an ability to improve.

Conservatives may well go back to Lincoln's words and deeds, not to seek for a phrase here or an act there that can be dragged in to prove some petty political point, but to observe a broad pattern of life and thought that was grounded on those hard but hopeful truths about man and history to which the good conservative has always sworn allegiance. If Lincoln was something more than a great conservative, this should not render him less appealing to conservatives.

The Civil War was the great divide of American conservatism. The victory of the northern armies assured the victory of northern sentiment on two issues, slavery and the nature of the Union that had fed the fires of political thought from the beginning of the Republic. Henceforth most thinking Americans would fix their attention on another great issue.

The war as conceived and fought by the Union also sealed the triumph of the Constitution as symbol of national unity and of democracy as secular religion. Henceforth they would debate this issue in one political language.

The major point of that debate, on which all other controversies turned, was the right and capacity of government to regulate business enterprise in the general interest of the community and in the specific interest of its less fortunate members, and the struggle between Right and Left, between those who opposed reform and those who favored it, was just about the whole history of politics in the Age of Enterprise. The root cause of this struggle over the future of America was industrial capitalism.

Today, Abraham Lincoln is remembered as a visionary leader, a gifted orator and one of America's greatest presidents. In his time, however, he faced harsh criticism for his handling of the Civil War and his expansion of executive power.

He was born in a Kentucky log cabin, the son of a typical pioneer family. Never prosperous, the family moved several times, and he grew up in Kentucky and Indiana. He later reckoned that his total schooling did not exceed one year, but being unusually ambitious he pursued self-improvement through reading and longed for a better life. Lincoln's identification with the Whig party and its program to promote economic opportunity grew out of his hard times as a youth.

When he came of age, Lincoln moved to New Salem, Illinois, where he held a variety of jobs, served in the legislature, and studied law. After receiving his attorney's license, he moved to the new capital of Springfield.

He retired from the legislature after four terms, served one term in Congress (1847-1849), and then devoted himself to his legal practice and became an important and prosperous attorney.

The repeal of the Missouri Compromise in 1854 rekindled Lincoln's political ambition. He spoke eloquently against the expansion of slavery in the West, became a leader of the new Republican Party, and gained national attention in 1858 from his debates with Stephen A. Douglas.

The Republican Party which grew out of the Whig tradition was not going to fall in the trap of dragging out old Generals to try to capture the Presidency. In 1856 John C Fremont was the Republican nominee but former president and Whig Millard Fillmore fractured the election as he ran a third party campaign which helped elect James Buchanan a Democrat from Pennsylvania who was an even worse president than either Fillmore or Pierce. Surely this period was a low point for leadership in America.

John C. Fremont ran as the first Republican nominee for President in 1856, using the political slogan: "Free soil, free labor, free speech, free men, Fremont." Although Fremont's bid was unsuccessful, the party showed a strong base. It dominated in New England, New York and the northern Midwest, and had a strong presence in the rest of the North. It had almost no support in the South, where it was roundly denounced in 1856-60 as a divisive force that threatened civil war.

John C. Fremont was one of most famous explorers of the American West and a towering figure in the history of California's 19th century gold rush. Among the second rank of explorers to follow Lewis & Clark into the American frontier, in the late 1830s and early 1840s he explored and surveyed much of the American west, in particular the Oregon Trail. He eventually settled in California and grew wealthy during the gold rush of 1848. Nationally famous as an explorer, soldier and politician, in 1850 Fremont became one of the state's first two senators.

In 1838 he helped Joseph Nicholas Nicollet survey and map the upper Mississippi and Missouri Rivers. Aided by Thomas Hart Benton, who became his sponsor and, in 1841, his father-in-law, he led government expeditions to map much of the area between the Mississippi River valley and the Pacific Ocean.

In 1845, on an expedition to California on which he may have carried secret instructions for action in case of war, he supported the Bear Flag Revolt. In the Mexican War he was appointed a major and with Robert F. Stockton helped conquer California; Stockton later appointed him military governor of the territory.

In a dispute with Gen. Stephen Kearny he was arrested and court-martialed; though his sentence of dismissal from the army was set aside by Pres. James K. Polk, he resigned. In the 1870s he embarked on railroad ventures and lost his fortune. He later served as governor of the Arizona Territory from 1878 – 83.

Historians have explored the ethnic and cultural foundations of the party, along the line that ethnic and religious groups set the moral standards for their members, who then carried those standards into politics. The churches also provided social networks that politicians used to sign up voters. The pietistic churches emphasized the duty of the Christian to purge sin from society. Sin took many forms alcoholism, polygamy and slavery became special targets for the Republicans. The Yankees, who dominated New England, much of upstate New York, and much of the upper Midwest were the strongest supporters of the new party.

The Democrats favored the status quo on slavery in 1860 and they nominated Stephen Douglas, while the fractured Democrats in the South endorsed John C Breckinridge. This monumental split of the Democratic Party paved the way for clear sailing for Lincoln and the new Republican Party. Republicans favored the rights of the central government and of men. Lincoln bit a bullet that no one else dares bite. In doing so the secession that had been coming for years finally did and thank god he was there to save our union. A more liberal philosophy would have been to allow states to leave the union, but the conservative mind couldn't abide treachery such as Jefferson Davis and his ilk performed.

Taking a broad view of the president's war powers, he proclaimed a blockade, suspended the writ of habeas corpus for disloyal activity, spent money without congressional authorization, and controlled the war effort. On most legislative matters he yielded to Congress, but he carefully preserved his independence on questions that he considered executive responsibility.

Despite his military inexperience, he displayed a shrewd grasp of military strategy, recognizing from the beginning the importance of the western theater and the necessity of taking advantage of the Union's superior resources. It took him several years, however, to find competent generals to implement this strategy.

Abraham Lincoln continues to have a unique appeal for his fellow countrymen and also for people of other lands. His distinctively human and humane personality as well as from his historical role as savior of the Union and emancipator of the slaves. His relevance endures and grows especially because of his eloquence as a spokesman for democracy. In his view, the Union was worth saving not only for its own sake but because it embodied an ideal, the ideal of self-government. In recent years, the political side to Lincoln's character and his racial views in particular, has come under close scrutiny, as scholars continue to find him a rich subject for research. In 1836, having passed the bar examination, he began to practice law. The next year he moved to Springfield, Illinois, the new state capital, which offered many more opportunities for a lawyer than New Salem did.

The coming of the railroads, especially after 1850, made travel easier and practice more remunerative. Lincoln served as a lobbyist for the Illinois Central Railroad, assisting it in getting a charter from the state, and thereafter he was retained as a regular attorney for that railroad. By the time he began to be prominent in national politics, about 20 years after launching his legal career, Lincoln had made himself one of the most distinguished and successful lawyers in Illinois.

He was noted not only for his shrewdness and practical common sense, which enabled him always to see to the heart of any legal case, but also for his invariable fairness and utter honesty.

Early in life Lincoln had been something of a skeptic and freethinker. His reputation had been such that, as he once complained, the "church influence" was used against him in politics. When running for Congress in 1846, he issued a handbill to deny that he ever had "spoken with intentional disrespect of religion." He went on to explain that he had believed in the doctrine of necessity "that is, that the human mind is impelled to action, or held in rest by some power over which the mind itself has no control."

Throughout his life he also believed in dreams and other enigmatic signs and portents. As he grew older, and especially after he became president and faced the soul-troubling responsibilities of the Civil War, he developed a profound religious sense, and he increasingly personified necessity as God. He came to look upon himself quite humbly as an "instrument of Providence" and to view all history as God's enterprise. "In the present civil war," he wrote in 1862, "it is quite possible that God's purpose is something different from the purpose of either party and yet the human instrumentalities, working just as they do, are of the best adaptation to affect His purpose."

Lincoln was fond of the Bible and knew it well. He also was fond of Shakespeare. In private conversation he used many Shakespearean allusions, discussed problems of dramatic interpretation with considerable insight, and recited long passages from memory with rare feeling and understanding.

When Lincoln first entered politics, Andrew Jackson was president. Lincoln shared the sympathies that the Jacksonians professed for the common man, but he disagreed with the Jacksonian view that the government should be divorced from economic enterprise. "The legitimate object of government," he was later to say, "is to do for a community of people whatever they need to have done, but cannot do at all, or cannot do so well, for themselves, in their separate and individual capacities." Among the prominent politicians of his time, he most admired Henry Clay and Daniel Webster. Clay and Webster advocated using the powers of the federal government to encourage business and develop the country's resources by means of a national bank, a protective tariff, and a program of internal improvements for facilitating transportation. In Lincoln's view, Illinois and the West as a whole desperately needed such aid for economic development. From the outset, he associated himself with the party of Clay and Webster, the Whigs.

During his single term in Congress (1847–49), Lincoln, as the lone Whig from Illinois, gave little attention to legislative matters. He proposed a bill for the gradual and compensated emancipation of slaves in the District of Columbia, but, because it was to take effect only with the approval of the "free white citizens" of the district, it displeased abolitionists as well as slaveholders and never was seriously considered.

Lincoln devoted much of his time to presidential politics to unmaking one president, a Democrat, and making another, a Whig. He found an issue and a candidate in the Mexican War. He challenged the statement of President James K. Polk that Mexico had started the war by shedding American blood upon American soil.

Along with other members of his party, Lincoln voted to condemn Polk and the war while also voting for supplies to carry it on. At the same time, he labored for the nomination and election of the war hero Zachary Taylor. After Taylor's success at the polls, Lincoln expected to be named commissioner of the general land office as a reward for his campaign services, and he was bitterly disappointed when he failed to get the job.

His criticisms of the war, meanwhile, had not been popular among the voters in his own congressional district. At the age of 40, frustrated in politics, he seemed to be at the end of his public career.

For about five years Lincoln took little part in politics, and then a new sectional crisis gave him a chance to re-emerge and rise to statesmanship. In 1854 his political rival Stephen A. Douglas maneuvered through Congress a bill for reopening the entire Louisiana Purchase to slavery and allowing the settlers of Kansas and Nebraska to decide for them whether to permit slaveholding in those territories. The Kansas-Nebraska Act provoked violent opposition in Illinois and the other states of the old Northwest. It gave rise to the Republican Party while speeding the Whig Party on its way to disintegration.

Along with many thousands of other homeless Whigs, Lincoln soon became a Republican (1856). Before long, some prominent Republicans in the East talked of attracting Douglas to the Republican fold, and with him his Democratic following in the West. Lincoln would have none of it.

Lincoln challenged the incumbent Douglas for the Senate seat in 1858, and the series of debates they engaged in throughout Illinois was political oratory of the highest order. Both men were shrewd debaters and accomplished stump speakers, though they could hardly have been more different in style and appearance the short and pudgy Douglas, whose powerful voice and graceful gestures swayed audiences, and the tall, homely, almost emaciated looking Lincoln, who moved awkwardly and whose voice was piercing and shrill. Lincoln's prose and speeches, however, were eloquent, pithy, powerful, and free of the verbosity so common in communication of his day.

In their basic views, Lincoln and Douglas were not as far apart as they seemed in the heat of political argument. Neither was abolitionist or proslavery. But Lincoln, unlike Douglas, insisted that Congress must exclude slavery from the territories. He disagreed with Douglas's belief that the territories were by nature unsuited to the slave economy and that no congressional legislation was needed to prevent the spread of slavery into them. In one of his most famous speeches, he said: "*A house divided against itself cannot stand. I believe the government cannot endure permanently half slave and half free.*"

In the end, Lincoln lost the election to Douglas. Although the outcome did not surprise him, it depressed him deeply. Lincoln had, nevertheless, gained national recognition and soon began to be mentioned as a presidential prospect for 1860.

On May 18, 1860, after Lincoln and his friends had made skillful preparations, he was nominated on the third ballot at the Republican National Convention in Chicago.
After Lincoln's election and before his inauguration, the state of South Carolina proclaimed its withdrawal from the Union. To forestall similar action by other Southern states, various compromises were proposed in Congress. The most important, the Crittenden Compromise included constitutional amendments guaranteeing slavery forever in the states where it already existed and dividing the territories between slavery and freedom.

Although Lincoln had no objection to the first of these amendments, he was unalterably opposed to the second and indeed to any scheme infringing in the slightest upon the free-soil plank of his party's platform. He feared that a territorial division, by sanctioning the principle of slavery extension, would only encourage planter imperialists to seek new slave territory south of the American border and thus would "put us again on the highroad to a slave empire." From his home in Springfield he advised Republicans in Congress to vote against a division of the territories, and the proposal was killed in committee. Six additional states then seceded and, with South Carolina, combined to form the Confederate States of America.

Thus, before Lincoln had even moved into the White House, a disunion crisis was upon the country. Attention, North and South, focused in particular upon Fort Sumter, in Charleston Harbor, South Carolina. This fort, still under construction, was garrisoned by U.S. troops under Major Robert Anderson. The Confederacy claimed it and, from other harbor fortifications, threatened it.

Foreseeing trouble, Lincoln, while still in Springfield, confidentially requested Winfield Scott, general in chief of the U.S. Army, to be prepared "to either *hold*, or *retake*, the forts, as the case may require, at, and after the inauguration."

No sooner was he in office than Lincoln received word that the Sumter garrison, unless supplied or withdrawn, would shortly be starved out. Still, for about a month, Lincoln delayed acting. He was beset by contradictory advice. On the one hand, General Scott, Secretary of State William H. Seward, and others urged him to abandon the fort; and Seward, through a go-between, gave a group of Confederate commissioners to understand that the fort would in fact be abandoned. On the other hand, many Republicans insisted that any show of weakness would bring disaster to their party and to the Union. Finally Lincoln ordered the preparation of two relief expeditions, one for Fort Sumter and the other for Fort Pickens, in Florida.

Without waiting for the arrival of Lincoln's expedition, the Confederate authorities presented to Major Anderson a demand for Sumter's prompt evacuation, which he refused. On April 12, 1861, at dawn, the Confederate batteries in the harbor opened fire.

"Then, and thereby," Lincoln informed Congress when it met on July 4, "the assailants of the Government, began the conflict of arms." The Confederates, however, accused him of being the real aggressor. They said he had cleverly maneuvered them into firing the first shot so as to put upon them the onus of war guilt. Although some historians have repeated this charge, it appears to be a gross distortion of the facts.

Lincoln was determined to preserve the Union, and to do so he thought he must take a stand against the Confederacy. He concluded he might as well take this stand at Sumter.

Lincoln's primary aim was neither to provoke war nor to maintain peace. In preserving the Union, he would have been glad to preserve the peace also, but he was ready to risk a war that he thought would be short.

From 1861 to 1864, while hesitating to impose his ideas upon his generals, Lincoln experimented with command personnel and organization. Accepting the resignation of Scott November of 1861, he put George B. McClellan in charge of the armies as a whole. After a few months, disgusted by the slowness of McClellan he demoted him to the command of the Army of the Potomac alone. He questioned the soundness of McClellan's plans for the Peninsular Campaign, repeatedly compelled McClellan to alter them, and, after the Seven Days' Battles to capture Richmond, Virginia June 25–July 1, 1862, failed, ordered him to give them up. Then he tried a succession of commanders for the army in Virginia John Pope, McClellan again, Ambrose E. Burnside, Joseph Hooker, and George Gordon Meade but was disappointed with each of them in turn.

Finally Lincoln looked to the West for a top general. He admired the Vicksburg Campaign of Ulysses S. Grant in Mississippi. Nine days after the Vicksburg surrender which occurred on July 4, 1863, he sent Grant a "grateful acknowledgment for the almost inestimable service" he had done the country. Lincoln sent also an admission of his own error.

He said he had expected Grant to bypass Vicksburg and go on down the Mississippi, instead of crossing the river and turning back to approach Vicksburg from the rear. "I feared it was a mistake," he wrote in his letter of congratulations. "I now wish to make the personal acknowledgment that you were right, and I was wrong."

On the issue of emancipation, Lincoln moved cautiously, insisting that his main priority was to save the Union. As the war continued, however, he became convinced that undermining slavery would weaken the Confederacy, and on January 1, 1863, he issued the Emancipation Proclamation. The proclamation applied only to areas under Confederate control, and its legal impact was uncertain, but it redefined the nature of the war and was of great symbolic significance.

Nevertheless, Lincoln seemed certain to be defeated in 1864. He faced a challenge from the former Union General whom had commanded the Union Army and failed, George C McClelan. Lincoln's record on civil liberties provoked protests, public opinion remained divided over emancipation, even Republicans lacked confidence in him, and most important, no end to the war was in sight. Sherman's capture of Atlanta in September, however, revived northern spirits and Lincoln was easily reelected. A few months later, in the hour of the Union's victory, he was cut down by an assassin's bullet.

Lincoln is justly considered our greatest president. He was a masterful politician, sensitive to and yet constantly shaping public opinion, skilled at balancing competing considerations, and extraordinarily adept at getting rival groups to work together toward a common goal.

His leadership qualities were demonstrated in his brilliant handling of the border slave states at the beginning of the fighting, in his defeat of a congressional attempt to reorganize his cabinet in 1862, and in his defusing of the peace issue in the 1864 campaign when he maneuvered the Confederacy into rejecting negotiations. Never losing sight of the larger aims of the war, he remained flexible in his approach to problems, as evidenced by his evolving policies on emancipation and Reconstruction. Nevertheless, the toll of the war was visible in his haggard face:

he stoically endured more than any other president personal slights, public ridicule, and criticism beyond the bounds of all decency, had his hopes dashed by one humiliating military defeat after another, and suffered deep personal anguish over the mounting casualty lists. Yet he never faltered in his resolve to persevere to save the union. After the war, the slaves freed by the proclamation would have risked re-enslavement had nothing else been done to confirm their liberty. But something else was done: the Thirteenth Amendment was added to the Constitution, and Lincoln played a large part in bringing about this change in the fundamental law.

Through the chairman of the Republican National Committee he urged the party to include a plank for such an amendment in its platform of 1864. The plank, as adopted, stated that slavery was the cause of the rebellion, that the president's proclamation had aimed a death blow at this great evil, and that a constitutional amendment was necessary to terminate and forever prohibit it.

When Lincoln was reelected on this platform and the Republican majority in Congress was increased, he was justified in feeling, as he apparently did, that he had a mandate from the people for the Thirteenth Amendment. The newly chosen Congress, with its overwhelming Republican majority, was not to meet until after the lame duck session of the old Congress during the winter of 1864–65. Lincoln did not wait. Using his resources of patronage and persuasion upon certain of the Democrats, he managed to get the necessary two-thirds vote before the session's end.

The civil war changed America from an agrarian based economy to an industrialized economy. Change, rapid, massive, and unsettling was now the dominant characteristic of the American scene. Leaders of the Right served as the chief agents of change, confident that their mines and mills could bring them power and riches without disrupting the established order.

Any discussion of conservatives should include a great friend of the Republican movement Horace White. White was one of the leading American journalists of his time and one of the last of the group of great New York editors. While he managed to keep a low profile, his influence was felt and respected by many of the personalities of his day. He knew John Brown and other militant Free-Soilers and helped his friend Abraham Lincoln achieve the highest political office in the land.

Always a crusader, he not only reported but also participated in some of the major events of his time, such as the Conservative Republican movement in the East in the 1870s.

He was an authority on finance and economics, and his editorials in the *New York Evening Post* for over twenty years were regarded as the most influential essays on finance in the country.

An editorial in the *New York Times* mourning his death observed that White "had exerted a strong influence upon the education of the public mind and the development of an understanding of the necessity of sound government finance." The editorial concluded that "as a newspaper editor, as a speaker, as a writer of books and pamphlets, Horace White was conspicuously instrumental in securing our financial salvation." White was instrumental in advising either directly or indirectly our presidents and congressional leaders of the late 19th century in America.

Another great conservative influence during the later 19th century was William Graham Sumner. Sumner grew up in Hartford, Connecticut, the son of a working-class English immigrant. After graduating from Yale University in 1863, he studied for the ministry and eventually became a priest in the Protestant Episcopal Church. In 1872, however, he left the ministry and returned to Yale as professor of political and social science. He quickly became a popular teacher known for his provocative ideas, rigorous intellectual standards and staunch moral conviction. He continued teaching at Yale until his death almost forty years later. In his lectures and writings, Sumner became one of the leading proponents of laissez-faire economics, opposing all government efforts to regulate business or to combat social inequality.

As one historian summarized this worldview, "Inequality, expressed in the ability of some men to accumulate substantial wealth by frugal living and hard work, was for him the mainspring of material progress in a society of open competition."

He criticized welfare programs for foolishly disrupting this rightful stratification and unfairly burdening what he called "the forgotten man," the autonomous citizen who worked hard and pulled his own weight. In many ways Sumner was a guiding force in the American Conservative movement. Seeing early on the welfare programs could in fact become a new form of slavery to a great segment of society.

His own father had been a working man, forced to flee England when he could find no work, but Sumner's arguments were against all forms of business regulation, labor unions, or public welfare. He was a lifelong Democrat but during this period the lines of party were not as ideologically based as before or after in America.

After the civil war Ulysses S. Grant the hero general of the war became the second Republican president of the United States. His philosophy was one of conservation and reconstruction during a very difficult time in our history. Coming into office, President Grant alienated party stalwarts by eschewing party politics. When he appointed his cabinet, he did not turn to Republicans for their advice. Instead, he chose people he thought he could trust and to whom he could delegate responsibility. This strategy led to some good cabinet appointments but also to a number of dubious ones. Grant was also loyal out of all proportion to anyone who had helped him or worked with him.

In his first inaugural address, Grant spoke of his desire for the ratification of the Fifteenth Amendment, which sought to grant citizens the right to vote regardless of race or previous servitude. He lobbied hard to get the amendment passed, angering many Southern whites in the process. He also, on occasion, sent in the military to protect African Americans from newly formed terrorist groups, such as the Ku Klux Klan, which tried to prevent blacks from participating in society. Grant incurred the wrath of citizens who blamed him for the economic woes that plagued the nation in the aftermath of the war. In 1872, however, Grant won reelection.

During his second term, a depression in Europe spread to the United States, resulting in high unemployment. Scandals also diverted attention from the administration's efforts. Although Grant was never personally implicated in any of the scandals, he did not disassociate himself from the members of his administration who were guilty. His inability to clean up his administration tarnished his reputation in the eyes of the American public. In 1875, he announced that he would not seek a third term.

After his presidency, Grant found himself in economic difficulties and dying of throat cancer. He lost his money in a financial scandal, yet he was determined to provide for his family after his death. After Century Magazine approached him to write articles about his Civil War experiences, Grant discovered that he enjoyed the process and decided to compile his memoirs. He approached this last battle as he had all others with grim and dogged determination. His final days were spent on his porch with pencil and paper in hand, wrapped in blankets and in fearsome pain, slowly scrawling out his life's epic tale.

He completed the book just days before his death. It was hugely successful and provided for his family's financial security.

At the Republican national nominating convention in 1876, the party was split between one faction who supported a third term for President Ulysses S. Grant and another faction who supported the nomination of Speaker of the House James G. Blaine of Maine.
As a compromise candidate, Hayes earned the party's nomination on the seventh ballot. His reputation for being honest, loyal and inclusive offered a departure from the charges of impropriety in Grant's administration.

In the 1876 presidential election between Hayes and Democrat Samuel J. Tilden, the governor of New York, Tilden won the popular vote. However, the Democratic and the Republican parties in Florida, Louisiana and South Carolina each sent their own conflicting ballot results to Washington. Because there were two sets of results from each state with each party's tally declaring its own candidate to be the victor Congress appointed a 15-member commission to determine the winner of each state's electoral votes.

The commission, which had a Republican majority, chose to award the disputed electoral votes to Hayes. Southern Democrats agreed to back the decision if the Republicans would recall the federal troops that were supporting Reconstruction. At the urging of the Southern Democrats, the Republicans also agreed to appoint at least one Southerner to Hayes' cabinet.
When the commission voted to award all the contested electoral votes to Hayes, he tallied 185 electoral votes to Tilden's 184.

Hayes was declared the winner on March 2, 1877. He took the presidential oath of office in a private ceremony at the White House the next day; a public inauguration followed on March 5. Northern Democrats who were unhappy with the outcome declared that Hayes had stolen the election.

In addition to party politics, Hayes experienced policy difficulties that arose outside Washington. Because of the economic downturn following the Civil War, Western and Southern states sought to strengthen the dollar.
They wanted to do this through the Bland-Allison Act , sponsored by Representative Richard P. Bland of Missouri and Representative William B. Allison of Iowa. The act allowed the federal government to resume minting silver coins, which had been halted five years earlier. With inflation a primary concern, Hayes and others who supported a gold standard for the nation's currency stood against the measure. However, Bland-Allison passed over Hayes' veto. Hayes declined to run for the presidency a second time, and retired from politics after his single term in the Oval Office ended.

While Hayes wasn't the most conservative choice of 1876 he was an effective and honest man who carried on nobly the new Republican revolution. After leaving the White House, Hayes and his wife Lucy returned to their estate, Spiegel Grove, in Fremont, Ohio, and the former president devoted himself to educational issues and prison reform, among other humanitarian causes.

Henry George was an American writer, politician and political economist, who was the most influential proponent of the land value tax, also known as the "single tax" on land.

He inspired the philosophy and economic ideology known as Georgism, which is that everyone owns what he or she creates, but that everything found in nature, most importantly land, belongs equally to all humanity. His most famous work is *Progress and Poverty* written during 1879; it is a treatise on inequality, the cyclic nature of industrial economies and possible remedies. His formal education ended at age 14 and he went to sea as a foremast boy at age 15 in April 1855 on the *Hindoo*, bound for Melbourne and Calcutta.

He returned to Philadelphia after 14 months at sea to become an apprentice typesetter before settling in California. After a failed attempt at gold mining he began work with the newspaper industry during 1865, starting as a printer, continuing as a journalist, and ending as an editor and proprietor. He worked for several papers, including four years (1871–1875) as editor of his own newspaper *San Francisco Daily Evening Post*.

George began as a Lincoln Republican, but then became a Democrat, once losing an election to the California State Assembly. He was a strong critic of railroad and mining interests, corrupt politicians, land speculators, and labor contractors. One day during 1871 George went for a horseback ride and stopped to rest while overlooking San Francisco Bay. Furthermore, on a visit to New York City, he was struck by the apparent paradox that the poor in that long established city were much worse off than the poor in less developed California. These observations supplied the theme and title for his 1879 book *Progress and Poverty*, which was a great success, selling over 3 million copies.

In it George made the argument that a sizeable portion of the wealth created by social and technological advances in a free market economy is possessed by land owners and monopolists via economic rents, and that this concentration of unearned wealth is the main cause of poverty. George considered it a great injustice that private profit was being earned from restricting access to natural resources while productive activity was burdened with heavy taxes, and indicated that such a system was equivalent to slavery, a concept somewhat similar to wage slavery.

George was in a position to discover this pattern, having experienced poverty himself, knowing many different societies from his travels, and living in California at a time of rapid growth. In particular he had noticed that the construction of railroads in California was increasing land values and rents as fast or faster than wages were rising.

During 1880, now a popular writer and speaker, George moved to New York City, becoming closely allied with the Irish nationalist community despite being of English ancestry. From there he made several speaking journeys abroad to places such as Ireland and Scotland where access to land was and still is a major political issue.

During 1886 George campaigned for mayor of New York City as the candidate of the United Labor Party, the short-lived political society of the Central Labor Union. He polled second, more than the Republican candidate Theodore Roosevelt. The election was won by Tammany Hall candidate Abram Stevens Hewitt by what many of George's supporters believed was fraud. In the 1887 New York state elections George came in a distant third in the election for Secretary of State of New York.

The United Labor Party was soon weakened by internal divisions: the management was essentially Georgist, but as a party of organized labor it also included some Marxist members who did not want to distinguish between land and capital, many Catholic members who were discouraged by the excommunication of Father Edward McGlynn, and many who disagreed with George's free trade policy. Against the advice of his doctors, George campaigned for mayor again during 1897, this time as an Independent Democrat. He died of a stroke four days before the election. An estimated 100,000 people attended his funeral.

Reconstruction came to an end when the contested election of 1876 was awarded by a special electoral commission to Republican Rutherford B. Hayes who promised, through the unofficial Compromise of 1877, to withdraw federal troops from control of the last three southern states. The region then became the Solid South, giving overwhelming majorities of its electoral votes and Congressional seats to the Democrats until 1964.

In terms of racial issues, "White Republicans as well as Democrats solicited black votes but reluctantly rewarded blacks with nominations for office only when necessary, even then reserving the more choice positions for whites. The results were predictable: these half-a-loaf gestures satisfied neither black nor white Republicans.

The fatal weakness of the Republican Party in Alabama, as elsewhere in the South, was its inability to create a bi-racial political party. And while in power even briefly, they failed to protect their members from Democratic terror. Alabama Republicans were forever on the defensive, verbally and physically."

Social pressure eventually forced most Scalawags to join the conservative/Democratic Redeemer coalition. A minority persisted and formed the "tan" half of the "Black and Tan" Republican Party, a minority in every southern state after 1877.

The Republican party split into two factions The "GOP" short for Grand Old Party, as it was now nicknamed split into factions in the late 1870s. The Stalwarts, followers of Senator Roscoe Conkling, defended the spoils system. The Half-Breeds, who followed Senator James G. Blaine of Maine, pushed for reform of the Civil service. Independents who opposed the spoils system altogether were called "Mugwumps." In 1884 Mugwumps rejected James G. Blaine as corrupt and helped elect Democrat Grover Cleveland; most returned to the party by 1888.

As the Northern post-war economy boomed with industry, railroads, mines, and fast-growing cities, as well as prosperous agriculture, the Republicans took credit and promoted policies to keep the fast growth going. The Democratic Party was largely controlled by pro-business Bourbon Democrats until 1896. The GOP supported big business generally, the gold standard, high tariffs, and generous pensions for Union veterans. By 1890, however, the Republicans had agreed to the Sherman Anti-Trust Act and the Interstate Commerce Commission in response to complaints from owners of small businesses and farmers. The high McKinley Tariff of 1890 hurt the party and the Democrats swept to a landslide in the off-year elections, even defeating McKinley himself.

Demographic trends aided the Democrats, as the German and Irish Catholic immigrants were Democrats, and outnumbered the English and Scandinavian Republicans. During the 1880s and 1890s, the Republicans struggled against the Democrats' efforts, winning several close elections and losing two to Grover Cleveland in 1884 and 1892.

Religious lines were sharply drawn. Methodists, Congregationalists, Presbyterians, Scandinavian Lutherans and other pietists in the North were tightly linked to the GOP. In sharp contrast, liturgical groups, especially the Catholics, Episcopalians, and German Lutherans, looked to the Democratic Party for protection from pietistic moralism, especially prohibition. Both parties cut across the class structure, with the Democrats more bottom-heavy.

Cultural issues, especially prohibition and foreign language schools became important because of the sharp religious divisions in the electorate. In the North, about 50% of the voters were pietistic Protestants, Methodists, Scandinavian, Lutherans, Presbyterians, Congregationalists, Disciples of Christ who believed the government should be used to reduce social sins, such as drinking. Liturgical churches Roman Catholics, German Lutherans, Episcopalians comprised over a quarter of the vote and wanted the government to stay out of the morality business.

The election of William McKinley in 1896 is widely seen as a resurgence of Republican dominance and is sometimes cited as a realigning election. McKinley promised that high tariffs would end the severe hardship caused by the Panic of 1893, and that the GOP would guarantee a sort of pluralism in which all groups would benefit.

He denounced William Jennings Bryan, the Democratic nominee, as a dangerous radical whose plans for "Free Silver" would bankrupt the economy. McKinley relied heavily on finance, railroads, industry and the middle classes for his support and cemented the Republicans as the party of business; his campaign manager, Ohio's Mark Hanna, developed a detailed plan for getting contributions from the business world, and McKinley outspent his rival William Jennings Bryan by a large margin.

This emphasis on business was in part mitigated by Theodore Roosevelt, McKinley's successor after assassination, who engaged in trust-busting. McKinley was the first president to promote pluralism, arguing that prosperity would be shared by all ethnic and religious groups. Theodore Roosevelt, who became president in 1901, had the most dynamic personality of the era in the nation. Roosevelt had to contend with men like Senator Mark Hanna, whom he outmaneuvered to gain control of the convention in 1904 that re nominated him and he won after promising to continue McKinley's policies.

More difficult to handle was conservative House Speaker Joseph Gurney Cannon. Roosevelt did endure over Speaker Cannon and Senator Hanna as well. He was brash, but articulate and very popular with the masses. The Republican party would win the Presidency and hold the office all but eight years out of forty from 1860 to 1900. Truly these days began a movement that would start with saving our union and see us through the greatest industrialization in world history.

From Lincoln through Roosevelt the Republican party shaped much of what became a thriving world power economically and financially.

Even the eight years that Democrat Grover Cleveland held office, though he was a Democrat he was a solid Conservative possibly more than most others of that time.

CHAPTER SIX - The Gilded Age

The Gilded Age was rooted in industrialization, especially heavy industry like factories, railroads and coal mining. The First Transcontinental Railroad opened in 1869, providing six-day service between the East Coast and San Francisco.

During the Gilded Age, American manufacturing production surpassed the combined total of Britain, Germany, and France. Railroad mileage tripled between 1860 and 1880, and tripled again by 1920, opening new areas to commercial farming, creating a truly national marketplace and inspiring a boom in coal mining and steel production. The voracious appetite for capital of the great trunk railroads facilitated the consolidation of the nation's financial market in Wall Street. By 1900, the process of economic concentration had extended into most branches of industry a few large corporations, called "trusts", dominated in steel, oil, sugar, meatpacking, and the manufacture of agriculture machinery. Other major components of this infrastructure were the new methods for fabricating steel, especially the Bessemer process. The first billion dollar corporation was United States Steel, formed by financier J. P. Morgan in 1901, who purchased and consolidated steel firms built by Andrew Carnegie and others.

J.P. Morgan was an American financier, banker and art collector who dominated corporate finance and industrial consolidation during his time.

In 1892 Morgan arranged the merger of Edison General Electric and Thomson-Houston Electric Company to form General Electric. After financing the creation of the Federal Steel Company he merged the Carnegie Steel Company and several other steel and iron businesses to form the United States Steel Corporation in 1901.

He died in Rome, Italy, in 1913 at the age of 75, leaving his fortune and business to his son, John Pierpont "Jack" Morgan, Jr., and bequeathing his mansion and large book collections to The Morgan Library & Museum in New York. By 1901, he was one of the wealthiest men in the world. At the height of Morgan's career during the early 1900s, he and his partners had financial investments in many large corporations and was accused by critics of controlling the nation's high finance. He directed the banking coalition that stopped the Panic of 1907.

He was the leading financier of the Progressive Era, and his dedication to efficiency and modernization helped transform American business. Morgan redefined conservatism in terms of financial prowess coupled with strong commitments to religion and to high culture.

During the early days of the American Civil War, U.S. forces in the field could not get enough rifles. Morgan financed the purchase and upgrading of old Hall carbines, which were quickly shipped to troops in Missouri. His profit was $5400, but after he ended his role the company that bought the rifles had to sue the government for the money it was due; it won in court but socialists for years accused Morgan falsely of selling defective guns. Morgan's ascent to power was accompanied by dynamic financial battles.

He wrested control of the Albany and Susquehanna Railroad from Jay Gould and Jim Fisk in 1869. He led the syndicate that broke the government-financing privileges of Jay Cooke, and soon became deeply involved in developing and financing a railroad empire by reorganizations and consolidations in all parts of the United States.

He raised large sums in Europe, but instead of only handling the funds, he helped the railroads reorganize and achieve greater efficiencies. He fought against the speculators interested in speculative profits, and built a vision of an integrated transportation system. In 1885, he reorganized the New York, West Shore & Buffalo Railroad, leasing it to the New York Central. In 1886, he reorganized the Philadelphia & Reading, and in 1888 the Chesapeake & Ohio. He was heavily involved with railroad tycoon James J. Hill and the Great Northern Railway.

After Congress passed the Interstate Commerce Act in 1887, Morgan set up conferences in 1889 and 1890 that brought together railroad presidents in order to help the industry follow the new laws and write agreements for the maintenance of "public, reasonable, uniform and stable rates." The conferences were the first of their kind, and by creating a community of interest among competing lines paved the way for the great consolidations of the early 20th century.

In 1895, at the depths of the Panic of 1893, the Federal Treasury was nearly out of gold. President Grover Cleveland arranged for Morgan to create a private syndicate on Wall Street to supply the U.S. Treasury with $65 million in gold, half of it from Europe, to float a bond issue that restored the treasury surplus of $100 million.

The episode saved the Treasury but hurt Cleveland with the agrarian wing of his Democratic party and became an issue in the election of 1896, when banks came under withering attack from William Jennings Bryan. Morgan and Wall Street bankers donated heavily to Republican William McKinley, who was elected in 1896 and re-elected in 1900 on a gold standard platform.

In 1901 U.S. Steel was as the first billion dollar company in the world with an authorized capitalization of $1.4 billion much larger than any other industrial firm, and comparable in size to the largest railroads. U.S. Steel aimed to achieve greater economies of scale, reduce transportation and resource costs, expand product lines, and improve distribution. It was also planned to allow the United States to compete globally with Britain and Germany. U.S. Steel's size was claimed by Charles M. Schwab and others to allow the company to pursue distant international markets-globalization. U.S. Steel was regarded as a monopoly by critics, as the business was attempting to dominate not only steel but also the construction of bridges, ships, railroad cars and rails, wire, nails, and a host of other products. With U.S. Steel, Morgan had captured two-thirds of the steel market, and Schwab was confident that the company would soon hold a 75 percent market share.

However, after 1901 the businesses' market share dropped. Schwab resigned from U.S. Steel in 1903 to form Bethlehem Steel, which became the second largest U.S. producer on the strength of such innovations as the wide flange "H" beam precursor to the I-beam widely used in construction.

While conservatives in the Progressive Era hailed Morgan for his civic responsibility, his strengthening of the national economy, and his devotion to the arts and religion, the left wing felt threatened by his enormous economic power.

Enemies of banking attacked Morgan for the terms of his loan of gold to the federal government in the 1895 crisis, for his financial resolution of the Panic of 1907, and for bringing on the financial ills of the New York, New Haven and Hartford Railroad. In December 1912, Morgan testified before the Pujo Committee, a subcommittee of the House Banking and Currency committee. The committee ultimately found that a group of financial leaders were abusing their public trust to consolidate control over many industries: the partners of J.P. Morgan & Co. along with the directors of First National and National City Bank controlled aggregate resources of $22.245 billion. Louis Brandeis, later a U.S. Supreme Court Justice, compared this sum to the value of all the property in the twenty-two states west of the Mississippi River.

The Panic of 1907 was a financial crisis that almost crippled the American economy. Major New York banks were on the verge of bankruptcy and there was no mechanism to rescue them until Morgan stepped in personally and took charge, resolving the crisis.- Treasury Secretary George B. Cortelyou earmarked $35 million of federal money to quell the storm but had no easy way to use it. Morgan now took personal charge, meeting with the nation's leading financiers in his New York mansion; he forced them to devise a plan to meet the crisis. James Stillman, president of the National City Bank, also played a central role.

Morgan organized a team of bank and trust executives which redirected money between banks, secured further international lines of credit, and bought plummeting stocks of healthy corporations. A delicate political issue arose regarding the brokerage firm of Moore and Schley, which was deeply involved in a speculative pool in the stock of the Tennessee Coal, Iron and Railroad Company. Moore and Schley had pledged over six million of the Tennessee Coal and Iron stock for loans among the Wall Street banks. The banks had called the loans, and the firm could not pay. If Moore and Schley should fail, a hundred more failures would follow and then all Wall Street might go to pieces.

Morgan decided they had to save Moore and Schley. TCI was one of the chief competitors of U.S. Steel and it owned valuable iron and coal deposits. Morgan controlled U.S. Steel and he decided it had to buy the TCI stock from Moore and Schley. Judge Gary, head of US Steel, agreed, but would there be antitrust implications that could cause grave trouble for US Steel, which was already dominant in the steel industry? Morgan sent Gary to see President Theodore Roosevelt, who promised legal immunity for the deal. U.S. Steel thereupon paid $30 million for the TCI stock and Moore and Schley was saved. The announcement had an immediate effect; by November 7, 1907, the panic was over. Vowing to never let it happen again, and realizing that in a future crisis there was not likely to be another Morgan, banking and political leaders, led by Senator Nelson Aldrich devised a plan that became the Federal Reserve System in 1913.

Increased mechanization of industry is a major mark of the Gilded Age's search for cheaper ways to create more product. Frederick Winslow Taylor observed that worker efficiency in steel could be improved through the use of machines to make fewer motions in less time. His redesign increased the speed of factory machines and the productivity of factories while undercutting the need for skilled labor. This mechanization made some factories an assemblage of unskilled laborers performing simple and repetitive tasks under the direction of skilled foremen and engineers. Machine shops grew rapidly, and they comprised highly skilled workers and engineers. Both the number of unskilled and skilled workers increased, as their wage rates grew Engineering colleges were established to feed the enormous demand for expertise. Railroads invented complex bureaucratic systems, using middle managers, and set up explicit career tracks. They hired young men at age 18-21 and promoted them internally until a man reached the status of locomotive engineer, conductor or station agent at age 40 or so. Career tracks were invented for skilled blue collar jobs and for white collar managers, starting in railroads and expanding into finance, manufacturing and trade. Together with rapid growth of small business, a new middle class was rapidly growing, especially in northern cities.

The United States became a world leader in applied technology. From 1860 to 1890, 500,000 patents were issued for new inventions over ten times the number issued in the previous seventy years. George Westinghouse invented air brakes for trains making them both safer and faster. Theodore Vail established the American Telephone & Telegraph Company.

Thomas A. Edison invented a remarkable number of electrical devices, as well as the integrated power plant capable of lighting multiple buildings simultaneously; he founded General Electric corporation. Oil became an important resource, beginning with the Pennsylvania oil fields. Kerosene replaced whale oil and candles for lighting. John D. Rockefeller founded Standard Oil Company to consolidate the oil industry which mostly produced kerosene before the automobile created a demand for gasoline in the 20th century.

Andrew Carnegie, John D. Rockefeller, and "Commodore" Cornelius Vanderbilt were among the most influential industrialists during the Gilded Age. Carnegie (1835–1919) was born into a poor Scottish family and came to Pittsburgh as a teenager. In 1870, Carnegie erected his first blast furnace and by 1890 dominated the fast growing steel industry. He preached the "Gospel of Wealth," saying the rich had a moral duty to engage in large-scale philanthropy. Carnegie did give away his fortune, creating many institutions such as the Carnegie Institute of Technology now part of Carnegie Mellon University to upgrade craftsmen into trained engineers and scientists. Carnegie built hundreds of public libraries and several major research centers and foundations.- Rockefeller built Standard Oil into a national monopoly, then retired from the oil business in 1897 and devoted the next 40 years of his life to giving away his fortune using systematic philanthropy, especially to upgrade education, medicine and race relations.

Cornelius Vanderbilt started out as a poor farm boy, then used his sharp wit and lethal business policies to build an empire in steamships and railroading, becoming the wealthiest man in the world in his day.

The "Commodore" believed in Jacksonian Democracy and shook off attacks by his conservative enemies for being too competitive. He was a visionary who pioneered modern business models.

His heirs became famous for their ability to both increase and spend their wealth, building gigantic and lavish mansions and dominating Gilded Age high society, as well as endowing a famous university.

Andrew Carnegie was born in Scotland, on November 25, 1835. While still employed by the Railroad, Carnegie invested in a new company to manufacture railway sleeping cars. From there, he expanded his business ventures to encompass the building of bridges, locomotives and rails. In 1865, he organized the first of his many companies, the Keystone Bridge Company, and in 1873, the first of his steel works.

Carnegie's companies were founded not as stock corporations but as partnerships, in line with his philosophy that "it shall be the rule for the workman to be Partner with Capital, the man of affairs giving his business experience, the working man in the mill his mechanical skill, to the company, both owners of the shares and so far equally interested in the success of their joint efforts." As associates, Carnegie attracted young men with exceptional talent for organization management. His steel company prospered, and when Carnegie sold the company to J.P. Morgan in 1901, the Carnegie Company was valued at more than $400 million.

Andrew Carnegie's philanthropic career began around 1870. He is best known for his gifts of free public library buildings.

His first such gift was to his native Dunfermline in 1881, and it was followed by similar gifts to 2,509 communities in the English-speaking world. In 1889, he wrote "The Gospel of Wealth" in which he boldly articulated his view that the rich are merely "trustees" of their wealth and are under a moral obligation to distribute it in ways that promote the welfare and happiness of the common man. Carnegie was a prolific writer, but the quotation for which he is most famous comes from "The Gospel of Wealth": "The man who dies thus rich dies disgraced."

When Carnegie retired from business in 1901, he set about in earnest to distribute his fortune. In addition to libraries, he provided hundreds of church organs to local communities. Carnegie's wealth helped to establish numerous colleges, schools, nonprofit organizations and associations both in his adopted country, as well as in Scotland and throughout the globe. His most significant contribution, both in terms of money and in terms of enduring influence, was the establishment of several endowed trusts or institutions bearing his name. By the time of his death in 1919, Andrew Carnegie had given away about $350 million, but the legacy of his generosity continues to unfold in the work of the trusts and institutions that he endowed.

John Davidson Rockefeller was born in Richford, New York in 1839. He attended the Cleveland Central High School and at 16 he became a clerk in a commission house. Determined to work for himself, Rockefeller saved all the money he could and in 1850 went into business with a young Englishman, Maurice Clark. The company, Clark & Rockefeller Produce and Commission, sold farm implements, fertilizers and household goods.

Rockefeller's company was fairly successful but did not bring him the wealth he desired. In 1862 Rockefeller heard that Samuel Andrews had developed a better and cheaper way of refining crude petroleum. Rockefeller sold his original business and invested it in a new company he set up with Andrews called Standard Oil.

One of the business problems that Rockefeller encountered was the high cost of transporting his oil to his Cleveland refineries 40 cents a barrel and the refined oil to New York $2 a barrel. Rockefeller negotiated an exclusive deal with the railway company where he guaranteed sixty car loads a day. In return the transport prices were reduced to 35 cents and $1.30. The cost of his oil was reduced and his sales increased dramatically.

Within a year four of his thirty competitors were out of business. Eventually Standard Oil monopolized oil refining in Cleveland. Rockefeller now bought out Samuel Andrews for a million dollars and turned his attentions to controlling the oil industry throughout the United States. His competitors were given the choice of being swallowed up by Standard Oil or being crushed. By 1890 Rockefeller's had swollen into an immense monopoly which could fix its own prices and terms of business because it had no competitors. In 1896 Rockefeller was worth about $200 million.

In November 1902, Ira Tarbell, one of the leading muckraking journalists in the United States, began a series of articles in *McClure's Magazine* on how Rockefeller had achieved a monopoly in refining, transporting and marketing oil. This material was eventually published as a book, *History of the Standard Oil Company* (1904).

Rockefeller responded to these attacks by describing Tarbell as "Miss Tarbarrel".

President Theodore Roosevelt, who had been elected on a program that included reducing the power of large corporations, attempted to use the Sherman Anti-Trust Act to deal with Rockefeller's monopoly of the oil industry. This was largely ineffective and it was not until 1911 that the Supreme Court dissolved the Standard Oil monopoly.

The various press campaigns against Rockefeller had turned him into one of America's most hated men. A devout Baptist, Rockefeller began giving his money away. He set up the Rockefeller Foundation to "promote the well-being of mankind". Over the next few years Rockefeller gave over $500 million in aid of medical research, universities and Baptist churches. He was also a major supplier of funds to organizations such as the Anti-Saloon League that was involved in the campaign for prohibition. By the time that he died on 23rd My, 1937, John Davidson Rockefeller had become a popular national figure.

Rockefeller had a long and controversial career in the industry followed by a long career in philanthropy. His image is an amalgam of all of these experiences and the many ways he was viewed by his contemporaries. These contemporaries include his former competitors, many of whom were driven to ruin, but many others of whom sold out at a profit or a profitable stake in Standard Oil, as Rockefeller often offered his shares as payment for a business, and quite a few of whom became very wealthy as managers as well as owners in Standard Oil.

They also include politicians and writers, some of whom served Rockefeller's interests, and some of whom built their careers by fighting Rockefeller and the "robber barons".

Cornelius Vanderbilt was an American entrepreneur. He built his wealth in shipping and railroads and was the patriarch of the Vanderbilt family. He was one of the richest Americans who ever lived.

When the American Civil War began in 1861, Vanderbilt attempted to donate his largest steamship, the *Vanderbilt*, to the Union navy. Secretary of the Navy Gideon Welles refused it, thinking its operation and maintenance too expensive for what he expected to be a short war. Vanderbilt had little choice but to lease it to the War Department, at prices set by ship brokers. When the Confederate ironclad *Virginia* popularly known in the North as the *Merrimack* wrought havoc with the Union blockading squadron at Hampton Roads, Virginia, Secretary of War Edwin Stanton and President Abraham Lincoln called on Vanderbilt for help. This time he succeeded in donating the *Vanderbilt* to the Union navy, equipping it with a ram and staffing it with handpicked officers. It helped bottle up the *Virginia,* after which Vanderbilt converted it into a cruiser to hunt for the Confederate commerce raider *Alabama*, captained by Raphael Semmes.

At the time of his death, aged 82, Cornelius Vanderbilt's fortune was estimated at $100 million. In his will, he left 95% of his $100 million estate to his son William and to William's four sons $5,000,000 to Cornelius Vanderbilt II, and $2 million apiece to William Kissam Vanderbilt, Frederick Vanderbilt, and George Washington Vanderbilt II.

The Commodore stated that he believed William Henry was the only heir capable of maintaining the business empire. He willed amounts ranging from $250,000 (approximate $4,950,000 in 2008 USD) to $500,000 ($9,920,000 in 2008 USD) to each of his eight daughters. His wife received US$500,000, their New York City home, and 2,000 shares of common stock in New York Central Railroad. To his younger surviving son, Cornelius Jeremiah Vanderbilt, who he regarded as a wasteful, he left the income from a $200,000 trust fund. The Commodore had lived in relative modesty considering his nearly unlimited means, splurging only on race horses, leaving his descendants to build the Vanderbilt houses that characterize America's Gilded Age.

It is worth noting that though trivial in comparison to the $90 million+ inherited by William Henry Vanderbilt and his sons, the bequests to his other children made them very wealthy by the standards of 1877 and were not subject to inheritance tax.

According to "The Wealthy 100" by Michael Klepper and Robert Gunther, Vanderbilt would be worth $143 billion in 2008 dollars, if his total wealth as a share of the nation's GDP in 1877 the year of his death were taken and applied in that same proportion in 2008. This would make him the second-wealthiest person in American history, after John D. Rockefeller. Another calculation, from 1998, puts him in third place, after Andrew Carnegie. Craft-oriented labor unions grew strong in the Northeast after 1870. One critical strike was the Great Railroad Strike of 1877, lasting 45 days and attended by violent attacks on railroad property until President Rutherford B. Hayes sent in federal troops.

In 1886, the Knights of Labor tried to unite both unskilled and skilled workers, but grew so fast it could not manage its affairs.

The failure of the Great Southwest Railroad Strike of 1886 and popular revulsion against the killing of police in the Haymarket Square Riot caused the collapse of support for the Knights.

The final major strike of the late 1800s was the Pullman Strike which was an effort to shut down the national railroad system in the face of federal court injunctions to desist. The strike was led by the upstart American Railway Union a few months old led by Eugene V. Debs, and collapsed totally.- These failures left the union field to the established railroad brotherhoods and the new American Federation of Labor, headed by Samuel Gompers. Gompers wanted better deals for his members, not revolution, and his AFL unions gained strength steadily down to 1919.

Americans' sense of civic virtue was shocked by the scandals associated with the Reconstruction era: corrupt state governments, massive fraud in cities controlled by political machines, political payoffs to secure government contracts through evidence of government corruption during the Ulysses S. Grant Administration.

This corruption divided the Republican party into two different factions, The Stalwarts led by Roscoe Conkling and the Half-Breeds led by James G. Blaine. Accordingly there were widespread calls for reform, such as Civil Service Reform led by the Bourbon Democrats and Republican Mugwumps supporting Democratic reform candidates such as Grover Cleveland.

There was a sense that government intervention in the economy inevitably led to favoritism, bribery, kickbacks, inefficiency, waste, and corruption. The Bourbon Democrats led the call for a free market, low tariffs, low taxes, less spending and, in general, a Laissez-Faire hands-off government. They specifically denounced imperialism and overseas expansion. Many business and professional people supported this approach, although to encourage rapid growth of industry and protect America's high wages against the low wage system in Europe most Republicans advocated a high protective tariff. Labor activists and agrarians expressed the same spirit but focused their attacks on monopolies and railroads as unfair to the little man.

Many Republicans also complained that high tariffs, for instance on British steel, benefited industrialists like Carnegie more than his employees who even at the time were regarded by many as being pitifully exploited. Large cities were dominated by political machines, in which constituents supported a candidate in exchange for anticipated patronage favors back from the government, once that candidate was elected and candidates were selected based on their willingness to play along.

The best known example of a political machine from this time period is Tammany Hall in New York City, led by Boss Tweed. Presidential elections between the two major parties the Republicans and Democrats, were closely contested, and Congress was marked by political stalemate. Mudslinging became an increasingly popular way of gaining advantage at the polls, and Republicans employed an election tactic known as "waving the bloody shirt".

Candidates, especially when combating corruption charges, would remind voters that the Republican Party had saved the nation in the Civil War. During the 1870s, voters were repeatedly reminded that the Democrats had been responsible for the bloody upheaval, an appeal that attracted many Union veterans to the Republican camp.

The Republicans consistently carried the North in presidential elections. The South, on the other hand, became the Solid South, nearly always voting Democratic. The political humiliations of Reconstruction were still fresh in many minds. Conversely, the Democrats invoked images of the "lost cause" and the glorious "stars and bars" in much the same way Republicans "waved the bloody shirt."

The corruption of the Republican organization led to the defection of a group of reformers called the Mugwumps that supported Democrat Grover Cleveland in 1884. This victory gave Democrats control of the presidency for the first time since the Civil War not counting the ascension of Andrew Johnson who was technically elected as part of the Union Party after Lincoln's assassination.
Overall, Republican and Democratic political platforms remained remarkably constant during the years before 1900. The negativity and ambiguity of politics began a shift in the press to yellow journalism, in which sensationalism and sentimental stories took as prominent a role as factual news.

Prior to the Gilded Age, the time commonly referred to as the old immigration saw the first real boom of new arrivals to the United States.

During the Gilded Age, approximately 10 million immigrants came to the United States in what is known as the new immigration, many in search of religious freedom and greater prosperity. The population surge in major U.S. cities as a result of immigration gave cities an even stronger impact on government, attracting power hungry politicians and entrepreneurs. Pressuring voters or falsifying ballots was commonplace for politicians, who often sought power only to exploit their constituents. To accommodate the influx of people into the U.S., the federal government built Ellis Island in 1892 near the Statue of Liberty. After 1892, a short physical examination was given; those with contagious diseases were not admitted. Few immigrants went to the poverty-stricken South.

Major American cities such as New York, Philadelphia and Chicago even saw populations grow in excess of one million people. These rapid changes in cities brought about modern architectural and transportation features. Louis Sullivan became a noted architect using steel frames to construct skyscrapers for the first time while pioneering the idea of "form follows function". One of his earliest works was the Wainwright Building in St. Louis, Missouri. Elisha Otis' introduction of safety measures on elevators also helped buildings reach newer heights. American cities also expanded with the introduction of new transportation technology. From horse cars to elevated railway and later electric streetcars and subways, the cities constantly pushed outward.

As immigration increased in cities, poverty rose as well. New immigrants were forced to live in the poorest urban areas including the Five Points and Hell's Kitchen in Manhattan.

These areas were quickly overridden with crime gangs such as the Five Points Gang and the Bowery Boys rose to prominence. Families were forced into crowded living conditions in the so-called "dumbbell tenements".

During the Gilded Age, many new social movements took hold in the United States. Many women abolitionists who were disappointed that the Fifteenth Amendment did not extend voting rights to them remained active in politics, this time focusing on issues important to them. Reviving the temperance movement from the Second Great Awakening, many women joined the Women's Christian Temperance Union (WCTU) in an attempt to bring morality back to America. Other women took up the issue of women's suffrage which had laid dormant since the Seneca Falls Convention. With leaders like Susan B. Anthony the National American Woman Suffrage Association (NAWSA) was formed in order to secure the right of women to vote.

Grover Cleveland who served as the 22nd and 24th U.S. president, was known as a political reformer. He is the only president to date who served two nonconsecutive terms, and also the only Democratic president to win election during the period of Republican domination of the White House that stretched from Abraham Lincoln's (1809-65) election in 1860 to the end of William Howard Taft's term in 1913. Cleveland worked as a lawyer and then served as mayor of Buffalo, New York, and governor of New York state before assuming the presidency in 1885. His record in the Oval Office was mixed. Not regarded as an original thinker, Cleveland considered himself a watchdog over Congress rather than an initiator.

In his second term, he angered many of his original supporters and seemed overwhelmed by the Panic of 1893 and the depression that followed. He declined to run for a third term.

Yet if you keep in mind the principles of Adams and Marshall and practices of Washington and Webster, you will probably decide that men like Grover Cleveland, Elihu Root, William Howard Taft, and Theodore Roosevelt were most successful in shaping the old truths of conservatism to the new facts of industrialism and democracy. John D. Rockefeller, Andrew Carnegie, and J. P. Morgan can be ruled out on a half-dozen obvious counts, not the least of these being the easily-forgotten fact that they were in one important sense radicals. Their experiments in finance and technology worked astonishing changes in the American way of life, and about these changes they were astonishingly casual.

William Graham Sumner, too, is a hard man for conservatives to canonize, since no American thinker ever went to such lengths in questioning at least half the accepted principles of the conservative tradition. In the end, Root and Roosevelt seem to be the most worthy candidates for membership in the select circle the former for his defense of old-fashioned constitutionalism against the advocates of "direct democracy"; the latter for his vigorous patrician leadership of a nation that was already showing too much fondness for vulgarity and mediocrity; both for their many acts of conservative statesmanship.

Although it is plainly too early to nominate candidates for conservative immortality out of our own generation, it would not be amiss to suggest that three men, one living and two recently dead, stand an excellent chance to be added eventually to the distinguished line that runs from Adams through Root. Adams, Hamilton, Marshall, Webster, Calhoun, Root, and Roosevelt these are the giants of American conservatism, and no conservative need ever feel reluctant to stack them up against the giants of American progressivism, especially since he may argue with some conviction that Washington and Lincoln can also be added to his list.

After spending the later half of the 19th century with presidents that had not exercised a large amount of executive power. Along came Theodore Roosevelt or TR as he would refer to himself. He became the most powerful exerciser of executive power since Abraham Lincoln. Theodore Roosevelt (1858-1919), the 26th president of the United States, guided the nation into a new century of innovation and power. Famous for his military leadership during the Spanish-American War, he became president at the age of 42 after the assassination of William McKinley. Roosevelt believed in an active foreign policy and pursued a conservative and progressive agenda. Born in New York City, Roosevelt graduated from Harvard in 1880. He emerged as the leader of reform Republicans in the New York State Assembly in the early 1880s. Thereafter, he pushed practical reforms as head of the U.S. Civil Service Commission (1889-1895), president of the New York City police commission (1895-1897), assistant secretary of the navy (1897-1898), and governor of New York (1899-1900). He vigorously advocated war against Spain in 1898 and then performed heroically in Cuba as colonel of a volunteer cavalry unit, the "Rough Riders."

Elected vice president of the United States in 1900, Roosevelt became president after the assassination of William McKinley in September 1901. For seven and a half years, Roosevelt strove to balance the interests of farmers, workers, and businesspeople. Despite his image as a trustbuster, he preferred continuous regulation of giant corporations to dissolution under the antitrust laws, and to that end he drove through Congress legislation creating the Bureau of Corporations and strengthening the regulation of railroads. He also supported regulation of the food and drug industries. But his most significant accomplishment was probably the transfer of 125 million acres of public land into the forest reserves, the doubling of national parks, the creation of sixteen national monuments such as California's Muir Woods, and the establishment of fifty-one wildlife refuges.

In 1904 Roosevelt won a full term by decisively defeating Democrat Alton B. Parker. He became increasingly progressive thereafter and by 1909 had endorsed proposals for very modest graduated income and inheritance taxes and other concepts then deemed radical.

In foreign affairs, Roosevelt willingly shouldered the responsibilities of world power. He broke precedents, acted independently of Congress, and held himself ready to invoke force in defense of the national interest if necessary. He arranged to construct a canal through Panama. "I took Panama," he boasted, with some cause. He faced down the Kaiser over German involvement in Venezuela. He assumed in the Roosevelt Corollary to the Monroe Doctrine the right to intervene in the affairs of Latin American states. And he facilitated, and to some extent mediated, the end of the Russo-Japanese War in 1905.

That same year he secretly recognized Japanese suzerainty in Korea and, in 1908, implicitly accepted Japan's economic ascendancy in Manchuria.

Roosevelt's views continued to evolve in retirement, and in 1910 he urged President William Howard Taft to abandon commercial ambitions in North China. Roosevelt also moved beyond the advanced progressive themes of the last years of his presidency. His commitment to an expanded regulatory and welfare program (the "New Nationalism") made conflict between him and Taft virtually inevitable; in 1912, running as the candidate of the Progressive, or Bull Moose party, Roosevelt outpolled his successor in the presidential campaign, which, however, Woodrow Wilson won.

TR is somewhat of a contradictory and complex leader. Conservative on many issues and a strict constructionist, but when matters called he had also a progressive side. Never losing sight of the importance of the constitution.

Overall, historians credit Roosevelt for changing the nation's political system by permanently placing the presidency at center stage and making character as important as the issues. His notable accomplishments include trust-busting and conservationism. However, he has been criticized for his interventionist and imperialist approach to nations he considered "uncivilized".

Even so, history and legend have been kind to him. His friend, historian Henry Adams, proclaimed, "Roosevelt, more than any other living man ....showed the singular primitive quality that belongs to ultimate matter – the quality that mediaeval theology assigned to God he was pure act."

Roosevelt's 1901 saying "Speak Softly and Carry a Big Stick" is still being occasionally quoted by politicians and columnists in different countries not only in English but also in translation to various other languages.

CHAPTER SEVEN - Wilsonian Democracy

Like Roosevelt before him, Woodrow Wilson regarded himself as the personal representative of the people. "No one but the President," he said, "seems to be expected ... to look out for the general interests of the country." Wilson had great faith in himself, too, bordering on arrogance. He developed a program of what he deemed progressive reform and asserted international leadership in building a new world order. In 1917 he proclaimed American entrance into World War I a crusade to make the world "safe for democracy." Perhaps our worst excuse for a president in history, more than any before or probably since he instituted fundamental liberal changes that have now been seen as the destruction of the constitutional republic our founding fathers began. Wilson grew the size of the federal government as no one previously had imagined.

After graduation from Princeton then the College of New Jersey and the University of Virginia Law School, Wilson earned his doctorate at Johns Hopkins University and entered upon an academic career. In 1885 he married Ellen Louise Axson. Wilson advanced rapidly as a young professor of political science and became president of Princeton in 1902.

His growing national reputation led some Democratic leaders to consider him Presidential timber. First they persuaded him to run for Governor of New Jersey in 1910.

In the campaign he asserted his independence of the conservatives and of the machine that had nominated him, endorsing a progressive platform, which he pursued as governor.

He was nominated for President at the 1912 Democratic Convention and campaigned on a program called the New Freedom, which stressed individualism and states' rights. In the three-way election he received only 42 percent of the popular vote but an overwhelming electoral vote.

Wilson maneuvered through Congress three major pieces of legislation. The first was a lower tariff, the Underwood Act; attached to the measure was a graduated Federal income tax. The passage of the Federal Reserve Act provided the Nation with the more elastic money supply. In 1914 antitrust legislation established a Federal Trade Commission to prohibit unfair business practices.

Another burst of legislation followed in 1916. One new law prohibited child labor; another limited railroad workers to an eight-hour day. By virtue of this legislation and the slogan "he kept us out of war," Wilson narrowly won re-election. But after the election Wilson concluded that America could not remain neutral in the World War. On April 2, 1917 he asked Congress for a declaration of war on Germany.

Massive American effort slowly tipped the balance in favor of the Allies. Wilson went before Congress in January 1918, to enunciate American war aims the Fourteen Points, the last of which would establish "A general association of nations…

affording mutual guarantees of political independence and territorial integrity to great and small states alike."

After the Germans signed the Armistice in November 1918, Wilson went to Paris to try to build an enduring peace. He later presented to the Senate the Versailles Treaty, containing the Covenant of the League of Nations, and asked, "Dare we reject it and break the heart of the world?" But the election of 1918 had shifted the balance in Congress to the Republicans. By seven votes the Versailles Treaty failed in the Senate.

The President, against the warnings of his doctors, had made a national tour to mobilize public sentiment for the treaty. Exhausted, he suffered a stroke and nearly died. Tenderly nursed by his second wife, Edith Bolling Galt, he lived until 1924.

Any standard US history text will at least mention, in passing, the suppression of American antiwar dissent in World War I. The great conservative sociologist, the late Robert Nisbet, wrote in 1988 that:

"The blunt fact is that when under Wilson America was introduced to the War State in 1917, it was introduced also to what would later be known as the total, or totalitarian, state." A bit harsh, ? American historians really hate coming to grips with what happened in America, starting in April 1917. They so fail because a fair reading would entail some responsibility for St. Woodrow, who oversaw the whole sorry show. But as Nisbet notes, Wilson "was an ardent prophet of the state, the state indeed as it was known to European scholars and statesmen.... He preached it....

From him supremely comes the politicization, the centralization, and the commitment to bureaucracy of American society during the past seventy-five years."

Woodrow Wilson's America was changing too. One of the most important changes occurred in 1898, namely the Spanish-American War. Wilson's contemporary and rival, Theodore Roosevelt, had become a national hero for his exploits in Cuba. This war is important in that unlike most other previous military interventions, the United States took the initiative and mounted a sustained foreign campaign. Up to that time the last major war on foreign soil was the Mexican-American War of 1848. The Mexican -American War involved the annexation of the Texas territory and the definition of the boarder between the United States and Mexico.

However, the war with Spain over the Cuba was not a boundary dispute. U.S. forces had to be transported over water, make an amphibious landing, and take the fight to the enemy. The Spanish-American War proved that America could fight and win a war away from its immediate borders.

The Spanish-American War also was surrounded by many claims of higher moral purposes. The overarching moral reason behind the war was to deliver the Cubans from their Spanish oppressors. The Spanish-American War and the strengthening of the presidency occurred less than two decades prior to Woodrow Wilson's taking office. He inherited a country with new interventionist mentality and a presidency that had reclaimed its prestige. These events, coupled with his own sense of destiny, set the stage for Woodrow Wilson to intervene into the affairs of other nations.

No, historians don't dwell on Woodrow's reign of terror. They imagine that reactionary subordinates and local bullies did it all, while Woodrow was busy running the war effort and planning the better world to come. Such a kindly man was our Woodrow. Historians, in short, would rather devote whole chapters to "McCarthyism," which inconvenienced a few Stalinists for a time, than deal with a real saga of repression and embarrassingly stupid violence.

Wilson asserted a new-found "presidential power" to arm the ships on his own motion. In April 1917, he asked for, and received, a declaration of war. During the rather tense, even hysterical debate, pro-war speakers began handing out accusations of "treason" to their fellow members of the great *deliberative* body. LaFollette and a few others voted No. On his way out of the chamber, a patriot handed LaFollette a coil of rope, underscoring, one supposes, the refined good manners to which warmongers adhere, especially when they have gotten their way.
The world of Woodrow Wilson was very similar to the world of today. In Wilson's day there were several major and emerging world powers: the United States, Great Britain, France, Russia, Germany, and Japan. Each nation had a series of treaties and alliances aimed at improving their own national interests. It was a fractious, multi polar world.

Those countries are still players in the world of today. The difference is that during the Cold War, the common enemy, the Soviet Union, united the America, Western Europe, and Japan to a great degree. With the disintegration of the Soviet Union, an even more multi-polar system has come into place.

As was true in Wilson's time, Russia is very unstable politically and economically.

The economies of the two eras are also similar. In Wilson's day a "second industrial revolution" was taking place with the advent of aircraft, oil-powered ships, radio communication, and the wide spread use of the internal combustion engine.

Today, information age technology is having a great impact on the world economy. In both eras new markets emerged and the subjects of trade agreements, tariffs, and protection for American workers arose. In both cases the haves employed cutting edge technology, while the have-nots tended to be left behind.

A sedition bill so insanely broad that it would have embarrassed the Federalist Party was quickly passed. It was now a federal crime entailing draconian penalties to question the war, its conduct, its costs, or anything. A great steel door shut down on the American mind, such as it was.

All free communication came to an end. People were arrested and indicted for casual remarks made in *private* conversation. It was not the New Left of the 1960s that actually invented the claim that the personal is the political it was the United States government.

A great wave of repression came down on the freest people in the world, as Americans liked to call themselves. Government gumshoes, federal, state, and local, delighted in following up idle charges of disloyalty, treason, pro-Germanism, and slacking.

Legislatures outlawed the teaching of the German language and the public performance of music by such dangerous Teutons as Beethoven. Wilson and the administration in charge of the enlarged federal apparatus of repression encouraged, aided, and abetted local efforts, including those of self-appointed, hyperthyroid patriotic snoops and bullies.

The Constitution specifically limited Congress' ability to impose direct taxes, by requiring Congress to distribute direct taxes in proportion to each state's census population. It was thought that head taxes and property taxes slaves could be taxed as either or both were likely to be abused, and that they bore no relation to the activities in which the federal government had a legitimate interest. The fourth clause of section 9 therefore specifies that, "No Capitation, or other direct, Tax shall be laid, unless in Proportion to the Census or enumeration herein before directed to be taken."

Taxation was also the subject of Federalist No. 33 penned secretly by the Federalist Alexander Hamilton under the pseudonym Publius. In it, he explains that the wording of the "Necessary and Proper" clause should serve as guidelines for the legislation of laws regarding taxation. The legislative branch is to be the judge, but any abuse of those powers of judging can be overturned by the people, whether as states or as a larger group.

The courts have generally held that direct taxes are limited to taxes on people variously called capitation, poll tax or head tax and property.- All other taxes are commonly referred to as indirect taxes, because they tax an event, rather than a person or property.

-What seemed to be a straightforward limitation on the power of the legislature based on the subject of the tax proved inexact and unclear when applied to an income tax, which can be arguably viewed either as a direct or an indirect tax.

The Wilson – Gorman Act allowed the first Federal income tax in America that still exists today. In fact, Wilson introduced the idea of a progressive tax. Actually when we think of progressives taxes should always come to mind first and foremost.

The Fourteen Points was a speech delivered by United States President Woodrow Wilson to a joint session of Congress on January 8, 1918. The address was intended to assure the country that the Great War was being fought for a moral cause and for postwar peace in Europe. People in Europe generally welcomed Wilson's intervention, but his Allied colleagues Georges Clemenceau, David Lloyd George and Vittorio Emanuele Orlando were skeptical of the applicability of Wilsonian idealism.

The speech was delivered 10 months before the armistice with the German Empire ended the Great War. The Fourteen Points became the basis for the terms of the German surrender, as negotiated at the Paris Peace Conference in 1919. The Treaty of Versailles had little to do with the Fourteen Points and so was never ratified by the U.S. Senate.

Wilson articulated what became known as the Fourteen Points before Congress on January 8, 1918. The Points were the only war aims clearly expressed by any belligerent nation and became the basis for the Treaty of Versailles following the war. The speech--mostly written by Walter Lippmann , was highly idealistic, translating Wilson's progressive domestic policy of democracy, self-determination, open agreements, and free trade into the international realm. The points were:

1. Abolition of secret treaties
2. Freedom of the seas
3. Free Trade
4. Disarmament
5. Adjustment of colonial claims (decolonization and national self-determination)
6. Russia to be assured independent development and international   withdrawal from occupied Russian territory
7. Restoration of Belgium to antebellum national status
8. Alsace-Lorraine returned to France from Germany
9. Italian borders redrawn on lines of nationality
10. Autonomous development of Austria-Hungary as a nation, as the Austro-Hungarian Empire dissolved
11. Romania, Serbia, Montenegro, and other Balkan states to be granted integrity, have their territories de-occupied, and Serbia to be given access to the Adriatic Sea
12. Sovereignty for the Turkish people of the Ottoman Empire as the Empire dissolved, autonomous development for other nationalities within the former Empire
13. Establishment of an independent Poland with access to the sea
14. General association of the nations – a multilateral international association of nations to enforce the peace (League of Nations)

The U.S. joined the Allies in fighting the Central Powers on April 6, 1917. By early 1918 it was clear that the war was nearing its end. The Fourteen Points in the speech were based on the research of the Inquiry, a team of about 150 advisors led by foreign-policy advisor Edward M. House into the topics likely to arise in the anticipated peace conference.

Wilson's speech on January 8, 1918, took many of the principles of progressivism that had produced domestic reform in the U.S. and translated them into foreign policy free trade, open agreements, democracy and self-determination. The Fourteen Points speech was the only explicit statement of war aims by any of the nations fighting in World War I, some belligerents gave general indications of their aims, others refused to state their aims. The speech also responded to Vladimir Lenin's Decree on Peace of October 1917, which proposed an immediate withdrawal of Russia from the war, calling for a just and democratic peace that was not compromised by territorial annexations, and led to the Treaty of Brest-Litovsk on March 3, 1918.
Opposition to the Fourteen Points among British and French leaders became clear after hostilities ceased: the British were against freedom of the seas; the French demanded war reparations. Wilson was forced to compromise on many of his ideals to ensure that his most important point, the establishment of the League of Nations, was accepted. In the end, the Treaty of Versailles went against many of the principles of the Fourteen Points, both in detail and in spirit. Rather than "peace without victory," the treaty sought harsh punishment of Germany both financially and territorially.

The resulting bitterness in Germany together with U.S. loans, laid the seeds for the rise of Nazism in the 1930s which resulted, in part, from the economic depression of the 1920s in Germany which the Versailles Treaty helped create.

Although the Fourteen Points declared that the peoples of Austria-Hungary should be accorded the freest opportunity to autonomous development, this principle was not generally applied to German-speaking or Hungarian populations. For instance, although Hungarians comprised 54% of the population of the Kingdom of Hungary, they were left with only 32% of their pre-war territory by the Treaty of Trianon with 3.3 million Hungarians left in successor states.

Similarly, although the very large German-speaking population of Bohemia and Moravia voted to remain with Austria, they were instead incorporated into Czechoslovakia against their will, and outnumbered Slovaks in the new state. The German-speaking population of southern Tyrol was cut off from the rest of Tyrol and incorporated into Italy, also against their will.

The United States Senate refused to consent to the ratification of the Treaty of Versailles, making it invalid in the U.S. and effectively hamstringing the nascent League of Nations envisioned by Wilson. The largest obstacle faced in the ratification of the Treaty of Versailles was the opposition of Henry Cabot Lodge. It has also been said that Wilson himself was the second-largest obstacle, not least because he kept the leaders of the Republican-led Congress in the dark during treaty deliberations, and refused to support the treaty with any of the alterations proposed by the United States Senate.

One of the largest obstacles was over the League of Nations; Congress believed that committing to the League of Nations also meant committing U.S. troops to any conflicts that might have arisen.

The last vote on the treaty occurred in the Senate on March 19, 1920, and fell short of the necessary two-thirds majority required for the Senate to consent to ratification. The U.S. did later sign a separate peace treaty with Germany, but never joined the League.

Henry Cabot Lodge was an American statesman, a Republican politician, and a noted historian. A Conservative of the highest order and great leader in the opposition to Wilson. While he did not claim the title, he is considered to be the first Senate majority leader.

As chairman of the Senate Foreign Relations Committee, Lodge led the successful fight against American participation in the League of Nations, which had been proposed by President Woodrow Wilson at the close of World War I. He also served as chairman of the Senate Republican Conference from 1918 to 1924. During his term in office, he and another powerful senator, Albert J. Beveridge, pushed for the construction of a new navy.

Lodge maintained that membership in the world peace-keeping organization would threaten the political freedom of the United States by binding the nation to international commitments it would not or could not keep.

Lodge perceived an open-ended commitment to deploy soldiers into conflict regardless of it being relevant to the national security interests of the United States. He did not want America to have this obligation.

Lodge was also motivated by political concerns; he strongly disliked Woodrow Wilson[1] and was eager to find an issue for the Republican Party to run on in 1920. Senator Lodge argued in 1919 against the League:

"The United States is the world's best hope, but if you fetter her in the interests and quarrels of other nations, if you tangle her in the intrigues of Europe, you will destroy her powerful good, and endanger her very existence. Leave her to march freely through the centuries to come, as in the years that have gone. Strong, generous, and confident, she has nobly served mankind. Beware how you trifle with your marvelous inheritance; this great land of ordered liberty. For if we stumble and fall, freedom and civilization everywhere will go down in ruin."

Lodge appealed to the patriotism of American citizens by objecting to what he saw as the weakening of national sovereignty: "I have loved but one flag and I can not share that devotion and give affection to the mongrel banner invented for a league." The League of Nations was established without U.S. participation in 1920. With headquarters in Geneva, Switzerland, it remained active until World War II.

The tyranny of Woodrow Wilson while lasting only eight years left the door open for future tyrants who pro-claimed Wilsonian attitudes toward their interpretation of our constitution. His domestic program expanded the role of the federal government in managing the economy and protecting the interests of citizens. His foreign policy established a new vision of America's role in the world. And he helped to make the White House the center of power in Washington.

Most historians rank him among the five most important American Presidents, along with Washington, Lincoln, and the two Roosevelts. Important doesn't always mean a positive thing, he was obviously important in establishing totalitarianism in the US.

Wilson secured passage of the Federal Reserve system in late 1913. He took a plan that had been designed by conservative Republicans, led by Senator Nelson W. Aldrich , and worked with the Democratic majority in Congress to pass a compromise bill.

After a successful academic career as an author and professor at Bryn Mawr, Wesleyan, and Princeton, Wilson was elected president of Princeton in 1902. In that office, his efforts to modernize the college brought him attention as a progressive reformer, and in 1910, New Jersey Democrats approached him about running for governor. Wilson accepted, but on the condition that their support came with "no strings attached."

Wilson's New Freedom platform was ambitious and thoroughly progressive. It called for tariff reduction, reform of the banking and monetary system, and new laws to weaken abusive corporations and restore economic competition. With a Presbyterian's confidence that God was guiding his course, Wilson pursued his New Freedom agenda with the zeal of a crusader, making use of his skill as an orator to galvanize the nation in support of his policies. Perhaps his greatest achievement was the passage of the Federal Reserve Act of 1913, which created the system that still provides the framework for regulating the nation's banks, credit, and money supply today. Other Wilson backed legislation put new controls on big business and supported unions to ensure fair treatment of working Americans.

Renominated in 1916, Wilson used as a major campaign slogan "He kept us out of the war", referring to his administration's avoiding open conflict with Germany or Mexico while maintaining a firm national policy. Wilson, however, never promised to keep out of war regardless of provocation. In his acceptance speech on September 2, 1916, Wilson pointedly warned Germany that submarine warfare that took American lives would not be tolerated:

The United Mexican States , commonly known as Mexico , is a federal constitutional republic in North America. It is bordered on the north by the United States; on the south and west by the Pacific Ocean; on the southeast by Guatemala, Belize, and the Caribbean Sea; and on the east by the Gulf of..."The nation that violates these essential rights must expect to be checked and called to account by direct challenge and resistance. It at once makes the quarrel in part our own."

Wilson narrowly won the election, defeating Republican candidate Charles Evans Hughes As governor of New York from 1907–1910, Hughes had a progressive record, strikingly similar to Wilson's as governor of New Jersey. Theodore Roosevelt would comment that the only thing different between Hughes and Wilson was a shave. Charles Evans Hughes Sr. was a lawyer and Republican politician from the State of New York. He served as Governor of New York , United States Secretary of State , Associate Justice of the Supreme Court of the United States and Chief Justice of the United States...

Theodore Roosevelt would comment that the only thing different between Hughes and Wilson was a shave. However, Hughes had to try to hold together a coalition of conservative Taft supporters and progressive Roosevelt partisans and so his campaign never seemed to take a definite form. Wilson ran on his record and ignored Hughes, reserving his attacks for Roosevelt. When asked why he did not attack Hughes directly, Wilson told a friend to "Never murder a man who is committing suicide."

In foreign affairs, Wilson was determined to revise the imperialist practices of earlier administrations, promising independence to the Philippines and making Puerto Ricans American citizens. But Wilson's own policies could sometimes be high-handed. His administration intervened militarily more often in Latin America than any of his predecessors.

Before entering the war in 1917, the U.S. had made a declaration of neutrality in 1914. During this time of neutrality, President Wilson warned citizens not to take sides in the war in fear of endangering wider U.S. policy. In his address to congress in 1914, Wilson states, "Such divisions amongst us would be fatal to our peace of mind and might seriously stand in the way of the proper performance of our duty as the one great nation at peace, the one people holding itself ready to play a part of impartial mediation and speak the counsels of peace and accommodation, not as a partisan, but as a friend."

To counter opposition to the war at home, Wilson pushed the Espionage Act of 1917 and the Sedition Act of 1918. which made it a crime for a person.

The Sedition Act of 1918 was an amendment to the Espionage Act of 1917 passed at the urging of President Woodrow Wilson, who was concerned that dissent, in time of war, was a significant threat to morale. The passing of this act forbade Americans to use "disloyal, profane, scurrilous, or abusive…

He welcomed socialists Socialism refers to various theories of economic organization advocating public or direct worker ownership and administration of the means of production and allocation of resources, and a society characterized by equal access to resources for all individuals with a method of compensation based on. who supported the war, such as Walter Lippmann. His wartime policies were strongly pro-labor; he worked closely with Samuel Gompers and the AFL, while suppressing antiwar groups trying to impede the war effort.

The American Federation of Labor , the railroad brotherhoods and other 'moderate' unions saw enormous growth in membership and wages during Wilson's administration. There was no rationing, so consumer prices soared. As income taxes increased, white-collar worker s suffered. Appeals to buy war bonds were highly successful, however. Bonds had the result of shifting the cost of the war to the affluent 1920s.

Theodore Roosevelt was the 26th President of the United States. He is well remembered for his energetic persona, his range of interests and achievements, his model of masculinity, and his "cowboy" image. He was a leader of the Republican Party and founder of the short-lived Bull Moose Party.

Future President Herbert Hoover was appointed to head the Food Administration which encouraged Americans to participate in "Meatless Mondays" and "Wheat less Wednesdays" to conserve food for the troops overseas. The Federal Fuel Administration run by Henry Garfield introduced daylight savings time and rationed fuel supplies such as coal and oil to keep the US military supplied. These and many other boards and administrations were headed by businessmen recruited by Wilson for a dollar a day salary to make the government more efficient in the war effort.

Robert Marion La Follette, Sr. nicknamed "Fighting Bob" La Follette was an American politician who served as a U.S. Congressman, the 20th Governor of Wisconsin , and Republican Senator from Wisconsin...

In the three to four days that Congress had to decide whether to declare war or not, several telegrams and petitions were wired to him in Washington expressing disagreement with going to war. Senator Robert La Follette was one of only six senators who voted against the decision to go to war. Republican Senator George W. Norris of Nebraska was also opposed to entry into the war. Norris stated:

"I am most emphatically and sincerely opposed to taking any step that will force our country into the useless and senseless war now being waged in Europe..." He provided reasonable examples of how the United States is unfair in declaring war on Germany. One of his examples was that the British had declared a war zone on November 4th and America had submitted to it, but when Germany declared a war zone on February 4th America had opposed it.

Both of them had violated international law and interfered with our neutral rights, and America only acts against Germany and not both.

Again, he finds evidence where there are "Many instances of cruelty and inhumanity that can be found on both sides". Norris believed that the government only wanted to take part in this war because the wealthy had already aided British financially in the war. He told Congress that the only people who would benefit from the war were "munitions manufacturers, stockbrokers, and bond dealers".

He presented evidence to the Congress as a letter written by a member of the New York Stock Exchange. He concluded from his evidence that "Here we have the man representing the class of people who will be made prosperous should we become entangled in the present war, who have already made millions of dollars, and who will make many hundreds of millions more if we get into the war". George W. Norris's concludes that it is not worth going to war just to benefit the rich and to "deliver munitions of war to belligerent nations". "War brings no prosperity to the great mass of common and patriotic citizens. It increases the cost of living of those who toil and those who already must strain every effort to keep soul and body together. War brings prosperity to the stock gambler on Wall Street--to those who are already in possession of more wealth than can be realized or enjoyed". Robert M. La Follette's main argument echoed Norris. LaFollette also believed the reputation of America would deteriorate:

"When we cooperate with those governments, we endorse their methods; we endorse the violations of international law by Great Britain; we endorse the shameful methods of warfare against which we have again and again protested in this war".

He also gave recognition to Woodrow Wilson's speech and how Wilson aimed towards his audience's feelings. He criticized Wilson that "In many places throughout the address is this exalted sentiment given expression. It is a sentiment peculiarly calculated to appeal to American hearts and, when accompanied by acts consistent with it, is certain to receive our support".

Despite what Norris and La Follette had to say, Congress had made a declaration of war on April 4, 1917. During the war, industrial production increased by 20 percent, daylight saving time was instituted to save fuel, the government took over the railroad system, and massive airplane and shipbuilding programs were launched. Americans began paying a new income tax and buying Liberty Bonds to pay for the war. Although most of the power the federal government acquired over the economy during the war was based on voluntary cooperation by businesses and individuals, conformity and aggressive patriotism became the order of the day. Private patriotic organizations persecuted dissenters and anyone suspected of political radicalism, and the administration sponsored Espionage and Sedition Acts that outlawed criticism of the government, the armed forces, and the war effort. Violators of the law were imprisoned or fined, and even mainstream publications were censored or banned.

Wilson had ignored the problems of demobilization after the war, and the process was chaotic and violent. Four million soldiers were sent home with little planning, little money, and few benefits. A wartime bubble in prices of farmland burst, leaving many farmers bankrupt or deeply in debt after they purchased new land. In 1919, major strikes in steel and meatpacking broke out.

Red Summer, a term coined by author James Weldon Johnson, is used to describe the bloody race riots that occurred during the summer and autumn of 1919. Race riots erupted in several cities in both the North and South of the United States. The three with the highest number of fatalities happened…

After a series of bombings by radical anarchist groups in New York and elsewhere, Wilson directed Attorney General A. Mitchell Palmer to put a stop to the violence. Palmer then ordered the Palmer Raids, with the aim of collecting evidence on violent radical groups, to deport foreign-born agitators, and jail domestic ones. The Justice Department brought Socialist leader Eugene Debs to trial for trying to block recruiting; he was convicted and sent to federal prison in Atlanta.

 The Palmer Raids were a series of controversial raids by the United States Department of Justice and Immigration and Naturalization Service from 1919 to 1921 on suspected radical leftist citizens and immigrants in the United States, the legality of which is now in question... The Chicago Race Riot of 1919 was a major racial conflict that began in on July 27, 1919 and ended on August 3. During the riot, dozens died and hundreds were injured.

It is considered the worst of the approximately 25 riots during the Red Summer of 1919, so named because of the violence and…

Wilson broke with many of his closest political friends and allies in 1918–20, including Colonel House. Historians speculate that a series of strokes may have affected his personality. He desired a third term, but his Democratic party was in turmoil, with German voters outraged at their wartime harassment, and Irish voters angry at his failure to support Irish independence.

Though he left office broken and defeated, Wilson believed firmly that his vision of America leading a world community of nations would eventually be embraced by the American people. Twenty-five years later, the United Nations built its headquarters in New York, a tangible symbol of his belief in bipartisan support that Wilsonian ideals had gained after a second world war.

But Wilson's legacy was not confined to foreign policy. His progressive domestic programs helped stabilize and humanize a huge industrial system, and his success in making the presidency the intellectual and political leader of the American government enabled the United States to deal effectively with the challenges and threats of the modern world.

CHAPTER EIGHT - The Roaring 20's

Albert Jay Nock was an influential American libertarian author, political theorist, and social critic of the early and middle 20th century. Throughout his life, Nock was a deeply private man who shared few of the details of his personal life with his working partners. He was born in Scranton, Pennsylvania, to a father who was both a steelworker and an Episcopal priest, and he was raised in Brooklyn, New York. After graduating from St. Stephen's College now known as Bard College (attended when he was 14–18 years of age), he had a brief career playing minor league baseball. He then attended a theological seminary and was himself ordained as an Episcopal priest in 1897. Nock married Agnes Grumbine in 1900 and had two children but separated from his wife after only a few years of marriage. In 1909 Nock left the clergy and became a journalist.

In 1914, Nock joined the staff of The Nation magazine, which was at the time supportive of liberal capitalism. Nock was an acquaintance of the influential politician and orator William Jennings Bryan, in 1915 even traveling to Europe on a special assignment for Bryan, who was then Secretary of State. Nock also maintained friendships with many of the leading proponents of the Georgist movement, one of whom had been his bishop in the Episcopal Church. However, while Nock was a lifelong admirer of Henry George, he was frequently at odds with the left-leaning movement that claimed his legacy.

Further, Nock was deeply influenced by the anti-collectivist writings of the German sociologist Franz Oppenheimer, whose most famous work, *Der Staat*, was published in English translation in 1915.
In his own writings, Nock would later build on Oppenheimer's claim that the pursuit of human ends can be divided into two forms: the productive or economic means and the parasitic, political means.

Nock was also a passionate opponent of war and what he considered the U.S. government's aggressive foreign policy. He believed that war could bring out only the worst in society, arguing that it led inevitably to collectivization and militarization and "fortified a universal faith in violence; it set in motion endless adventures in imperialism, endless nationalist ambitions," while, at the same time, costing countless human lives. During the First World War, Nock wrote for *The Nation*, which was censored by the Wilson administration for opposing the war.
Charles Evans Hughes Sr. was a lawyer and Republican politician from the State of New York. He served as the 36th Governor of New York (1907-1910), United States Secretary of State (1921-1925), Associate Justice of the Supreme Court of the United States (1910-1916) and Chief Justice of the United States (1930-1941). He was the Republican candidate in the 1916 U.S. Presidential election, losing to Woodrow Wilson. He was also a significant influence on conservative politics in America until his death in 1948.

Before his nomination, Warren G. Harding declared, "America's present need is not heroics, but healing; not nostrums, but normalcy; not revolution, but restoration;

not agitation, but adjustment; not surgery, but serenity; not the dramatic, but the dispassionate; not experiment, but equipoise; not submergence in internationality, but sustainment in triumphant nationality...."

A Democratic leader, William Gibbs McAdoo, called Harding's speeches "an army of pompous phrases moving across the landscape in search of an idea." Their very murkiness was effective, since Harding's pronouncements remained unclear on the League of Nations, in contrast to the impassioned crusade of the Democratic candidates, Governor James M. Cox of Ohio and Franklin D. Roosevelt. On the other hand Cox put together a lot of words that sounded really great, but no one could figure out what he said.

Thirty-one distinguished Republicans had signed a manifesto assuring voters that a vote for Harding was a vote for the League. But Harding interpreted his election as a mandate to stay out of the League of Nations. Republicans in Congress easily got the President's signature on their bills. They eliminated wartime controls and slashed taxes, established a Federal budget system, restored the high protective tariff, and imposed tight limitations upon immigration.

By 1923 the postwar depression seemed to be giving way to a new surge of prosperity, and newspapers hailed Harding as a wise statesman carrying out his campaign promise "Less government in business and more business in government." Looking wan and depressed, Harding journeyed westward in the summer of 1923, taking with him his upright Secretary of Commerce, Herbert Hoover.

"If you knew of a great scandal in our administration," he asked Hoover, would you for the good of the country and the party expose it publicly or would you bury it?" Hoover urged publishing it, but Harding feared the political repercussions. He did not live to find out how the public would react to the scandals of his administration. In August of 1923, he died in San Francisco of a heart attack.

Harding ran on a promise to "Return to Normalcy", a seldom-used term he popularized. The slogan called an end to the abnormal era of the Great War, along with a call to reflect three trends of his time: a renewed isolationism in reaction to the War, a resurgence of nativism, and a turning away from the government activism of the reform era. Harding calmed the 1919-1920 Bolshevik scare and released election opponent, Socialist leader Eugene Debs, from prison. Debs had been convicted under charges brought by the Wilson administration for his opposition to the draft during World War I. Despite many political differences between the two candidates, Harding commuted Debs' sentence to time served.

Harding pushed for the establishment of the Bureau of Veterans Affairs, the first permanent attempt at answering the needs of those who had served the nation in time of war-He created the the Office of Management and Budget , becoming the first president to have the executive branch take a role in federal expenditures.

In April 1921, speaking before a joint session of Congress, Harding called for peacemaking with Germany and Austria, emergency tariffs, new immigration laws, regulation of radio and trans cable communications retrenchment in government, tax reduction, repeal of wartime excess profits tax, reduction of railroad rates, promotion of agricultural interests, a national budget system, a great merchant marine and a department of public welfare. He called for measures to bring an end to lynching, but he didn't want to make enemies in his own party and with the Democrats, and did not fight for his program.

According to biographers, Harding got along well with the press more than any other President, being a former newspaper man. Reporters admired his frankness, candor, and his confessed limitations. He took the press behind the scenes and showed them the inner circle of the presidency. Harding, in November 1921, also implemented a policy of taking written questions from reporters during a press conference. Hardings relationship with Congress, however, was strained and he did not receive the traditional honeymoon given to new Presidents.

Prior to Harding's election the nation was adrift; President Woodrow Wilson had been ill by a debilitating stroke for eighteen months and before that Wilson had been in Europe for several months attempting to negotiate a peace settlement after WWI. By contrast on the March 4, 1921 Inaugural; Harding looked strong; with grey hair and a commanding physical presence.

On June 12, 1921 President Harding signed the Budget and Accounting Act of 1921 establishing the Bureau of the Budget. The Budget director was directly responsible to the President, rather than the Secretary of Treasury. The General Accounting Office was created to assure oversight in the federal budget expenditures.

Harding appointed Charlie Dawes, known for being a fiscal conservative, as the first director of the Bureau of the Budget. Dawes reduced government spending by 1.5 billion his first year as director.

Initially, Harding's death in 1923 was mourned by the nation and his presidency was popularly viewed by both the press and the nation. However, as the many scandals during the Harding Administration were exposed, his presidential reputation was destroyed and he became a defenseless target relegated among historians to a legacy of scandal, greed, and corruption. Although traditionally viewed as one of the worst Presidents, one Harding biographer, John W. Dean, points out that his actual Presidential record has been overlooked. Harding had officially ended WWI; overcame the Depression of 1920-1921; and established a conference system to solve international disputes rather than militarization and war.

Harding encouraged civil rights for African Americans; supported an anti lynching law at a time when membership in the KKK was at its highest; and signed into law a progressive child welfare program. Harding also did much to regulate and protect farm interests and cooperatives. Although Harding had many presidential accomplishments; he was unable to resolve contentious disputes between industrial corporations and labor unions that plagued his administration. Harding had chosen his friends poorly and was unable to stop criminal activity during his administration. The legacy of Warren G. Harding's unfinished presidency is incomplete; how he would have reacted to the exposed scandals remains historical speculation.

The Harding presidency represented a return to conservative values and though marred by scandals over trivial matters in which he of course wasn't implicated. It was rather small minded men who were cabinet members. For many years his presidency was seen as unsuccessful however recently we're discovering that Warren Harding actually put our nation back on it's right track.
At 2:30 on the morning of August 3, 1923, while visiting in Vermont, Calvin Coolidge received word that he was President. By the light of a kerosene lamp, his father, who was a notary public, administered the oath of office as Coolidge placed his hand on the family Bible.

As President, Coolidge demonstrated his determination to preserve the old moral and economic precepts amid the material prosperity which many Americans were enjoying. He refused to use Federal economic power to check the growing boom or to ameliorate the depressed condition of agriculture and certain industries. His first message to Congress in December 1923 called for isolation in foreign policy, and for tax cuts, economy, and limited aid to farmers.

He rapidly became popular. In 1924, as the beneficiary of what was becoming known as Coolidge prosperity, he polled more than 54 percent of the popular vote.
In his Inaugural he asserted that the country had achieved "a state of contentment seldom before seen," and pledged himself to maintain the status quo. In subsequent years he twice vetoed farm relief bills, and killed a plan to produce cheap Federal electric power on the Tennessee River.

The political genius of President Coolidge, Walter Lippmann pointed out in 1926, was his talent for effectively doing nothing: "This active inactivity suits the mood and certain of the needs of the country admirably. It suits all the business interests which want to be let alone.... And it suits all those who have become convinced that government in this country has become dangerously complicated and top-heavy...."

Coolidge was both the most negative and remote of Presidents, and the most accessible. He once explained to Bernard Baruch why he often sat silently through interviews: "Well, Baruch, many times I say only 'yes' or 'no' to people. Even that is too much. It winds them up for twenty minutes more." But no President was kinder in permitting himself to be photographed in Indian war bonnets or cowboy dress, and in greeting a variety of delegations to the White House.

Both his dry Yankee wit and his frugality with words became legendary. His wife, Grace Goodhue Coolidge, recounted that a young woman sitting next to Coolidge at a dinner party confided to him she had bet she could get at least three words of conversation from him. Without looking at her he quietly stated, "You lose." And in 1928, while vacationing in the Black Hills of South Dakota, he issued the most famous of his legendry statements, "I do not choose to run for President in 1928."

Coolidge restored public confidence in the White House after the scandals of his predecessor's administration, and left office with considerable popularity. As a Coolidge biographer put it, "He embodied the spirit and hopes of the middle class, could interpret their longings and express their opinions.

That he did represent the genius of the average is the most convincing proof of his strength."- Many later criticized Coolidge as part of a general criticism of laissez-faire government.- His reputation underwent a renaissance during the Ronald Reagan Administration, but the ultimate assessment of his presidency is still divided between those who approve of his reduction of the size of government programs and those who believe the federal government should be more involved in regulating and controlling the economy.

During Coolidge's presidency the United States experienced the period of rapid economic growth known as the "Roaring Twenties". He left the administration's industrial policy in the hands of his activist Secretary of Commerce, Herbert Hoover, who energetically used government auspices to promote business efficiency and develop airlines and radio. With the exception of favoring increased tariffs, Coolidge disdained regulation, and carried about this belief by appointing commissioners to the Federal Trade Commission and the Interstate Commerce Commission who did little to restrict the activities of businesses under their jurisdiction.- The regulatory state under Coolidge was, as one biographer described it, "thin to the point of invisibility."

Coolidge's economic policy has often been misquoted as "generally speaking, the business of the American people is business". Some have criticized Coolidge as an adherent of the laissez-faire ideology, which they claim led to the Great Depression.- On the other hand, historian Robert Sobel offers some context based on Coolidge's sense of federalism:

As Governor of Massachusetts, Coolidge supported wages and hours legislation, opposed child labor, imposed economic controls during World War I, favored safety measures in factories, and even worker representation on corporate boards. Did he support these measures while president? No, because in the 1920s, such matters were considered the responsibilities of state and local governments.

Coolidge's taxation policy was that of his Secretary of the Treasury, Andrew Mellon: taxes should be lower and that fewer people should have to pay them.- Congress agreed, and the taxes were reduced in Coolidge's term. In addition to these tax cuts, Coolidge proposed reductions in federal expenditures and retiring some of the federal debt. Coolidge's ideas were shared by the Republicans in Congress, and in 1924 Congress passed the Revenue Act of 1924, which reduced income tax rates and eliminated all income taxation for some two million people.-They reduced taxes again by passing the Revenue Acts of 1926 and 1928, all the while continuing to keep spending down so as to reduce the overall federal debt.- By 1927, only the richest 2% of taxpayers paid any income tax.- Although federal spending remained flat during Coolidge's administration, allowing one-fourth of the federal debt to be retired, state and local governments saw considerable growth, surpassing the federal budget in 1927.

Perhaps the most contentious issue of Coolidge's presidency was that of relief for farmers. Some in Congress proposed a bill designed to fight falling agricultural prices by allowing the federal government to purchase crops to sell abroad at lowered prices.

-Agriculture Secretary Henry Wallace and other administration officials favored the bill when it was introduced in 1924, but rising prices convinced many in Congress that the bill was unnecessary, and it was defeated just before the elections that year.- In 1926, with farm prices falling once more, Senator Charles L. McNary and Representative Gilbert N. Haugen both Republicans proposed the McNary-Haugen Farm Relief Bill. The bill proposed a federal farm board that would purchase surplus production in high-yield years and hold it when feasible for later sale, or sell it abroad. Coolidge opposed McNary-Haugen, declaring that agriculture must stand "on an independent business basis," and said that "government control cannot be divorced from political control."- He favored instead Herbert Hoover's proposal to modernize agriculture to create profits, instead of manipulating prices. Secretary Mellon wrote a letter denouncing the McNary-Haugen measure as unsound and likely to cause inflation, and it was defeated.

While he was not an isolationist, Coolidge was reluctant to enter into foreign alliances. Coolidge saw the landslide Republican victory of 1920 as a rejection of the Wilsonian idea that the United States should join the League of Nations.- While not completely opposed to the idea, Coolidge believed the League, as then constituted, did not serve American interests, and he did not advocate membership in it.

Coolidge's best-known initiative was the Kellogg-Briand Pact of 1928, named for Coolidge's Secretary of State, Frank B. Kellogg, and French foreign minister Aristide Briand.

The treaty, ratified in 1929, committed signatories including the U.S., the United Kingdom, France, Germany, Italy, and Japan to "renounce war, as an instrument of national policy in their relations with one another."

In 1925 Kellogg succeeded Charles Evans Hughes as secretary of state in Coolidge's cabinet, holding the position until 1929. His policy toward Mexico on critical problems of oil and land expropriation which were solved by legal rather than military means, toward Nicaragua despite armed intervention at one point, and toward the Caribbean and South American nations has been described as one of retreat from imperialism; his policy toward China with whom relations were troubled by outbreaks against foreigners in Shanghai and Nanking and by problems of tariff autonomy and abolition of extraterritoriality was one of goodwill ; and, in general, his policy toward Europe was one of isolationism, in part because there were few significant diplomatic problems with European nations.

In pursuance of his faith in the efficacy of the legal arbitration of international disputes, Kellogg arranged for the signing of bilateral treaties with nineteen foreign nations. Of the eighty treaties of various kinds which he signed while in office a total breaking the record set by William Jennings Bryan from 1913 to 1915 none was so important to him as the Pact of Paris, commonly called the Kellogg-Briand Pact.

Negotiations for the pact originated with Aristide Briand, the French foreign minister, who released for publication on April 6, 1927, the tenth anniversary of America's entry into World War I, an open letter proposing a bilateral Franco-American treaty of perpetual friendship denouncing war between the two nations. Kellogg, at first cool to the proposal, countered on December 28, 1927, by suggesting to Briand the adoption of a multilateral treaty renouncing war as an instrument of national policy.

Calvin Coolidge was a small government conservative probably not seen again until Ronald Reagan. Like Harding his administration was one of prosperity at home and prestige abroad.

Herbert Clark Hoover was the 31st President of the United States (1929–1933). Hoover was a professional mining engineer and author. As the United States Secretary of Commerce in the 1920s under Presidents Warren Harding and Calvin Coolidge, he promoted government intervention under the slogan "economic modernization". In the presidential election of 1928, Hoover easily won the Republican nomination, despite having no previous elected office experience. To date, Hoover is the last cabinet secretary to be directly elected President of the United States, as well as one of only two Presidents along with William Howard Taft to have been elected President without electoral experience or high military rank. The nation was prosperous and optimistic at the time, leading to a landslide victory for Hoover over Democrat Al Smith.

Hoover, a trained engineer, deeply believed in the Efficiency Movement, which held that government and the economy were riddled with inefficiency and waste, and could be improved by experts who could identify the problems and solve them. When the Wall Street Crash of 1929 struck less than eight months after he took office, Hoover tried to combat the ensuing Great Depression with volunteer efforts, none of which produced economic recovery during his term. The consensus among historians is that Hoover's defeat in the 1932 election was caused primarily by failure to end the downward economic spiral.

No small task for me here to try to convince brainwashed masses to believe that Herbert Hoover was not only equipped to be president but also probably did mostly the right things. The great depression began with the crash of 1929 and it happened while Herbert Hoover was president. That's where the significance begins and ends, the fact is it would have happened regardless of who was president. The reason it lasted so long is for debate.

After the United States entered the war, President Wilson appointed Hoover head of the Food Administration. He succeeded in cutting consumption of foods needed overseas and avoided rationing at home, yet kept the Allies fed.

After the Armistice, Hoover, a member of the Supreme Economic Council and head of the American Relief Administration, organized shipments of food for starving millions in central Europe. He extended aid to famine stricken Soviet Russia in 1921. When a critic inquired if he was not thus helping Bolshevism, Hoover retorted, "Twenty million people are starving. Whatever their politics, they shall be fed!"

In 1931 repercussions from Europe deepened the crisis, even though the President presented to Congress a program asking for creation of the Reconstruction Finance Corporation to aid business, additional help for farmers facing mortgage foreclosures, banking reform, a loan to states for feeding the unemployed, expansion of public works, and drastic governmental economy. At the same time he reiterated his view that while people must not suffer from hunger and cold, caring for them must be primarily a local and voluntary responsibility.

His opponents in Congress, who he felt were sabotaging his program for their own political gain, unfairly painted him as a callous and cruel President. Hoover became the scapegoat for the depression and was badly defeated in 1932. In the 1930's he became a powerful critic of the New Deal, warning against tendencies toward statism.

Hoover entered office with a plan to reform the nation's regulatory system, believing that a federal bureaucracy should have limited regulation over a country's economic system. A self-described Progressive and Reformer, Hoover saw the presidency as a vehicle for improving the conditions of all Americans by regulation and by encouraging volunteerism. Long before entering politics, he had denounced *laissez-faire* thinking. As Commerce Secretary, he had taken an active pro-regulation stance. As President, he helped push tariff and farm subsidy bills through Congress.

Hoover expanded civil service coverage of Federal positions, canceled private oil leases on government lands, and by instructing the Justice Department and the Internal Revenue Service to pursue gangsters for tax evasion, he enabled the prosecution of Al Capone.

He appointed a commission that set aside 3 million acres of national parks and 2.3 million acres of national forests; advocated tax reduction for low-income Americans not enacted; closed certain tax loopholes for the wealthy; doubled the number of veterans' hospital facilities; negotiated a treaty on St. Lawrence Seaway which failed in the U.S. Senate; wrote a Children's Charter that advocated protection of every child regardless of race or gender; created an antitrust division in the Justice Department; required air mail carriers to adopt stricter safety measures and improve service; proposed federal loans for urban slum clearances ; organized the Federal Bureau of Prisons; reorganized the Bureau of Indian Affairs; instituted prison reform; proposed a federal Department of Education which was not enacted; advocated $50-per-month pensions for Americans over 65 not enacted; chaired White House conferences on child health, protection, homebuilding and homeownership; began construction of the Boulder Dam later renamed Hoover Dam; and signed the Norris-La Guardia Act that limited judicial intervention in labor disputes.

The depth of the financial crisis so affected our nation that Hoover used government intervention to try to stem the crisis. His efforts of course failed, our economy was red hot and it overheated and the bubble burst. Now it needed time to recover as it did in the panics of 1873 and 1893. It needed time not government programs. By 1932, the Great Depression had spread across the globe. In the U.S., unemployment had reached 24.9%,- a drought persisted in the agricultural heartland, businesses and families defaulted on record numbers of loans, and more than 5,000 banks had failed.

167

Tens of thousands of Americans who found themselves homeless and began congregating in the numerous Hoovervilles also known as shanty towns or tent cities that had begun to appear across the country. The name 'Hoover Ville' was coined by their residents as a sign of their disappointment and frustration with the perceived lack of assistance from the federal government. In response, Hoover and the Congress approved the Federal Home Loan Bank Act, to spur new home construction, and reduce foreclosures. The plan seemed to work, as foreclosures dropped, but it was seen as too little, too late.

To pay for these and other government programs and to make up for revenue lost due to the Depression, Hoover agreed to roll back previous tax cuts his Administration had effected on upper incomes. In one of the largest tax increases in American history, the Revenue Act of 1932 raised income tax on the highest incomes from 25% to 63%. The estate tax was doubled and corporate taxes were raised by almost 15%. Also, a "check tax" was included that placed a 2-cent tax (over 30 cents in today's dollars) on all bank checks. Economists William D. Lastrapes and George Selgin,- conclude that the check tax was "an important contributing factor to that period's severe monetary contraction." Hoover also encouraged Congress to investigate the New York Stock Exchange, and this pressure resulted in various reforms.

National debt expressed as a fraction of gross national product climbs from 20% to 40% under Hoover; levels off under FDR; soars during World War II. For this reason, years later libertarians argued that Hoover's economics were statist.

Franklin D. Roosevelt blasted the Republican incumbent for spending and taxing too much, increasing national debt, raising tariffs and blocking trade, as well as placing millions on the dole of the government. If that's not ironic I don't know what irony is. Roosevelt attacked Hoover for "reckless and extravagant" spending, of thinking "that we ought to center control of everything in Washington as rapidly as possible."- Some of you must be thinking, WHAT???? Roosevelt's running mate, John Nance Garner, accused the Republican of "leading the country down the path of socialism".

Ironically, these policies pale beside the more drastic steps taken under Franklin D. Roosevelt's administration later as part of the New Deal. Hoover's opponents charge that his policies came too little, and too late, and did not work. Even as he asked Congress for legislation, he reiterated his view that while people must not suffer from hunger and cold, caring for them must be primarily a local and voluntary responsibility.

Even so, New Dealer Rexford Tugwell- later remarked that although no one would say so at the time, "practically the whole New Deal was extrapolated from programs that Hoover started."

Hoover was nominated by the Republicans for a second term. He had originally planned to make only one or two major speeches, and to leave the rest of the campaigning to proxies, but when polls showed the entire Republican ticket facing a resounding defeat at the polls, Hoover agreed to an expanded schedule of public addresses. In his nine major radio addresses Hoover primarily defended his administration and his philosophy.

The apologetic approach did not allow Hoover to refute Democratic Party nominee Franklin Roosevelt's charge that he was personally responsible for the depression.

In his campaigns around the country, Hoover was faced with perhaps the most hostile crowds any sitting president had ever faced. Besides having his train and motorcades pelted with eggs and rotten fruit, he was often heckled while speaking, and on several occasions, the Secret Service halted attempts to kill Hoover by disgruntled citizens, including capturing one man nearing Hoover carrying sticks of dynamite, and another already having removed several spikes from the rails in front of the President's train. He lost the election by a huge margin, winning only six out of 48 states.

Hoover suffered a large defeat at the election, obtaining 39.7% of the popular vote to Roosevelt's 57.4%. Hoover's popular vote was reduced by 26% from his result in the 1928 election. In the electoral college he carried only Pennsylvania, Delaware, and four other Northeast states to lose 59–472.

The Democrats also extended their control over the U.S. House and gained control of the U.S. Senate. After the defeat, Hoover's attempts to reach out to Roosevelt to help calm investors and begin to resolve the economic problems facing the country were rebuffed; since Roosevelt was not inaugurated until March 1933, this "guaranteed that Roosevelt took the oath of office amid such an atmosphere of crisis that Hoover had become the most hated man in America."

CHAPTER NINE - The New Deal & FDR

The 1920s "boom" enriched only a fraction of the American people. Earnings for farmers and industrial workers stagnated or fell. While this represented lower production costs for companies, it also precluded growth in consumer demand. Thus, by the mid 1920s the ability of most Americans to purchase new automobiles, new houses and other durable goods was beginning to weaken.

This weakening demand was masked, however, by the great bull market in stocks on the New York Stock Exchange. The ever-growing price for stocks was, in part, the result of greater wealth concentration within the investor class. Eventually the Wall Street stock exchange began to take on a dangerous aura of invincibility, leading investors to ignore less optimistic indicators in the economy. Over-investment and speculating in stocks further inflated their prices, contributing to the illusion of a robust economy.

The crucial point came in the 1920s when banks began to loan money to stock-buyers since stocks were the hottest commodity in the marketplace. Banks allowed Wall Street investors to use the stocks themselves as collateral. If the stocks dropped in value, and investors could not repay the banks, the banks would be left holding near-worthless collateral.

Banks would then go broke, pulling productive businesses down with them as they called in loans and fore-
closed mortgages in a desperate attempt to stay afloat.

But that doomsday scenario was laughed off by analysts
and politicians who argued the U.S. stock market had
entered a new era where stock values and prices would
always go up. That, of course, did not happen. Stock
prices were seriously over-priced when measured in the
actual productivity of the companies they represented
making a market correction inevitable.

 In October 1929 the New York Stock Exchange's house
of cards collapsed in the greatest market crash seen up
to that time. Students are often surprised to learn that
the stock market crash itself did not cause the rest of the
economy to collapse. But, because American banks had
loaned so heavily for stock purchases, falling stock
prices began endangering local banks whose stock-
buying borrowers began defaulting on their loans.

Banks are the pumping stations or hearts of the capitalist
organism. Not only do banks circulate money, they create new money through the making of loans.   Bank-
created credit represents the most elastic element in the
supply of money. As hundreds then thousands of banks
failed between 1929 and 1933, the economy's credit and
money supply began to dry up. Also, as banks went
down, they often took local businesses with them as they
called in business loans in a desperate effort to stay
afloat. All of this rippled outward in ever-widening circles
of bankruptcies, job lay-offs and curtailed consumption.
Conservative historians place a high value on the ideal of
laissez-faire.

Thus, the Depression was simply a painful but necessary market correction which would have corrected itself if left alone. To conservatives, small government means maximum freedom; and, the New Deal means the beginnings of an irresponsible and/or over-regulatory welfare state.

For liberal historians the Depression represents the failure of *laissez-faire*, but not capitalism itself. Liberals value democracy, asserting that democratic governments must be responsive to the social needs of the people. For many liberals the New Deal represents another American Revolution leading to the empowerment of previously powerless and oppressed groups and laying the foundation for a humane welfare state.

Roosevelt remained vague on the campaign trail, promising only that under his presidency government would act decisively to end the Depression. Once in office, FDR said yes to almost every plan put forward by advisors and the Congress said yes to almost every program proposed by the president. In the frantically-paced first few months of his administration, Congress passed scores of new legislation at the president's request. Historians tend to categorize these efforts as either measures for relief short-term programs designed to alleviate immediate suffering, recovery long-term programs to strengthen the economy back to its pre crash level, or, reform permanent structures meant to prevent future depressions.

Another way of understanding FDR's Depression-fighting efforts is to analyze the politics of the New Deal. Generally speaking, the overall aim of the New Deal was essentially conservative.

The New Deal sought to save capitalism and the fundamental institutions of American society from the disaster of the Great Depression. Within that framework, however, significant differences between New Deal programs existed. The first New Deal (1933-35) tended toward a continuation of trickle down policies, albeit better funded and executed more creatively. Even in the early first New Deal, exceptional programs pointed toward the second New Deal's tendency toward "Keynesian" economic policies of revitalizing a mass consumption based economy by revitalizing the masses ability to consume.

English economist John Maynard Keynes sought both to explain why depressions occurred and what might be done to prevent them. Simply put, he thought government should use its massive financial power taxing and spending as a sort of ballast to stabilize the economy. Depressions, then, should be attacked with increased government spending at the bottom of the income pyramid. This position is the opposite of trickle down. Keynesian economists call this counter-cyclical demand management, believing that the government's massive financial impact can be used as a counterweight to current market forces.

For a more detailed explanation of Keynesian theory, visit this well-written British site. Yet, as your text points out, Roosevelt never fully subscribed to Keynes' counter-intuitive argument that government's should spend more during hard times. Roosevelt was a faint-hearted Keynesian, at best. A favorite economist of the left Keynes haunts us to this day. In fact both parties have been overtaken by his throw money at the problem solution to economic crisis.

The Agricultural Adjustment Act, passed in 1933, accepted the long-held premise that low farm prices resulted from overproduction. Thus, the government sought to stimulate increased farm prices by paying farmers to produce less. While the original act was declared unconstitutional by the Supreme Court, a new act correcting for the Court's concerns was passed in 1935. Critics pointed out the irony of reducing food production in a society where children already went hungry. Of course, those children's hunger did not represent demand in the marketplace. Indeed there were agricultural surpluses; as usual, the problem of the American farm was demand and distribution, not supply. Acreage allotment the backbone of the crop reduction program helped the largest and best capitalized farmers. It did little for smaller farmers and led to the eviction and homelessness of tenants and sharecroppers whose landlords hardly needed their services under a system that paid them to grow less. Further, it failed to address the fundamental problem of the Depression: weak consumer demand due to falling wages and unemployment. In the long run the effect of the AAA was beneficial to moderate to large operators.

The 1933 National Industrial Recovery Act (NIRA) set up the New Deal's fundamental strategy of centralized planning as a means of combating the Depression. Industrial sectors were encouraged to avoid cutthroat competition selling below cost to attract dwindling customers and drive weaker competitors out of business which may have been good for individual businesses in the short run, but resulted in increased unemployment and an even smaller customer pool in the long-run.

The government temporarily suspended enforcement of anti monopoly laws and sponsored what amounted to price-fixing as an emergency measure. Similar efforts were made to stabilize wages within industries as well. Again, the basic problem left unanswered was overall weak consumer demand. The NIRA did address this in a limited way with the Public Works Administration which funded various public employment schemes; however, the number of jobs created by the PWA were miniscule compared to the number of jobless workers.

The First New Deal's Tennessee Valley Authority (TVA) reflected the future liberal methods of the Second New Deal. The TVA (1933) provided millions of dollars to transform the economies of seven depressed, rural Southern states along the Tennessee River. The program included dam-building, electric power-generation, flood and erosion control. It provided relatively high-wage jobs in construction in a region the president called "the nation's number one economic problem." Critics saw creeping socialism in this venture; liberals saw it as a successful example of government solving social and economic problems.

The right-wing of American politics convinced Roosevelt he had nothing to lose on that end of the spectrum. Chief among his critics on the right was the Liberty League, a speaker's bureau funded by the Du Pont family and other business interests. The League leadership sought to fuse a partnership between the segregationist governor of Georgia Eugene Talmadge and other conservative leaders to create a grassroots opposition to the New Deal. Liberty League speakers toured the country accusing Roosevelt of instituting creeping socialism.

Right-wing radio personality Father Charles Coughlin denounced recipients of government assistance and claimed the New Deal led the country toward a Communist dictatorship. The Liberty League convinced Roosevelt that he had lost any hope of support from the business right and Coughlin's popularity convinced him that people must be suffering indeed to listen to such rhetoric. In a sense, both the Liberty League and Coughlin for different reasons pushed FDR further to the left. Roosevelt was pulled toward the left by both the traditional Left (The Socialist Party of America) and the unconventional left (Dr. Francis Townsend and Sen. Huey P. Long of Louisiana). In 1932 the Socialists' presidential candidate Norman Thomas had tripled his 1928 showing as hard times rejuvenated the Socialist critique of the system. Nobody thought Thomas posed an electoral threat to FDR; the president was sensitive, however, to the Socialists' rising popularity.

The second New Deal attempted to end the Depression by spending at the bottom of the economy where government funds attempted to turn non-consumers into consumers again. Many of the programs lasted only until World War II while others became permanent fixtures in American life. Here are three to illustrate the central thrust of the second New Deal. The Works Progress Administration was a huge federal jobs program that sought to hire unemployed breadwinners for the purpose strengthening their family's well-being as well as boosting consumer demand. The jobs varied but consisted of mainly of construction of public roads, buildings and parks. Over the course of its life (1935-43) over eight million Americans worked on WPA projects.

Responding in part to "Townsendites," the 1935 Social Security Act set up a modest worker funded but federally guaranteed pension system. Not on the princely scale Townsend had advocated, nevertheless, Social Security did act as a safety net for older workers, promote increased consumer demand and earned a place as a fixture on the American political and social landscape. Finally, another significant component of the second New Deal was the National Labor Relations Act of 1935. Usually called the Wagner Act after its sponsor, Senator Robert Wagner of New York, this law attempted to prevent employers' use of intimidation and coercion in breaking up unions. It set up the National Labor Relations Board to guarantee the right of collective bargaining for American workers. The results were immediately discernable: the formation of the Congress of Industrial Organizations whose auto worker and coal miner units soon saw their wages increase significantly.

Again, higher wages among the masses of the working class is an example of the second New Deal's attempt to restore the economy from the bottom up.
World War II ended both the temporary New Deal programs and the Depression they were attempting to cure. Keep in mind that many facets of the New Deal Social Security, the Federal Deposit Insurance Corporation and the Securities and Exchange Commission to name only three have remained features of American life from the 1930s until the present. Important in the 30's for providing security and good feelings to a skittish public, but become out molded relics kept in place by the left.

War ended the Depression simply because of increased government spending, an intensified version of what Roosevelt was already doing with the WPA and similar programs. Responding to the external threats posed by the Axis Powers Germany, Japan and Italy. Roosevelt and the Congress threw fiscal caution to the wind and spent what was necessary to win the war. In so doing, they also achieved pre-Depression levels of employment and prosperity.

What then is the legacy of the New Deal as a whole? Would it have ended the Depression? The best answer to that is that it went a long way toward alleviating the worst suffering of the Depression while still being captive to the conventional thinking political, fiscal, racial of the day. We cannot answer that question of whether it could have ended the Depression based on historical facts. World War II interrupted the process. The depression would have ended as part of a normal business cycle according to long standing conservative business models.

What are the other long-term consequences of the Depression and New Deal? The rise of the Roosevelt Coalition of farmers, union members, working class people, northern blacks and liberals made the Democratic Party the nation's dominant party for almost sixty years. The real lesson from the New Deal is how politicians on the left could garner the support of these coalitions to keep power.

Further, the political consensus that developed after World War II held that never again should the government allow another depression to take hold.

Thus, there followed an unprecedented level of federal economic intervention. This huge expansion in the role, size and power of government in American social and economic life is aptly summed up in Republican President Richard Nixon's famous 1971 remark, "We're all Keynesians now."

John W Davis was an American politician, diplomat and lawyer. He served as a United States Representative from West Virginia (1911–1913), then as Solicitor General of the United States and U.S. Ambassador to the UK under President Woodrow Wilson. Over a 60-year legal career, he argued 140 cases before the U.S. Supreme Court.

Davis is best known as the Democratic Party nominee for President of the United States during the 1924 presidential election, losing to Republican incumbent Calvin Coolidge. He is regarded as the last conservative nominated by the Democratic Party for President. This distinction is very noteworthy since the Democratic party still awaits a conservative voice on the national stage.

Davis was one of the most prominent and successful lawyers of the first half of the twentieth century, arguing 140 cases before the U.S. Supreme Court. His firm, variously titled Stetson Jennings Russell & Davis, then Davis Polk Wardwell Gardiner & Reed then Davis Polk Wardwell Sunderland & Kiendl represented many of the largest companies in the United States in the 1920s and following decades.

The last twenty years of Davis's practice included representing large corporations before the United States Supreme Court challenging the constitutionality and application of New Deal legislation. Davis lost many of these battles.

The American Liberty League was an American political organization formed in 1934 by conservative Democrats to oppose the New Deal of Franklin Roosevelt and other liberal Democrats. Jouett Shouse, a prominent Democrat, was the League's president. Other leaders included prominent Democrats and businessmen, such as Al Smith the 1928 Democratic presidential nominee, John W. Davis and John Jacob Raskob former Democratic National Chairman and the foremost opponent of prohibition, Dean Acheson future Secretary of State under Harry Truman and Bainbridge Colby, a former secretary of state. It attracted many industrialists.

Regarding the controversial NRA, the League was ambivalent. Jouett Shouse, the League president commented that "the NRA has indulged in unwarranted excesses of attempted regulation"; on the other, he added that "in many regards [the NRA] has served a useful purpose."- Shouse said that he had "deep sympathy" with the goals of the NRA, explaining, "While I feel very strongly that the prohibition of child labor, the maintenance of a minimum wage and the limitation of the hours of work belong under our form of government in the realm of the affairs of the different states, yet I am entirely willing to agree that in the case of an overwhelming national emergency the Federal Government for a limited period should be permitted to assume jurisdiction of them."

The League labeled Roosevelt's Agricultural Adjustment Administration a trend toward Fascist control of agriculture. Social Security was said to mark the end of democracy. Lawyers for the American Liberty League challenged the validity of the Wagner Act National Labor Relations Act, but in 1937, the United States Supreme Court upheld the constitutionality of the statute. The League faded away and disbanded in 1940.

Al Smith, was an American politician who was elected the 42nd Governor of New York four times, and was the Democratic U.S. presidential candidate in 1928. He was the first Roman Catholic to run for President as a major party nominee. He lost the election to Herbert Hoover. He then became president of the Empire State, Inc. and was instrumental in getting the Empire State Building built at the onset of the Great Depression.
Smith became critical of Roosevelt's New Deal policies and joined the American Liberty League, an anti-Roosevelt group. Smith believed the New Deal was a betrayal of good government Progressive ideals, and ran counter to the goal of close cooperation with business. Smith's antipathy of Roosevelt and his policies was so great that he supported Republican presidential candidates Alfred M. Landon in the 1936 election and Wendell Wilkie in the 1940 election.

Although personal resentment was a motivating factor in Smith's break with Roosevelt and the New Deal, Smith was consistent in his beliefs and politics. Smith always believed in social mobility, economic opportunity, religious tolerance, and individualism. Strangely enough, Smith and Eleanor Roosevelt remained close.

Although most of the Democratic party and a fair share of the Republicans backed Roosevelt and his new deal Davis and Smith are representative of a minority of conservative Democrats that felt the policy was a betrayal to American business.

At the other end of the spectrum stood leftist radicals like Huey Pierce Long, Jr. nicknamed The Kingfish, served as the 40th Governor of Louisiana from 1928 to 1932 and as a U.S. senator from 1932 to 1935. A Democrat, he was noted for his radical populist policies. Though a backer of Franklin D. Roosevelt in the 1932 presidential election, Long split with Roosevelt in June 1933 and allegedly planned to mount his own presidential bid.

Long created the Share Our Wealth program in 1934, with the motto "Every Man a King", proposing new wealth redistribution measures in the form of a net asset tax on corporations and individuals to curb the poverty and crime resulting from the Great Depression. To stimulate the economy, Long advocated federal spending on public works, public education, old age pensions and other social programs. He was an ardent critic of the Federal Reserve System's policies to reduce lending. Charismatic and immensely popular for his social reform programs and willingness to take forceful action, Long was accused by his opponents of dictatorial tendencies for his near total control of the state government.
At the height of his popularity, Long was shot on September 8, 1935, at the Louisiana State Capitol in Baton Rouge. He died two days later at the age of 42. It is unclear whether he was assassinated, or accidentally killed by bodyguards who believed an assassination attempt was in progress. His last words were reportedly, "God, don't let me die, I have so much left to do."

Long's three-year term in the Senate overlapped an important time in American history as the Franklin Delano Roosevelt administration attempted to deal with the Great Depression. Long often attempted to upstage the president and the congressional leadership by mounting populist appeals of his own, most notably his "Share Our Wealth" program.

Long arrived in Washington, D.C., to take his seat in the United States Senate in January 1932, although he was absent for more than half the days in the 1932 session. With the backdrop of the Great Depression, he made characteristically fiery speeches which denounced the concentration of wealth in the hands of a few. He also criticized the leaders of both parties for failing to address the crisis adequately, most notably attacking Senate Democratic Leader Joseph Robinson of Arkansas for his apparent closeness with President Herbert Hoover. Robinson had been the vice-presidential candidate in 1928 on the Democratic ticket opposite Hoover and his running-mate, Senator Charles Curtis of Kansas.

Aware that Roosevelt had no intention to radically redistribute the country's wealth, Long became one of the few national politicians to oppose Roosevelt's New Deal policies from the left. He considered them inadequate in the face of the escalating economic crisis. Long sometimes supported Roosevelt's programs in the Senate, saying that "whenever this administration has gone to the left I have voted with it, and whenever it has gone to the right I have voted against it."

To discredit Long and damage his support base, in 1934 Roosevelt had Long's finances investigated by the Internal Revenue Service.

Though they failed to link Long to any illegality, some of Long's lieutenants were charged with income tax evasion, but only one had been convicted by the time of Long's death.

Long's radical populist rhetoric and his aggressive tactics did little to endear him to his fellow senators. Not one of his proposed bills, resolutions or motions was passed during his three years in the Senate despite an overwhelming Democratic majority. During one debate, another senator told Long, "I do not believe you could get the Lord's Prayer endorsed in this body."

Charles Edward Coughlin began to criticize the government of President Herbert Hoover. CBS, concerned by this development, warned him to tone down his broadcasts. When Coughlin refused, CBS decided not to renew his contract when it expired in April 1931. Coughlin responded by organizing his own radio network which eventually grew to over 30 stations.

During the 1932 presidential election, Coughlin advocated that his listeners should vote for Franklin D. Roosevelt. After the election Coughlin gave his support to Roosevelt's New Deal. He continued with his radio broadcasts where he advocated the nationalization of gold and the revaluation of the dollar. Coughlin continued to be extremely popular and the first edition of his complete radio discourses, published in 1933, quickly sold over a million copies.

In 1935 Coughlin started a campaign to restructure the Federal Reserve System and urged Roosevelt to take full government control over the nation's banking system and to establish a Central Bank.

Coughlin also became involved in trade unions. He established the Automotive Industrial Workers Association (AIWA) in Detroit in direct competition with the more radical United Auto Workers. Coughlin also joined Huey Long in the campaign to persuade President Franklin D. Roosevelt to support the paying of the Bonus Bill, a large sum of money owed to the American veterans of the First World War.

Coughlin gradually grew disillusioned with Roosevelt and on 11th November, 1934, he announced the formation of the National Union of Social Justice. At this time some observers claimed that Father Coughlin was the second most important political figure in the United States. It was estimated that Coughlin's radio broadcasts were getting an audience of 30 million people. He was also having to employ twenty six secretaries to deal with the 400,000 letters a week he was receiving from his listeners.

According to Wallace Stegner "Father Coughlin had a voice of such mellow richness, such manly, heart-warming, confidential intimacy, such emotional and in-gratiating charm, that anyone tuning past it on the radio dial almost automatically returned to hear it again." As well as his radio broadcasts, Coughlin also began publishing *Social Justice Weekly*, a journal which soon achieved a circulation of over one million copies.

In May 1935 Coughlin began having talks with Huey Long, Francis Townsend, Gerald L. K. Smith, Milo Reno and Floyd B. Olson about a joint campaign to take on President Franklin D. Roosevelt in the 1936 presidential elections. Long was expected to be the candidate but he was assassinated on 8th September, 1935.

After this defeat Coughlin's replaced the National Union of Social Justice with the Christian Front and concentrated on the dangers of communism. Coughlin also became an isolationist and one of his campaign slogans was: "Less care for internationalism and more concern for national prosperity."

Alfred (Alf) Mossman Landon was born in West Middlesex, Pennsylvania on September 9, 1887. He grew up in Ohio and moved with his family to Kansas in 1904 when he was seventeen. The move to Kansas was the result of the emerging oil and gas business in Kansas.
He became Governor of Kansas in 1932 and again in 1934. Alf Landon was the only Republican Governor elected in 1934 in the United States. He was the Republican Party presidential candidate in 1936. He retained ownership of the house throughout his presidential campaign and used pictures of the house in his presidential campaign literature. He died at the age of 100, October 12, 1987 in Topeka, KS.

Republican national leaders saw Landon as a promising candidate to oppose Franklin D. Roosevelt's re-election bid in 1936. Few members of the party had the stature or voter appeal to seriously contest the popular president, and Landon's folksy image and common-sense political stands made him an early favorite for the nomination. After expressing disbelief that anyone saw him as presidential material, he pursued the nomination in earnest, tapping Kansas national committeeman John D. M. Hamilton as his campaign manager. His candidacy was officially launched at the 1935 American Legion Convention.

Among his early supporters was powerful newspaper mogul William Randolph Hearst, whose publications hailed Landon as the "Horse and Buggy Governor" and the "Kansas Coolidge."

He did feel that the New Deal's programs were poorly executed, showing "too much of the slap-dash, jazzy method." Instead of condemning them completely, he favored eliminating the waste and inefficiency in specific programs. Unlike the Republican Old Guard, Landon didn't seek a return to the unfettered capitalism of an earlier era. "I do not believe the Jeffersonian theory that the best government is the one that governs the least can be applied today," he told a Kansas audience. "I think that as civilization becomes more complex, government power must increase."

In October the highly regarded *Liberty Digest* straw poll predicted a Landon victory. The results on election day proved to be far different: the incumbent Roosevelt carried 46 states worth 523 electoral votes, leaving only Maine and Vermont 8 electoral votes in his opponent's column. Roosevelt also overwhelmed Landon in the popular vote, garnering 27,757,333 to the Kansan's 16,684,231. Landon took the defeat philosophically, remarking to a friend: "I don't think that it would have made any difference what kind of a campaign I made as far as stopping this avalanche is concerned. That is one consolation you get out of a good licking."

Surviving most of his political peers, Landon lived to see his daughter Nancy Landon Kassebaum elected to the U.S. senate in 1978. Ronald and Nancy Reagan were among the visitors who helped him celebrate his 100th birthday.

On October 12, 1987, Landon died peacefully at his Topeka home, having put his political wins and losses far behind him. Kansas Senator Robert Dole was among those who eulogized Landon, hailing him as "a legendary Republican who taught generations of politicians what integrity and leadership were all about."

Robert Alphonso Taft of the Taft political family of Cincinnati, was a Republican United States Senator and a prominent conservative statesman. As the leading opponent of the New Deal in the Senate from 1939 to 1953, he led the successful effort by the conservative coalition to curb the power of labor unions, and was a major proponent of the foreign policy of non-interventionism. However, he failed in his quest to win the presidential nomination of the Republican Party in 1940, 1948 and 1952. From 1940 to 1952 he battled New York Governor Thomas E. Dewey, the leader of the GOP's moderate Eastern Establishment for control of the Republican Party. In 1957, a Senate committee chaired by John F. Kennedy named Taft as one of the five greatest senators in American history.

Cooperating with conservative southern Democrats, he led the Conservative Coalition that opposed the New Deal. The Republican gains in the 1938 congressional elections, combined with the creation of the Conservative Coalition, had stopped the expansion of the New Deal. However, Taft saw his mission as not only stopping the growth of the New Deal, but also as eliminating many of the government programs that had already come from it.

During his first term in the Senate, Taft criticized what he believed was the inefficiency and waste of many New Deal programs, and of the need to let private enterprise and businesses restore the nation's economy instead of relying upon government programs to end the Great Depression. He condemned the New Deal as socialist and attacked deficit spending, high farm subsidies, governmental bureaucracy, the National Labor Relations Board, and nationalized health insurance.

Taft set forward a conservative program that promoted economic growth, individual economic opportunity, adequate social welfare, strong national defense primarily the Navy and Air Force, and non involvement in European wars. He also strongly opposed the military draft on the principle that it limited a young man's freedom of choice. Broadly speaking, in terms of political philosophy Taft was a libertarian; he opposed nearly all forms of governmental interference in both the national economy and in the private lives of citizens.

As the 1940 presidential election loomed large, the question of whether or not Franklin Roosevelt would break the two term tradition became a popular one within Washington and in the media. On the one hand, the nation was still recovering from the Great Depression and the war in Europe began to rage to the point where increased American involvement might become necessary. Franklin Roosevelt's leadership had proven invaluable symbolically and practically during the 1930s depression and may prove necessary in the case of war. On the other hand, great presidents like Theodore Roosevelt and George Washington had adhered to an unspoken two term limit, in order to prevent the type of tyranny that the first settlers to America were running away from.

Roosevelt's decision to run for a third term was embraced by many in the Democratic rank and file, who saw his political fortitude as an asset more valuable than the two term tradition. However, some Democratic leaders were upset with Roosevelt's decision, in part because he consulted few people about it and also because there were several Democratic leaders that were presidential hopefuls.

John Nance Garner, the vice president and a 1932 presidential hopeful, became estranged from the president over his two terms due to the president's liberal use of the executive powers and abstained from running as the vice president in 1940. Instead, Roosevelt chose Henry Wallace, his secretary of agriculture, to run in the second spot. His decision to seek a third term broke an unwritten rule that went back to George Washington who saw the two term limit as needed. As well, Postmaster General James Farley, a key member of the Democratic leadership structure, resigned in protest of Roosevelt's decision to run for a third term. Despite the tumult, Roosevelt won easy renomination to the Democratic ticket.

The Republican party was kidnapped by the eastern liberal faction and endorsed Wendell Wilkie who was born in Elwood, Indiana, on February 18, 1892. The Republican party tapped Wilkie, a lawyer and utilities executive, to run against FDR in 1940, even though Wilkie was a former Democrat.

Wilkie campaigned against the New Deal and the government's lack of military preparedness. During the election, Roosevelt preempted the military issue by expanding military contracts.

Wilkie then reversed his approach and accused FDR of warmongering. On election day, FDR received 27 million votes to Wilkie's 22 million, and in the Electoral College, Roosevelt buried Wilkie 449 to 82.

As World War II loomed after 1938, with the Japanese invasion of China and the aggressions of Nazi Germany, FDR gave strong diplomatic and financial support to China and Britain, while remaining officially neutral. His goal was to make America the "Arsenal of Democracy" which would supply munitions to the Allies. In March 1941, Roosevelt, with Congressional approval, provided Lend-Lease aid to the countries fighting against Nazi Germany with Great Britain. He secured a near-unanimous declaration of war against Japan after the Japanese attack on Pearl Harbor on December 7, 1941, calling it a "date that will live in infamy". He supervised the mobilization of the US economy to support the Allied war effort which saw unemployment evaporate and the industrial economy soar to heights no one ever expected.

Roosevelt dominated the American political scene, not only during the twelve years of his presidency, but for decades afterward. He orchestrated the realignment of voters that created the Fifth Party System. FDR's New Deal Coalition united together labor unions, big city machines, white ethnics, African Americans and rural white Southerners. Roosevelt's diplomatic impact also resonated on the world stage long after his death, with the United Nations and Bretton Woods as examples of his administration's wide-ranging impact.

Roosevelt's third term was dominated by World War II, in Europe and in the Pacific. Roosevelt slowly began re armament in 1938 since he was facing strong isolationist sentiment from leaders like Senators William Borah and Robert Taft.

By 1940, it was in high gear, with bipartisan support, partly to expand and re-equip the United States Army and Navy and partly to become the "Arsenal of Democracy" supporting Britain, France, China and after June 1941, the Soviet Union. As Roosevelt took a firmer stance against the Axis Powers, American isolationists including Charles Lindbergh and America First vehemently attacked the President as an irresponsible warmonger.

The military buildup spurred economic growth. By 1941, unemployment had fallen to under 1 million. There was a growing labor shortage in all the nation's major manufacturing centers, accelerating the African Americans from farms in the South, and of underemployed farmers and workers from all rural areas and small towns. The home front was subject to dynamic social changes throughout the war, though domestic issues were no longer Roosevelt's most urgent policy concerns.

When Nazi Germany invaded the Soviet Union in June 1941, Roosevelt extended Lend-Lease to the Soviets. During 1941, Roosevelt also agreed that the U.S. Navy would escort Allied convoys as far east as Great Britain and would fire upon German ships or submarines U-boats of the German Navy if they attacked Allied shipping within the U.S. Navy zone.

Thus, by mid-1941, Roosevelt had committed the U.S. to the Allied side with a policy of all aid short of war. Roosevelt met with Winston Churchill, Prime Minister of the United Kingdom on August 14, 1941, to develop the Atlantic Charter in what was to be the first of several wartime conferences. In July 1941, Roosevelt ordered Henry Stimson, Secretary of War to begin planning for total American military involvement. The resulting Victory Program, under the direction of Albert Wedemeyer, provided the President with the estimates necessary for the total mobilization of manpower, industry, and logistics to defeat the potential enemies of the United States.

When the war began the danger of a Japanese attack on the coast led to growing pressure to remove people of Japanese descent away from the coastal region. This pressure grew due to fears of terrorism, espionage, and/or sabotage.

On February 19, 1942, President Roosevelt signed an Executive Order which relocated the first generation of Japanese immigrants who did not have US citizenship and their children, who had dual citizenship. After both Nazi Germany and Fascist Italy declared war on the United States in December 1941, German and Italian citizens who had not taken out American citizenship and who spoke out for Hitler and Mussolini were often arrested or interned.

William E Borah was a prominent Republican attorney and longtime United States Senator from Idaho noted for his oratorical skills and isolationist views. One of his nicknames later in life was "The Lion of Idaho."

In 1906, the Idaho Legislature elected William Borah to the U.S. Senate over the controversial Democratic incumbent, Fred Dubois. Borah was reelected by the Idaho Legislature in 1912, and four more times by popular vote (1918, 1924, 1930 and 1936). He remains the longest-serving member of the United States Congress in Idaho history.

A member of the Republican National Committee from 1908 to 1912, he was a delegate to the 1912 Republican National Convention. As a senator Borah was dedicated to principles rather than party loyalty, a trait which earned him the nickname "the Great Opposer." He disliked entangling alliances in foreign policy and became a prominent anti-imperialist and nationalist, favoring a continued separation of American liberal and European Great Power politics. He encouraged the formation of a series of world economic conferences and favored a low tariff.

In 1919 Borah and other Senate Republicans, notably Henry Cabot Lodge of Massachusetts and Hiram W. Johnson of California, clashed with President Woodrow Wilson over Senate ratification of the Treaty of Versailles ending World War I and establishing the League of Nations. Borah emerged as leader of the Irreconcilables, a group of senators noted for their uncompromising opposition to the treaty and the League. During 1919 Borah and Johnson toured the country speaking against the treaty in response to Wilson's own speaking tour supporting it. Borah's impassioned November 19, 1919, speech on the Senate floor in opposition to the treaty and League of Nations was contributive to the Senate's ultimate rejection of it.

After Hoover's defeat by Democrat Franklin D. Roosevelt, Borah, now the Dean of the United States Senate, supported certain components of the New Deal, such as old-age pensions and the confiscation of U.S. citizens' gold by executive order, but opposed others, including the National Industrial Recovery Act and the Agricultural Adjustment Act.

Robert Taft was an ardent isolationist and felt we should not enter the foreign war. Taft's greatest prominence during his first term came not from his fight against the New Deal and President Franklin Roosevelt, but rather from his vigorous and outspoken opposition to U.S. involvement in the Second World War.

A staunch non-interventionist, Taft believed that America should avoid any involvement in European or Asian wars and concentrate instead on solving its domestic problems. He believed that a strong U.S. military, combined with the natural geographic protection of the broad Atlantic and Pacific Oceans, would be adequate to protect America even if the Nazis overran all of Europe. Between the outbreak of war in September 1939 and the Japanese attack on Pearl Harbor in December 1941 Taft opposed nearly all attempts to aid Allied forces fighting the Nazis in Europe.

His outspoken opposition to aiding the Allied forces earned him strong criticism from many liberal Republicans, such as Wendell Wilkie and Thomas E. Dewey, who felt that America could best protect itself by fully supporting the British and their allies.

Although Taft fully supported the American war effort after Pearl Harbor and the declaration of war on Japan by the U.S. congress on December 8, 1941, he continued to harbor a deep suspicion of American involvement in postwar military alliances with other nations, including NATO. His stance was foreign alliances was not only prophetic for our nation but also a position that American conservatives still hold today.

In 1944 Taft was nearly defeated in his bid for a second term in the Senate; his Democratic opponent, William G. Pickrel, received major support from Ohio's labor unions and internationalists and nearly won the upset victory. He became chairman of the Senate Republican Conference in 1944.

Taft first sought the Republican presidential nomination in 1940, but lost to Wendell Wilkie. Taft was regarded as a strong contender, but his outspoken opposition support of non interventionist foreign policies, and his opposition to the New Deal in domestic policy led many liberal Republicans to reject his candidacy. At the 1940 GOP Convention Willkie a onetime Democrat and corporate executive who had never run for political office came from behind to beat Taft and several other candidates for the nomination. In the 1944 presidential campaign Taft was not a candidate, instead he supported Governor John Bricker of Ohio, a fellow conservative, for the GOP nomination. However, Bricker was defeated by New York Governor Thomas E. Dewey; Bricker then became Dewey's running mate.

The period during World War II the country rallied around their president and nation. While Roosevelt prosecuted the war there was little conservative decent of our basic mission to end Hitler and Japan's world conquest.

Roosevelt, who turned 62 in 1944, had been in declining health since at least 1940. The strain of his paralysis and the physical exertion needed to compensate for it for over 20 years had taken their toll, as had many years of stress and a lifetime of chain-smoking. By this time, Roosevelt had numerous ailments including chronic high blood pressure, emphysema, systemic atherosclerosis, coronary artery disease with angina pectoris, and myopathic hypertensive heart disease with congestive heart failure. Though not yet confirmed, it has been speculated that he also had a melanoma removed from above his left eye, although this was not known publicly. Dr. Emanuel Libman, then an assistant pathologist at Mount Sinai Hospital in New York City, reacting to Roosevelt's appearance in newsreels, remarked in 1944 that "It doesn't matter whether Roosevelt is re-elected or not, he'll die of a cerebral hemorrhage within 6 months" which he did, five months later.

Aware of the risk that Roosevelt would die during his fourth term, the party regulars insisted that Henry A. Wallace, who was seen as too pro-Soviet, be dropped as Vice President. After considering James F. Byrnes of South Carolina, and being turned down by Indiana Governor Henry F. Schricker, Roosevelt replaced Wallace with the little known Senator Harry S. Truman.

In the 1944 election, Roosevelt and Truman won 53% of the vote and carried 36 states, against New York Governor Thomas E. Dewey.

Thomas E Dewey the crusading Governor of New York had wrestled the Republican nomination in 1944. When the convention opened, Governor Dewey was the front-runner for the nomination. Former presidential candidate Wendell Wilkie again vied for the nomination, but when he lost the Wisconsin primary, the lack of support from the Republican Party became evident. Dewey was nominated on the first ballot. He became the first Republican candidate to accept his party's nomination in person at the convention.

On March 29, 1945, Roosevelt went to Warm Springs to rest before his anticipated appearance at the founding conference of the United Nations. On the afternoon of April 12, Roosevelt said, "I have a terrific pain in the back of my head." He then slumped forward in his chair, unconscious, and was carried into his bedroom. The president's attending cardiologist, Dr. Howard Bruenn, diagnosed a massive cerebral hemorrhage (stroke). At 3:35 p.m. that day, Roosevelt died.

Following months of uncertainty over the president's preference for a running mate, Truman was selected as Franklin Roosevelt's vice presidential candidate in 1944 as the result of a deal worked out by Hannegan, who was Democratic National Chairman that year.

Although his public image remained that of a robust, engaged world leader, Roosevelt's physical condition was in fact rapidly deteriorating in mid 1944. A handful of key FDR advisers, including outgoing Democratic National Committee Chairman Frank C. Walker, incoming Chairman Robert Hannegan, party treasurer Edwin W. Pauley, strategist Ed Flynn, and lobbyist George E. Allen closed ranks in the summer of 1944 to keep Henry Wallace off the ticket. They considered Wallace, the incumbent vice president, too liberal, and had grave concerns about the possibility of his ascension to the presidency. Allen would later recall that each of these men "realized that the man nominated to run with Roosevelt would in all probability be the next President.

On April 12, 1945, Truman was urgently called to the White House, where Eleanor Roosevelt informed him that the president had died after suffering a massive cerebral hemorrhage. Truman's first concern was for Mrs. Roosevelt. He asked if there was anything he could do for her, to which she replied, "Is there anything *we* can do for *you*? You are the one in trouble now!"

CHAPTER TEN - Post War America

Many Americans feared that the end of World War II and the subsequent drop in military spending might bring back the hard times of the Great Depression. But instead, pent-up consumer demand fueled exceptionally strong economic growth in the postwar period. The automobile industry successfully converted back to producing cars, and new industries such as aviation and electronics grew by leaps and bounds. A housing boom, stimulated in part by easily affordable mortgages for returning members of the military, added to the expansion. The nation's gross national product rose from about $200,000 million in 1940 to $300,000 million in 1950 and to more than $500,000 million in 1960. At the same time, the jump in postwar births, known as the "baby boom," increased the number of consumers. More and more Americans joined the middle class.

The need to produce war supplies had given rise to a huge military industrial complex. It did not disappear with the war's end. As the Iron Curtain descended across Europe and the United States found itself embroiled in a cold war with the Soviet Union, the government maintained substantial fighting capacity and invested in sophisticated weapons such as the hydrogen bomb. Economic aid flowed to war ravaged European countries under the Marshall Plan, which also helped maintain markets for numerous U.S. goods. And the government itself recognized its central role in economic affairs.

The Employment Act of 1946 stated as government policy "to promote maximum employment, production, and purchasing power."

The United States also recognized during the postwar period the need to restructure international monetary arrangements, spearheading the creation of the International Monetary Fund and the World Bank institutions designed to ensure an open, capitalist international economy.

Business, meanwhile, entered a period marked by consolidation. Firms merged to create huge, diversified conglomerates. International Telephone and Telegraph, for instance, bought Sheraton Hotels, Continental Banking, Hartford Fire Insurance, Avis Rent-a-Car, and other companies.

The American work force also changed significantly. During the 1950s, the number of workers providing services grew until it equaled and then surpassed the number who produced goods. And by 1956, a majority of U.S. workers held white-collar rather than blue-collar jobs. At the same time, labor unions won long-term employment contracts and other benefits for their members.

Other Americans moved, too. Growing demand for single-family homes and the widespread ownership of cars led many Americans to migrate from central cities to suburbs. Coupled with technological innovations such as the invention of air conditioning, the migration spurred the development of Sun Belt cities such as Houston, Atlanta, Miami, and Phoenix in the southern and southwestern states. As new, federally sponsored highways created better access to the suburbs, business patterns began to change as well. Shopping centers multiplied, rising from eight at the end of World War II to 3,840 in 1960.

Many industries soon followed, leaving cities for less crowded sites.

The Cold War began after World War Two. The main enemies were the United States and the Soviet Union. The Cold war got its name because both sides were afraid of fighting each other directly. In such a hot war, nuclear weapons might destroy everything. So, instead, they fought each other indirectly. They played havoc with conflicts in different parts of the world. They also used words as weapons. They threatened and denounced each other. Or they tried to make each other look foolish. The United States and the Soviet Union were the only two superpowers following the Second World War. The fact that, by the 1950s, each possessed nuclear weapons and the means of delivering such weapons on their enemies, added a dangerous aspect to the Cold War.

The Cold War world was separated into three groups. The United States lead the West. This group included countries with democratic political systems. The Soviet Union led the East. This group included countries with communist political systems. The non-aligned group included countries that did not want to be tied to either the West or the East.

The Soviet Union had been invaded via Eastern Europe in both the First and Second World Wars. In both conflicts, some of the nations of Eastern Europe had participated in those invasions. Both Wars had devastated the Soviet Union. An estimated twenty-five million Russians were killed during the Second World War. The Soviet Union was determined to install friendly regimes throughout Eastern Europe following the War.

The strategic goal was to protect its European borders from future invasions. Since the Soviet Union was a communist state, the Soviet government was determined to install communist regimes throughout Eastern Europe. The Red Army was liberating the nations of Eastern Europe and therefore, the Soviet Union was in a position to influence the type of governments that would emerge following the War.

The Soviets believed that they had an agreement with the western democracies that made Eastern Europe a Soviet sphere of influence, the Soviet Union would have dominant influence in that region. In 1945 Joseph Stalin pronounced that any freely elected governments in Poland, Czechoslovakia and other Eastern European states would be anti-Soviet and he refused to allow this. In March 1946 Winston Churchill referred to an iron curtain descending across the continent. The cold war began because of this struggle for control of the politics of these nations. By 1948, pro-Soviet regimes were in power in Poland, Bulgaria, Hungary, Romania, and Czechoslovakia.

The Western democracies, led by the United States, were determined to stop the spread of communism and Soviet power. While not being able to stop the Soviets in Eastern Europe, the U.S. and Britain were determined to prevent communist regimes from achieving power in Western Europe. During the Second World War, communist parties throughout Western Europe, had gained popularity in their resistance to Nazi occupation. There was a real possibility the communist parties would be elected in both France and Italy.

Harry Truman was the first American president to fight the Cold War. Probably the most important, certainly the most forgotten, and surely the most controversial, was the decision to concentrate on the European theater, rather than the Pacific. Avoiding a two front war has long been a fundamental strategic choice. Germany during the 20th Century was bedeviled by two front wars, and the Allies gave preference to the European theater where the Soviet Union was engaged with Germany over the Pacific theater where the Soviets remained at peace with Japan. Truman was in a sense re-affirming the geographical preferences of the struggle against the Axis in his priorities in the struggle against Communism. General George C. Marshall was chief of staff of the United States Army from 1939 through 1945 and the principal American military architect of Allied victory. Marshall was special representative of the president to China, from 1945 until 1947. He concluded that no describable amount of American aid could save Chiang Kai Chek from the communists, and returned to Washington to propose a strategy that concentrated on Europe. Marshall retired from active service February 1947, and served as Secretary of State from 21 January 1947 until 21 January 1949.

In March 1947, President Truman asked Congress for $400 million in aid for Greece and Turkey. "It must be the policy of the United States," he argued in what became known as the Truman Doctrine, "to support free peoples who are resisting attempted subjugation by armed minorities or by outside pressures." The Truman Doctrine was a plan to give money and military aid to countries threatened by communism.

The Truman Doctrine effectively stopped communists from taking control of Greece and Turkey. And in April 1948 the Marshall Plan was announced, to provide financial and economic assistance to the nations of Western Europe. This strengthened the economies and governments of countries in western Europe, and as the economies of Western Europe improved, the popularity of communist parties declined.

The conflict came to center on the future of Germany, and the Soviet Union blockaded all surface transport into West Berlin in June 1948. In June 1948 the Soviets blocked all ways into the western part of Berlin, Germany. President Truman quickly ordered military planes to fly coal, food, and medicine to the city. The planes kept coming, sometimes landing every few minutes, for more than a year. The United States received help from Britain and France. Together, they provided almost 2.5 million tons of supplies on about 280,000 flights. Gradually there was a massive build up of an airlift of supplies into that city through until September 1949, although the blockade was officially lifted in May 1949.

The United States also led the formation of the North Atlantic Treaty Organization in 1949. NATO was a joint military group. Its purpose was to defend against Soviet forces in Europe or, as the saying went, to keep Russia out, America in and Germany down. The first members of NATO were Belgium, Britain, Canada, Denmark, France, Iceland, Italy, Luxembourg, the Netherlands, Portugal, and the United States. The Soviet Union and its east European allies formed their own joint military group the Warsaw Pact six years later.

Mao's only visit to Moscow to meet Stalin, which he made following the Communist victory in the Chinese civil war in 1949, culminated in the proclamation of a Sino-Soviet alliance in February 1950. The alliance peaked during the Korean War as China intervened for almost three years on behalf of North Korea. Declassified documents show the initiative for the North attacking the South came not from Stalin but from Kim Il Sung, who pleaded with Moscow unsuccessfully in 1947 and 1949 for permission to attack. The attack came only after the North Korean dictator received permission from both Mao and Stalin to attack, essentially daring the Soviets or the Chinese to appear weak.

During his few weeks as Vice President, Harry S Truman scarcely saw President Roosevelt, and received no briefing on the development of the atomic bomb or the unfolding difficulties with Soviet Russia. Suddenly these and a host of other wartime problems became Truman's to solve when, on April 12, 1945, he became President. He told reporters, "I felt like the moon, the stars, and all the planets had fallen on me."

As President, Truman made some of the most crucial decisions in history. Soon after V-E Day, the war against Japan had reached its final stage. An urgent plea to Japan to surrender was rejected. Truman, after consultations with his advisers, ordered atomic bombs dropped on cities devoted to war work. Two were Hiroshima and Nagasaki. Japanese surrender quickly followed.

In June 1945 Truman witnessed the signing of the charter of the United Nations, hopefully established to preserve peace.

Thus far, he had followed his predecessor's policies, but he soon developed his own. He presented to Congress a 21-point program, proposing the expansion of Social Security, a full-employment program, a permanent Fair Employment Practices Act, and public housing and slum clearance. The program, Truman wrote, "symbolizes for me my assumption of the office of President in my own right." It became known as the Fair Deal.

In 1947 as the Soviet Union pressured Turkey and, through guerrillas, threatened to take over Greece, he asked Congress to aid the two countries, enunciating the program that bears his name the Truman Doctrine.

In November 1947, the United Nations voted in favor of the partition of Palestine, proposing the creation of a Jewish state, an Arab state, and a UN-administered Jerusalem. The newly created United Nations approved the Partition Plan for Palestine United Nations General Assembly Resolution 181 on November 29, 1947, which sought to divide the country into two states one Arab and one Jewish. Jerusalem was to be designated an international city administered by the UN.

The Jewish community accepted the plan,- but the Arab League and Arab Higher Committee rejected it. On December 1, 1947, the Arab Higher Committee proclaimed a three-day strike, and Arab bands began attacking Jewish targets.-Jews were initially on the defensive as civil war broke out, but they gradually moved onto the offensive.

The Palestinian Arab economy collapsed and 250,000 Palestinian-Arabs fled or were expelled on May 14, 1948, the day before the expiration of the British Mandate, the Jewish Agency proclaimed independence, naming the country Israel.

The following day, the armies of four Arab countries Egypt, Syria, Lebanon and Iraq attacked Israel, launching the 1948 Arab-Israeli War;- Saudi Arabia sent a military contingent to operate under Egyptian command; Yemen declared war but did not take military action.- After a year of fighting, a ceasefire was declared and temporary borders, known as the Green Line, were established.- Jordan annexed what became known as the West Bank and East Jerusalem, and Egypt took control of the Gaza Strip. Meanwhile, Israel was accepted as a member of the United Nations by majority vote on May 11, 1949.- According to UN estimates, 711,000 Arabs, or about 80% of the initial Arab population of the area that became Israel, were expelled or fled the country during the conflict.- The fate of these Palestinian refugees remains a major point of contention in the Israeli–Palestinian conflict.

United States support for the partition of Palestine was crucial to the adoption of the UN partition plan and to the creation of the state of Israel. During World War II, the USA was anxious to maintain good relations with Saudi Arabia. President Roosevelt had promised King Saud that the USA would make no policy decisions about Palestine without consulting the Arabs, though Roosevelt tried to enlist Saud's support for allowing Jewish immigration to Palestine. Following Roosevelt's verbal promise to Saud to consult the Arabs about Palestine policy, he reiterated the promise in writing on April 5, 1945.

However, a week later, Roosevelt was dead, replaced by Vice President Harry S. Truman, and the end of the war created a different political reality as well as bringing the revelation of massive murder of Jews in the Holocaust.

Despite his plainspoken ways, Harry S. Truman had a sweeping grasp of geopolitical realities. He was also a friend of the Jews who had made clear his support for the Zionist cause before WWII. He was strengthened in his resolve to help the Jews following the revelations of Nazi atrocities.

On May 25, 1939, following the British White Paper of 1939 that limited Jewish immigration, Truman inserted a remark in the Congressional Record condemning the White paper as a repudiation of British obligations. At a Chicago rally in 1944, then Senator Truman said, *"Today, not tomorrow, we must do all that is humanly possible to provide a haven for all those who can be grasped from the hands of Nazi butchers. Free lands must be opened to them."*

Truman wrote in his memoirs, *"The question of Palestine as a Jewish homeland goes back to the solemn promise that had been made to them the Jews by the British in the Balfour Declaration of 1917 - a promise which had stirred the hopes and the dreams of these oppressed people. This promise, I felt, should be kept, just as all promises made by responsible, civilized governments should be kept."*

Truman was inexperienced in foreign affairs and initially felt he was out of his league and crushed by the burden of his new office and responsibilities. Nonetheless, he did not forget the Palestine question as soon as World War II was over.

Truman's support for a Jewish state had evolved over time, shaped by a number of factors. Though Loy Henderson and others in the State Department had insisted that a Jewish state would compromise the position of the US in the Middle East, the opposite position was equally tenable. The notion that Henderson and Marshall advocated, that the Zionists were communists and would therefore side with the USSR was founded on personal prejudice rather than fact, and backfired when the possibility was raised that the USSR would intervene on behalf of Israel, absent US support. The idea that Truman had initially entertained, and that the State Department encouraged, that a Jewish state could only be defended by hundreds of thousands of US troops, proved to be groundless. It is probably this realization more than any that turned the tide, and overcame the single greatest objection.

The policy was undoubtedly influenced by electoral considerations. Loy Henderson admitted, "Many of the leaders of the Republican Party, including Dewey...were almost constantly criticizing Truman for failure to give full support to the Zionists. If Truman had taken positions that would have resulted in a failure to establish the Jewish State, he would almost certainly have been defeated in the November 1948 elections since the Zionists had almost the full support of the Congress, the United States media, and most of the American people. The new Republican Administration would then have gone along with the Zionists."

From the point of view of the Americans, and world opinion, the creation of Israel was a more or less conscious and willful act that was meant to compensate for the Holocaust.

This view has been accepted by the Arabs, who protest that the Palestinians should not have been made to pay for the Holocaust. For his part in the drama, Harry S Truman is revered by Zionists and hated by Arab partisans.

This view ignores some pertinent facts. After the British Mandate was established, the Jewish Agency came into being as the expression of the administrative arm of the Zionist organization in Palestine. The state had begun to become a reality in the 30s, with its own government institutions, tax system, economic policy, labor unions, embryonic armies, school system and health facilities. The dissolution of the British mandate, like all colonial holdings, was only a matter of time. While the Jews were still a minority in population and land ownership, they already had the major part of the economy of Palestine in their hands, and they were the only well organized national force, and in fact, probably only the Jews had the potential to control the destiny of Palestine, as was shown decisively by the Israeli War of Independence.

In June 1950, when the Communist government of North Korea attacked South Korea, Truman conferred promptly with his military advisers. There was, he wrote, "complete, almost unspoken acceptance on the part of everyone that whatever had to be done to meet this aggression had to be done. There was no suggestion from anyone that either the United Nations or the United States could back away from it."

A long, discouraging struggle ensued as U.N. forces held a line above the old boundary of South Korea. Truman kept the war a limited one, rather than risk a major conflict with China and perhaps Russia.

Harold Stassen ran for U.S. president nine times between 1948 and 1992. Stassen was originally a wonder kid of Minnesota politics, having been elected governor at age 31 in 1938. He resigned the office in 1943 to join the U.S. Navy during World War II. He ran for president in 1948, 1952, 1964, 1968, 1976, 1980, 1984, 1988, and 1992, never winning the office or the nomination of the Republican party.

At the 1952 convention he released Minnesota's delegates to Dwight Eisenhower, helping him defeat Robert Taft on the first ballot. Stassen's later campaigns were considered symbolic, even humorous, and his name became a catch phrase for political futility. He along with Thomas Dewey had kidnapped the spotlight in the Republican party as it moved away from it's conservative principles.

Robert Taft remained and challenged for the right in the party. When the Republicans took control of Congress in 1947, Taft focused on labor-management relations as Chair of the Senate Labor Committee. Decrying the effect of the Wagner Act in tilting the balance toward labor unions, he wrote the 1947 Taft Hartley Act, which remains the basic labor law. It bans unfair union practices, outlaws closed shops, and authorizes the President to seek federal court injunctions to impose an eighty day cooling off period if a strike threatened the national interest. Taft displayed all of his parliamentary skills in getting the bill through Congress; when President Harry Truman vetoed it, Taft then convinced both houses of Congress to overturn the veto.

From 1947 to 1949, when the Republicans controlled the Senate, Taft was his party's leading voice in domestic policy. He was reluctant to support farm subsidies, a position that hurt the GOP in rural areas especially in the Midwest in the 1948 elections. Moving a bit to the left, he supported federal aid to education which did not pass and cosponsored the Taft-Wagner-Ellender Housing Act to subsidize public housing in inner cities. In terms of foreign policy he was non interventionist and did not see Stalin's Soviet Union as a major threat.

Nor did he pay much attention to internal Communism. The true danger, he believed, was big government and runaway spending. He supported the Truman Doctrine, reluctantly approved the Marshall Plan, and opposed NATO as unnecessary and provocative to the Soviets. He took the lead among Republicans in condemning President Harry S. Truman's handling of the Korean War. In 1950 Taft ran a more effective campaign in which he wooed factory workers; he won a third term by a wide margin. By the start of his third term in the Senate, Taft had been given the nickname "Mr. Republican"; he was the chief ideologue and spokesperson for the conservatism of the Republican Party of that era, and he was the acknowledged national leader of the GOP's conservative faction.

In 1948 Taft made a second try for the GOP nomination, but was defeated by his arch-rival, Governor Dewey, who led the GOP's moderate/liberal wing. Dewey of course went down to defeat to Truman in 1948 after a hotly contested race. Give em hell Harry was his own man not owned by any faction of the Democratic party and was a moderate force and rest from the tyranny of the extreme left that represented King Roosevelt.

Although Truman had his own left leanings he truly was his own man.

Joseph Raymond McCarthy was born on a farm in the Town of Grand Chute, near Appleton, Wisconsin, on November 15, 1908. Initially, McCarthy was given little chance of defeating incumbent Robert M. La Follette, Jr. for the Republican Senate nomination in 1946. La Follette, the son of the famous "Fighting Bob" La Follette, was well known in Wisconsin, having served as senator for 21 years. But La Follette had only recently rejoined the Republican Party after years as a leader of the Progressive Party, and many Republicans resented his return. Aided by the support of the Republican organization, McCarthy ran a typically energetic campaign and beat La Follette by a tiny margin. In the general election, McCarthy easily defeated his Democratic opponent and went to Washington at age 38, the youngest member of the new Senate.

Throughout the early 1950s, McCarthy continued to make accusations of communist infiltration of the U. S. government, though he failed to provide evidence. McCarthy himself was investigated by a Senate panel in 1952. That committee issued the "Henning's Report," which uncovered unethical behavior in McCarthy's campaigns and tax returns, but found no basis for legal action. Despite that report, McCarthy was re-elected in 1952 with 54% of the vote, although he ran behind all other statewide Republicans and had a lower vote total than in 1946.

Liberals love to point out that McCarthy was a conservative. While that maybe true he was a kook and had a short fling in the spotlight.

Even though he was a demagogue he did keep our national focus on the enemy that international communism actually was.

In 1952 Taft made his third and final try for the GOP nomination; it also proved to be his strongest effort. He had the solid backing of the party's conservative wing, and with Dewey no longer an active candidate many political pundits regarded him as the frontrunner. However, the race changed when Dewey and other GOP moderates were able to convince Dwight D. Eisenhower, the most popular general of World War II, to run for the nomination. According to biographer Stephen Ambrose, Eisenhower agreed to run in part because of his fear that Taft's non interventionist views in foreign policy might unintentionally benefit the Soviet Union in the Cold War.

The fight between Taft and Eisenhower for the GOP nomination was one of the closest and most bitter in American political history. When the Republican Convention opened in July 1952, Taft and Eisenhower were neck-and-neck in delegate votes, and the nomination was still up for grabs as neither had a majority. On the convention's first day, Eisenhower's managers complained that Taft's forces had unfairly denied Eisenhower supporters delegate slots in several Southern states, including Texas, where the state chairman, Orville Bullington, was committed to Taft, and also in Georgia.

The Eisenhower partisans proposed to remove pro-Taft delegates in these states and replace them with pro-Eisenhower delegates; they called their proposal "Fair Play".

Although Taft angrily denied having stolen any delegate votes, the convention voted to support Fair Play 658 to 548, and the Texans voted 33-5 for Eisenhower as a result. In addition, several uncommitted state delegations, such as Michigan and Pennsylvania, agreed to support Eisenhower.

There were rumors after the convention that the chairmen of these uncommitted states, such as Arthur Summerfield of Michigan, were secretly pressured by Dewey and the GOP's Eastern Establishment to support Eisenhower; however, these rumors were never proved.
The addition of these formerly uncommitted state delegations, combined with Taft's loss of many Southern delegates due to the Fair Play proposal, decided the nomination in Eisenhower's favor. Despite his bitterness at his narrow defeat and his belief that he had been unfairly ambushed by the Eisenhower forces including Governor Dewey, after the convention Taft issued a brief statement conveying his congratulations and support to Eisenhower.

Thereafter, however, he brooded in silence at his summer home in Quebec. As the weeks passed, Eisenhower's aides worried that Taft and his supporters would sit on their hands during the campaign, and that as a result Eisenhower might lose the election. In September 1952 Taft finally agreed to meet with Eisenhower, at Morningside Heights in New York City. There, in order to gain Taft's support in the campaign, Eisenhower promised he would take no reprisals against Taft partisans, would cut federal spending, and would fight "creeping socialism in every domestic field."

In fact, Eisenhower and Taft agreed on most domestic issues; their disagreements were primarily in foreign policy. Eisenhower firmly believed in NATO and was committed to the U.S. supporting anti Communism in the Cold War.

Following Eisenhower's election and the GOP takeover of Congress, Taft served as Senate Majority Leader in 1953, and he strongly supported Eisenhower's domestic proposals.

He worked hard to assist the inexperienced new officials of the administration. He even tried with little success to curb the excesses of red-baiting U.S. Senator Joseph McCarthy. By April the President and Taft were friends and golfing companions, and Taft was praising his former adversary. Defeat in 1952, it seemed, had softened Taft. No longer burdened by presidential ambitions, he had become less partisan, less abrasive, and more conciliatory; during this time he was widely regarded as the most powerful man in Congress.

In early 1953 Taft began to feel pain in his hips, and after a painful golf outing with President Eisenhower in April 1953 he entered Walter Reed Hospital for initial tests which led doctors to suspect a tumor or arthritis.
Tests in May at Holmes Memorial Hospital near Cincinnati revealed that his body was full of cancer.- In late May 1953, Taft transferred his duties as Senate Majority Leader to Senator William Knowland of California, but he did not resign his Senate seat and told reporters that he expected to recover and return to work. However, his condition rapidly worsened, and Taft returned to New York Hospital for surgery on July 4 during a Senate recess.

He died on July 31, suffering a final brain hemorrhage just hours after his wife Martha's final visit.- President Eisenhower and many prominent politicians from both parties attended his funeral.

In 1957, a committee led by Senator John F. Kennedy selected Taft as one of five of their greatest Senate predecessors whose oval portraits would adorn the President's Room off the Senate floor. Kennedy would profile him in his book *Profiles in Courage*, and Taft continues to be regarded by historians as one of the most powerful U.S. Senators of the twentieth century. Bringing to the Presidency his prestige as commanding general of the victorious forces in Europe during World War II, Dwight D. Eisenhower obtained a truce in Korea and worked incessantly during his two terms to ease the tensions of the Cold War. Born in Texas in 1890, brought up in Abilene, Kansas, Eisenhower was the third of seven sons. He excelled in sports in high school, and received an appointment to West Point. Stationed in Texas as a second lieutenant, he met Mamie Geneva Doud, whom he married in 1916.

Negotiating from military strength, he tried to reduce the strains of the Cold War. In 1953, the signing of a truce brought an armed peace along the border of South Korea. The death of Stalin the same year caused shifts in relations with Russia.

New Russian leaders consented to a peace treaty neutralizing Austria. Meanwhile, both Russia and the United States had developed hydrogen bombs. With the threat of such destructive force hanging over the world, Eisenhower, with the leaders of the British, French, and Russian governments, met at Geneva in July 1955.

The President proposed that the United States and Russia exchange blueprints of each other's military establishments and "provide within our countries facilities for aerial photography to the other country." The Russians greeted the proposal with silence, but were so cordial throughout the meetings that tensions relaxed.

In domestic policy the President pursued a middle course, continuing most of the New Deal and Fair Deal programs, emphasizing a balanced budget. As desegregation of schools began, he sent troops into Little Rock, Arkansas, to assure compliance with the orders of a Federal court; he also ordered the complete desegregation of the Armed Forces. "There must be no second class citizens in this country," he wrote.

Eisenhower concentrated on maintaining world peace. He watched with pleasure the development of his atoms for peace program the loan of American uranium to have not nations for peaceful purposes.

Before he left office in January 1961, for his farm in Gettysburg, he urged the necessity of maintaining an adequate military strength, but cautioned that vast, long-continued military expenditures could breed potential dangers to our way of life. He concluded with a prayer for peace "in the goodness of time." Both themes remained timely and urgent when he died, after a long illness, on March 28, 1969.

Richard Nixon was born on January 9, 1913, Nixon's early life was marked by hardship, and he would later quote a saying of Eisenhower to describe his boyhood, "We were poor, but the glory of it was, we didn't know it.

Nixon first gained national attention in 1948 when his investigation on the House Un-American Activities Committee (HUAC) broke the impasse of the Alger Hiss spy case. While many doubted Whittaker Chambers' allegations that Hiss, a high State Department official, was a Soviet spy, Nixon believed the allegations to be true. He discovered that Chambers saved microfilm reproductions of incriminating documents by hiding the film in a pumpkin.- They were alleged to be accessible only to Hiss and to have been typed on his personal typewriter. Hiss was convicted of perjury in 1950 for statements he made to the HUAC. The discovery that Hiss committed perjury and thus may well have been a Soviet spy thrust Nixon into the spotlight for the first time. This case turned the young Congressman into a controversial figure.- He was easily reelected in 1948.

39-year-old Nixon was selected by Republican party nominee General Dwight D. Eisenhower to be the Vice Presidential candidate at the Republican National Convention in July 1952.

As Vice President, Nixon expanded the office into an important and prominent post. Nixon would conduct National Security meetings in the president's absence.-As President of the Senate, he intervened to make procedural rulings on filibusters to assure the passage of Eisenhower's 1957 civil rights bill, which created the United States Commission on Civil Rights and protected voting rights. Although he had little formal power, Nixon had the attention of the media and the Republican Party.

Clearly the Republican party with the death of Senator Robert Taft was adrift in it's need for a real Conservative leader.

Since Calvin Coolidge the country was without a Conservative president.

Russell Kirk (October 19, 1918 – April 29, 1994) was an American political theorist, moralist, historian, social critic, literary critic, and fiction author known for his influence on 20th century American conservatism. His 1953 book, *The Conservative Mind*, gave shape to the amorphous post-World War II conservative movement. It traced the development of conservative thought in the Anglo-American tradition, giving special importance to the ideas of Edmund Burke. Kirk was also considered the chief proponent of traditionalist conservatism.
Russell Kirk was born in Plymouth, Michigan. He was the son of Russell Andrew Kirk, a railroad engineer, and Marjorie Pierce Kirk. Kirk obtained his B.A. at Michigan State University and a M.A. at Duke University. During World War II, he served in the American armed forces and corresponded with libertarian writer, Isabel Paterson, who helped to shape his early political thought. After the war, he attended the University of St. Andrews in Scotland. In 1953, he became the only American to be awarded the degree of Doctor of Letters by that university.

Kirk grounded his Burkean conservatism in tradition, political philosophy, creative writing and the strong religious faith of his later years; rather than libertarianism and free market economic reasoning. *The Conservative Mind* hardly mentions economics at all.

In a polemic essay, Kirk quoting T. S. Eliot called libertarians "chirping sectaries," adding that they and conservatives have nothing in common despite his early correspondence with the libertarian Paterson.

He called the libertarian movement "an ideological clique forever splitting into sects still smaller and odder, but rarely conjugating."

He said a line of division exists between believers in "some sort of transcendent moral order" and "utilitarian admitting no transcendent sanctions for conduct." He included libertarians in the latter category.- Kirk, therefore, questioned the fusionism between libertarians and traditional conservatives that marked much of post World War II conservatism in the United States.

Kirk's view of classical liberals is positive though; he agrees with them on ordered liberty as they make common cause with regular conservatives against the menace of democratic despotism and economic collectivism. Kirk developed six "canons" of conservatism:

1. A belief in a transcendent order, which Kirk described variously as based in tradition, divine revelation, or natural law;
2 .An affection for the "variety and mystery" of human existence;
3. A conviction that society requires orders and classes that emphasize "natural" distinctions;
4. A belief that property and freedom are closely linked;
5. A faith in custom, convention, and prescription, and
6. A recognition that innovation must be tied to existing traditions and customs, which entails a respect for the political value of prudence.

Kirk said that Christianity and Western Civilization are "unimaginable apart from one another." and that "all culture arises out of religion.

When religious faith decays, culture must decline, though often seeming to flourish for a space after the religion which has nourished it has sunk into disbelief." Russell Kirk would be perhaps the greatest influence on Conservatives in the 1950's and 60's. Leading to the emergence of people like William F Buckley and Barry Goldwater and Ronald Reagan.

Current baby-boomer nostalgia has, for the most part, washed over and sanitized the political history of the 1950s. When compared to the turbulent decades that would follow and the world war that had preceded in the 1940s, the 1950s would appear from the present, popular perspective to represent a peaceful interlude in twentieth-century power politics a kind of return to innocence from which the American people would emerge the children of Eisenhower. Indeed, two-term president Dwight D. Eisenhower, the decade's dominant political presence, was a paternal figure. Running on the 1952 Republican platform at the age of sixty-two, he was an international hero who had organized the Allied victory over the Nazis and briefly served as president of Columbia University.

He had a kind face and a smile that beamed confidence and optimism. A high handicapper, he spent a good deal of time at the golf course more time there, contended some political wags, than in the Oval Office. But if he had a weakness for play, it was something the American people were more than willing to forgive in him as a fatherly indulgence; for, as a young Jack Kerouac and an equally drunk fellow Beat poet once sarcastically phrased it in an obscene letter meant for the White House, Eisenhower *was* the "Great White Father."

But Eisenhower was much more than a golf-playing figurehead: he was a shrewd and savvy politician, as his more current biographers and many historians convincingly argue. A state of relative peace and prosperity likewise camouflaged a highly charged, rough-and-tumble political landscape. Politics in the 1950s were driven by immediate fears that the American way of life was being threatened by a philosophy that ran counter to, and called for the destruction of, democracy. American's fear of communism during the 1950s is often looked back on as having been fueled by naive generalization and paranoia. When understood in the context of the times, however, American fears were hardly naive. After World War II the Soviets had acted quickly to annex most of Eastern Europe.

In 1949 China had fallen to the Communists. In June 1950 the United Nations intervened in the Korean border conflict, and the United States once again sent troops to war this time to contain Communist aggression.
Tired of New Deal bureaucracy and war and scared of the Communist presence that had engulfed Eastern Europe and China and that had supposedly infiltrated their government Americans entered the 1950s a beleaguered people yet politicized as they had never been before in the twentieth century. They voted in record numbers in the 1952 elections, and, in proclaiming an electoral majority for Eisenhower over Democratic opponent Adlai Stevenson, they ushered in a watershed moment in American politics.

Out were twenty years of Democratic control of the White House. Out was Truman the last American president without a college degree whom the Republicans had portrayed as the last vestige of New Deal, partisan policy making and final reminder of Franklin D. Roosevelt's alleged appeasement of the Soviets at the 1945 Yalta Conference. It was an era of governing that was to appeal to Middle America's political sensibilities.

Eisenhower Republicans pledged to cut defense spending while simultaneously engaging Communist aggression both abroad and at home; limit the federal government's role in the business and private sectors; and invigorate a maturing sense of America's role as a superpower.

CHAPTER ELEVEN - The Cultural Revolution of the 1960's

The 1960's was as close to a second civil war that our country has probably ever experienced. In my opinion the 60's also was a time that Conservatism in America came of age in the modern era. With men like Russell Kirk making the case for conservatives others would be added such as William F Buckley, Frank Meyer, Barry Goldwater and Ronald Reagan.

The presidential election of 1960 marked the end of Dwight D. Eisenhower's two terms as President. Eisenhower's Vice President, Richard Nixon, who had transformed his office into a national political base, was the Republican candidate, whereas the Democrats nominated Massachusetts Senator John F. Kennedy.

The electoral vote was the closest in any presidential election since 1916. In the popular vote, Kennedy's margin of victory was among the closest ever in American history. The 1960 election also remains a source of debate among some historians as to whether vote theft in selected states aided Kennedy's victory. Machine politics in Chicago was claimed by some that voter fraud stole votes from Nixon in favor of Kennedy which led to him carrying Illinois and ultimately winning the presidency. Nixon didn't protest officially but always believed that Kennedy had stolen the election.

The major candidates for the 1960 Democratic presidential nomination were Kennedy, Senator Wayne Morse of Oregon, Senator Lyndon Johnson of Texas, Senator Hubert Humphrey of Minnesota, Senator Stuart Symington of Missouri, Governor Edmund G. Brown of California and former Illinois Governor Adlai Stevenson.

Kennedy was initially dogged by suggestions from some Democratic Party elders such as former President Harry Truman, who was supporting Symington that he was too youthful and inexperienced to be president; these critics suggested that he should agree to be the running mate for a "more experienced" Democrat.
Realizing that this was a strategy touted by his opponents to keep the public from taking him seriously, Kennedy stated frankly, "I'm not running for vice president, I'm running for president."

Kennedy won the nomination on the first ballot. Then, in a move which surprised many, Kennedy asked Johnson to be his running mate. To this day there is much debate regarding the details of Johnson's nomination, why it was offered and why he agreed to take it. Some historians speculate that Kennedy actually wanted someone else such as Senators Stuart Symington or Henry Jackson to be his running mate, and that he offered the nomination to Johnson first only as a courtesy to the powerful Senate Majority Leader. According to this theory, Kennedy was then surprised when Johnson accepted second place on the Democratic ticket. Another related story is that, after Johnson accepted the offer, Robert Kennedy went to Johnson's hotel suite to pressure Johnson into declining the vice-presidential offer. Johnson was offended that JFK's kid brother would brashly tell him to stay off the ticket.

In response to his blunt confrontation with Robert Kennedy, Johnson called JFK to confirm that the vice presidential nomination was his; JFK claimed that his brother Robert "wasn't aware of recent developments" and clearly stated that he wanted Johnson as his running mate. Both Johnson and Robert Kennedy became so embittered by the experience that they began a fierce personal and political feud that would have grave implications for the Democratic Party in the 1960s.

In 1959, it looked as if Vice President Richard Nixon might face a serious challenge for the GOP nomination from New York Governor Nelson Rockefeller, the leader of the GOP's moderate-liberal wing. However, Rockefeller announced that he would not be a candidate for president after a national tour revealed that the great majority of Republicans favored Nixon.

After Rockefeller's withdrawal, Nixon faced no significant opposition for the Republican nomination. At the 1960 Republican National Convention in Chicago, Nixon was the overwhelming choice of the delegates, with conservative Senator Barry Goldwater of Arizona receiving 10 votes from conservative delegates.

Nixon then chose former Massachusetts Senator and United Nations Ambassador Henry Cabot Lodge, Jr. as his Vice Presidential candidate. Nixon chose Lodge because his foreign-policy credentials fit into Nixon's strategy to campaign more on foreign policy than domestic policy, which he believed favored the Democrats. Nixon had previously sought Rockefeller as his running mate, but the governor had no ambitions to be Vice President. William F. Buckley Jr. was a prominent conservative American political commentator.

His grandfather made millions in the oil business, and his father made many millions more with ownership of the Catawba Corporation, using the extended Buckley family's almost-complete control of six giant oil companies to ensure that all six companies relied on Catawba for lucrative geological, geophysical, accounting, and technical services.

Like his nine brothers and sisters, Buckley had Latin American nursemaids and French governesses, and he grew up trilingual. As a young boy, on his father's recommendation, Buckley read the works of Albert Jay Nock. He was drafted into the Army in 1944, and upon his discharge in 1946 worked for the Central Intelligence Agency, where three of his siblings have also been employed.

At Yale, Buckley was the star of the debating team, and earned his bachelor's degree in 1950. Upon graduation, Buckley promptly wrote *God and Man at Yale*, a book criticizing his alma mater for straying from its original, Christian mission. He was an editor at *The American Mercury* for several years, before his aggravation at the liberal policies of the Eisenhower administration led him to start his conservative magazine, *National Review*. *National Review* quickly found its audience, making Buckley a political force. It was cited as influential by conservative leaders such as Barry Goldwater and Ronald Reagan.

In 1960, Young Americans for Freedom or YAF, as it was widely known through the 1960s was founded in a meeting at Buckley's Connecticut estate. During the Watergate scandal, Buckley underwrote his former CIA boss Hunt's legal defense.

Buckley's newspaper column, accurately titled "On the Right", was syndicated beginning in 1962, and in 1965 he ran for mayor of New York on the Conservative Party ticket, receiving about 13% of the vote.

In 1966, Buckley began hosting *Firing Line*, a political talk show on National Educational Television, the fore-runner of PBS. 1,429 weekly episodes were produced over the next 33 years, until Buckley stepped down in 2000. He resigned from management of *National Review*, but continued writing for the magazine until his death.

When Attorney General Robert F. Kennedy rejected re-peated invitations to appear on *Firing Line*, Buckley quipped: "Why does baloney reject the grinder?" He also once threatened to punch Gore Vidal in the face, after an exchange of insults. As AIDS became a topic of conversation in the 1980s, Buckley suggested that those diagnosed with the disease should be tattooed on their backsides, presumably to protect uninfected Americans. George H. Nash, a historian of the modern American conservative movement, believed that Buckley was "arguably the most important public intellectual in the United States in the past half century". "For an entire generation he was the preeminent voice of American conservatism and its first great ecumenical figure.

Buckley's primary change to politics was the fusion of traditional American political conservatism with laissez-faire economic theory and anti-communism, laying the groundwork for the modern American conservatism of U.S. presidential candidates Barry Goldwater and President Ronald Reagan.

Buckley referred to himself as either a libertarian or conservative. He resided in New York City and Stamford, Connecticut. He was a practicing Roman Catholic, regularly attending the traditional Latin Mass in Connecticut. Frank S. Meyer was born to a prominent business family in Newark, New Jersey. He attended Princeton University for one year but was displeased by the anti-Semitism and snobbery he found there. He then transferred to Oxford University. He later studied at the London School of Economics.

Meyer was an active communist early in life before his conversion to conservatism and his joining of *National Review*. As a conservative, Meyer like many of the magazine's founding senior editors an ex-Communist was a close adviser to and confidant of founder/editor William F. Buckley, Jr.

Meyer is best known for his theory of fusionism a political philosophy that unites elements of libertarianism and conservatism. Murray Rothbard argued, however, that Meyer's fusionism was actually the natural law-natural rights branch of libertarian thought that Rothbard and others followed.

Known in conservative and libertarian circles for his nocturnal lifestyle Buckley among others has recalled in *Miles Gone By: A Literary Autobiography* that Meyer would sleep by day and be on the phone by night on behalf of his journalism and activism. Meyer married the former Elsie Bown. They had two sons, John and Eugene. The latter is president of the Federalist Society. Frank Meyer converted to Catholicism before he died of lung cancer in 1972.

From Meyer's pen came "In Defense of Freedom: A Conservative Credo," a work designed to prove that order and virtue is concomitant with freedom. The use of concomitance as a noun is telling. What he was saying was that traditionalism can occur with libertarianism in a lesser way.

He was awarding the likes of Kirk, Voegelin, and Weaver the coveted title of "Miss Congeniality." Not that he hid the fact. He acknowledges that the traditionalists "staunchly held the line against the assault of utilitarianism, positivism, and scientism, but on another level they failed philosophically, deeply misreading the nature of man."

Barry M Goldwater (January 1, 1909 – May 29, 1998) was a five-term United States Senator from Arizona (1953–1965, 1969–1987) and the Republican Party's nominee for President in the 1964 election. An articulate and charismatic figure in the 1960-64 era, he was known as "Mr. Conservative".

Goldwater is the politician most often credited for sparking the resurgence of the American conservative political movement in the 1960s. He also had a substantial impact on the libertarian movement. Goldwater rejected the legacy of the New Deal and fought through the conservative coalition to defeat the New Deal coalition.

Goldwater was born on January 1, 1909 in Phoenix, in what was then the Arizona Territory, the son of Baron Goldwater and his wife, Hattie Josephine Williams. His father's Jewish American family had founded Goldwater's, the largest department store in Phoenix.

Goldwater's mother came from an old Yankee family that included the famous theologian, Roger Williams of Rhode Island.-Goldwater's father converted to Christianity and was shunned by his family; he and Josephine were married in an Episcopal church in Phoenix. For his entire life, Goldwater was an Episcopalian, though on rare occasions he referred to himself as Jewish. While he did not often attend church, he stated that "If a man acts in a religious way, an ethical way, then he's really a religious man and it doesn't have a lot to do with how often he gets inside a church".

Goldwater soon became most associated with labor-union reform and anti-communism; he was an active supporter of the conservative coalition in Congress. However, he rejected the wilder fringes of the anti-communist movement; in 1956 he sponsored the passage through the Senate of the final version of the Alaska Mental Health Enabling Act, despite vociferous opposition from opponents who claimed that the Act was a communist plot to establish concentration camps in Alaska.

His work on labor issues led to Congress passing major anti-corruption reforms in 1957, and an all-out campaign by the AFL-CIO to defeat his 1958 reelection bid. He voted against the censure of Senator Joseph McCarthy in 1954, but he was much more prudent than McCarthy and never actually charged any individual with being a communist/Soviet agent. Goldwater emphasized his strong opposition to the worldwide spread of communism in his 1960 book *The Conscience of a Conservative*. The book became an important reference text in conservative political circles.

Ronald Reagan was born in an apartment on the second floor of a commercial building in Tampico, Illinois, on February 6, 1911, to John Edward Reagan and Nelle Wilson Reagan. Reagan's father was of Irish Catholic ancestry, while his mother had Scots-English ancestors. Reagan had one older brother, Neil "Moon" Reagan (1908–1996), who became an advertising executive.- As a boy, Reagan's father nicknamed his son "Dutch", due to his "fat little Dutchman"-like appearance, and his "Dutch boy" haircut;- the nickname stuck with him throughout his youth.

Reagan began as a liberal Democrat, admirer of Franklin D. Roosevelt, and active supporter of New Deal policies, but in the early 1950s he shifted to the right and endorsed the presidential candidacies of Dwight D. Eisenhower in 1952 and 1956 as well as Richard Nixon in 1960 while remaining a Democrat.- His many GE speeches which he wrote himself were non-partisan but carried a conservative, pro-business message; he was influenced by Lemuel Boulware, a senior GE executive. Boulware, known for his tough stance against unions and his innovative strategies to win over workers, championed the core tenets of modern American conservatism: free markets, anticommunism, lower taxes, and limited government.- Eventually, the ratings for Reagan's show fell off and GE dropped Reagan in 1962.- Reagan formally switched to the Republican Party in 1962, complaining, "I didn't leave the Democratic Party the party left me."

Reagan opposed certain civil rights legislation, although he later reversed his opposition to voting rights and fair housing laws. He strongly denied having racist motives.

When legislation that would become Medicare was introduced in 1961, Reagan created a recording for the
American Medical Association warning that such legislation would mean the end of freedom in America.
Reagan said that if his listeners did not write letters to
prevent it, "we will awake to find that we have socialism.
And if you don't do this, and if I don't do it, one of these
days, you and I are going to spend our sunset years telling our children, and our children's children, what it once
was like in America when men were free."

In the United States, "The Sixties", as they are known in
popular culture, is a term used by historians, journalists,
and other objective academics; in some cases nostalgi-
cally to describe the counterculture and social revolution
near the end of the decade; and pejoratively to describe
the era as one of irresponsible excess and flamboyance.
The decade was also labeled the Swinging Sixties because of the social attitudes that emerged during this
decade.

The 1960s have become synonymous with all the new,
exciting, radical, and subversive events and trends of the
period, which continued to develop in the 1970s, 1980s,
1990s and beyond.

John F. Kennedy was sworn in as the 35th President at
noon on January 20, 1961. In his inaugural address he
spoke of the need for all Americans to be active citizens,
famously saying, "Ask not what your country can do for
you; ask what you can do for your country." He also
asked the nations of the world to join together to fight
what he called the "common enemies of man: tyranny,
poverty, disease, and war itself."

On April 17, 1961, Kennedy ordered the previously planned invasion of Cuba to proceed. With support from the CIA, in what is known as the Bay of Pigs Invasion, 1,500 U.S.-trained Cuban exiles, called "Brigade 2506," returned to the island in the hope of deposing Castro. However, Kennedy ordered the invasion to take place without U.S. air support. By April 19, 1961, the Cuban government had captured or killed the invading exiles, and Kennedy was forced to negotiate for the release of the 1,189 survivors.

The failure of the plan originated in a lack of dialog among the military leadership, a result of which was the complete lack of naval support in the face of organized artillery troops on the island who easily incapacitated the exile force as it landed on the beach.

The Cuban Missile Crisis began on October 14, 1962, when CIA U-2 spy planes took photographs of a Soviet intermediate-range ballistic missile site under construction in Cuba. The photos were shown to Kennedy on October 16, 1962. The United States would soon be posed with a serious nuclear threat. Kennedy faced a dilemma: if the U.S. attacked the sites, it might lead to nuclear war with the U.S.S.R., but if the U.S. did nothing, it would endure the threat of nuclear weapons being launched from close range. Because the weapons were in such proximity, the U.S. might have been unable to retaliate if they were launched pre emptively. Another consideration was that the U.S. would appear to the world as weak in its own hemisphere.

Many military officials and cabinet members pressed for an air assault on the missile sites, but Kennedy ordered a naval quarantine in which the U.S. Navy inspected all ships arriving in Cuba. He began negotiations with the Soviets and ordered the Soviets to remove all defensive material that was being built on Cuba. Without doing so, the Soviet and Cuban peoples would face naval quarantine. A week later, he and Soviet Premier Nikita Khrushchev reached a basically cordial, lasting agreement.

Khrushchev agreed to remove the missiles subject to U.N. inspections if the U.S. publicly promised never to invade Cuba and quietly remove its Jupiter missiles stationed in Turkey. The removal of the Jupiter missiles was not a great concession as they were viewed as obsolete and Kennedy believed the US Navy Polaris subs could fill their role. This crisis had brought the world closer to nuclear war than at any point before or since. In the end, the humanity of the two men prevailed.

Kennedy sought to contain communism in Latin America by establishing the Alliance for Progress, which sent foreign aid to troubled countries in the region and sought greater human rights standards in the region. He worked closely with Governor of Puerto Rico Luis Muñoz Marín for the development of the Alliance of Progress, as well as developments in the autonomy of the Commonwealth of Puerto Rico.

One of his first presidential acts, Kennedy asked Congress to create the Peace Corps.- Through this program, Americans volunteer to help underdeveloped nations in areas such as education, farming, health care, and construction.

In Southeast Asia, Kennedy followed Eisenhower's lead by using limited military action as early as 1961 to fight the Communist forces led by Ho Chi Minh. Proclaiming a fight against the spread of Communism, Kennedy enacted policies providing political, economic, and military support for the unstable French installed South Vietnamese government, which included sending 16,000 military advisors and U.S. Special Forces to the area. Kennedy also authorized the use of free-fire zones, napalm and jet planes.

Nevertheless, given the stated reason for the overthrow of the Diem government, such action would have been a policy reversal, but Kennedy was generally moving in a less hawkish direction in the Cold War since his acclaimed speech about World Peace at American University the previous June 10, 1963.

According to historian Lawrence Freedman, regarding Kennedy's statements about withdrawing from Vietnam, it was, "less of a definite decision than a working assumption, based on a hope for stability rather than an expectation of chaos".

Under simultaneous and opposing pressures from the Allies and the Soviets, Germany was divided. The Berlin Wall separated West and East Berlin, the latter being under the control of the Soviets. On June 26, 1963, Kennedy visited West Berlin and gave a public speech criticizing communism. Kennedy used the construction of the Berlin Wall as an example of the failures of communism: "Freedom has many difficulties and democracy is not perfect, but we have never had to put a wall up to keep our people in." The speech is known for its famous phrase *"Ich bin ein Berliner"*.

Nearly five-sixths of the population was on the street when Kennedy said the famous phrase. He remarked to aides afterwards: "We'll never have another day like this one."

Troubled by the long-term dangers of radioactive contamination and nuclear weapons proliferation, Kennedy pushed for the adoption of a Limited or Partial Test Ban Treaty, which prohibited atomic testing on the ground, in the atmosphere, or underwater, but did not prohibit testing underground. The United States, the United Kingdom, and the Soviet Union were the initial signatories to the treaty. Kennedy signed the treaty into law in August 1963. The turbulent end of state sanctioned racial discrimination was one of the most pressing domestic issues of Kennedy's era. The United States Supreme Court had ruled in 1954 in *Brown v. Board of Education* that racial segregation in public schools was unconstitutional. However, many schools, especially in southern states, did not obey the Supreme Court's judgment. Segregation on buses, in restaurants, movie theaters, bathrooms, and other public places remained. Kennedy supported racial integration and civil rights, and during the 1960 campaign he telephoned Coretta Scott King, wife of the jailed Reverend Martin Luther King, Jr., which perhaps drew some additional black support to his candidacy. John and Robert Kennedy's intervention secured the early release of King from jail.

As President, Kennedy initially believed the grass roots movement for civil rights would only anger many Southern whites and make it even more difficult to pass civil rights laws through Congress, which was dominated by conservative Southern Democrats, and he distanced himself from it.

As a result, many civil rights leaders viewed Kennedy as unsupportive of their efforts.

On June 11, 1963, President Kennedy intervened when Alabama Governor George Wallace blocked the doorway to the University of Alabama to stop two African American students, Vivian Malone and James Hood, from enrolling. Wallace moved aside after being confronted by federal marshals, Deputy Attorney General Nicholas Katzenbach and the Alabama National Guard. That evening Kennedy gave his famous civil rights address on national television and radio.

President Kennedy was assassinated in Dallas, Texas, at 12:30 p.m. Central Standard Time on November 22, 1963, while on a political trip to Texas to smooth over factions in the Democratic Party between liberals Ralph Yarborough and Don Yarborough (no relation) and conservative John Connally. He was shot once in the upper back and was killed with a final shot to the head. He was pronounced dead at 1:00 p.m. Only 46, President Kennedy died younger than any U.S. president to date. Lee Harvey Oswald, an employee of the Texas School Book Depository from which the shots were suspected to have been fired, was arrested on charges of the murder of a local police officer and was subsequently charged with the assassination of Kennedy.

Lyndon B. Johnson was sworn in as President on *Air Force One* at Love Field Airport in Dallas on November 22, 1963 two hours and eight minutes after President Kennedy was assassinated in Dealey Plaza in Dallas. He was sworn in by Federal Judge Sarah T. Hughes, a family friend, making him the first President sworn in by a woman. He is also the only President to have been sworn in on Texas soil.

Johnson did not swear on a Bible, as there were none on *Air Force One*; a Roman Catholic missal was found in Kennedy's desk and was used for the swearing-in ceremony.

 In the days following the assassination, Lyndon B. Johnson made a moving address to Congress: "No memorial oration or eulogy could more eloquently honor President Kennedy's memory than the earliest possible passage of the Civil Rights Bill for which he fought so long."
The Republican primaries of 1964 featured liberal Nelson Rockefeller of New York and conservative Barry Goldwater of Arizona as the two leading candidates.

Shortly before the California primary, Rockefeller's wife, whom he had just married the previous year soon after divorcing his previous wife, gave birth; this drew renewed attention to his family life which hurt his popularity among conservatives and led to Goldwater winning the primary.

The Republican National Convention of 1964 was a tension-filled contest. Goldwater's conservatives were openly clashing with Rockefeller's moderates. Goldwater was regarded as the conservatives' leading spokesman. As a result, Goldwater was not as popular with the moderates and liberals of the Republican party. When Rockefeller attempted to deliver a speech, he was booed by the convention's conservative delegates, who regarded him as a member of the "eastern liberal establishment." Despite the infighting, Goldwater was easily nominated.

He chose William E. Miller, a Congressman from Buffalo, New York as his running mate. In his acceptance speech, he declared communism as a "principal disturber of the peace in the world today" and said, "I would remind you that extremism in the defense of liberty is no vice. And let me remind you also that moderation in the pursuit of justice is no virtue."

Some people, including those within his own campaign staff, believed this weakened Goldwater's chances, as he effectively severed ties with the moderates and liberals of the Republican Party. Former GOP presidential nominee Richard M. Nixon introduced the Arizonan as "Mr. Conservative" and "Mr. Republican" and he continued that "he is the man who, after the greatest campaign in history will be Mr. President Barry Goldwater".

Goldwater lost the 1964 presidential election to incumbent Democrat Lyndon B. Johnson by one of the largest landslides in history, bringing down many Republican candidates as well. The Johnson campaign and other critics painted him as a reactionary, while supporters praised his crusades against the Soviet Union, labor unions, and the welfare state.

His defeat allowed Johnson and the Democrats in Congress to pass the liberal Great Society programs, but the defeat of so many older Republicans in 1964 also cleared the way for a younger generation of American conservatives to mobilize. Goldwater was much less active as a national leader of conservatives after 1964; his supporters mostly rallied behind Ronald Reagan, who became governor of California in 1967.

Goldwater returned to the Senate in 1968, and specialized in defense policy, bringing to the table his long experience as a senior officer in the Air Force Reserve. His main accomplishment was passage of the Goldwater-Nichols Act of 1986 restructuring the higher levels of the Pentagon by increasing the power of the Chairman of the Joint Chiefs of Staff to direct military action.

By the 1980s, the increasing influence of the Christian right on the Republican Party so conflicted with Goldwater's libertarian views that he became a vocal opponent of the religious right on issues such as abortion, gay rights, and the role of religion in public life.

Goldwater entered Phoenix politics in 1949 when he was elected to the City Council as part of a nonpartisan group of candidates who focused on "cleaning up" widespread prostitution and gambling-. As a Republican he won a seat in the US Senate in 1952, when he upset veteran Democrat and Senate majority leader Ernest McFarland. He defeated McFarland again in 1958, but would step down from the Senate in 1964 for his presidential campaign. Goldwater had a strong showing in his first reelection in 1958, a year in which the Democrats picked up thirteen seats in the Senate.

While Goldwater had been depicted by his opponents in the Republican primaries as a representative of a conservative philosophy that was extreme and alien, his Congressional voting records show that his positions were in harmony with those of his fellow Republicans in the Congress. What distinguished him from his predecessors was, according to Hans J. Morgenthau, his firmness of principle and determination, which did not allow him to be content with rhetoric.

Goldwater fought in 1971 to stop U.S. funding of the United Nations after the People's Republic of China was admitted to the body. He said:

I suggested on the floor of the Senate today that we stop all funds for the United Nations. Now, what that'll do to the United Nations, I don't know. I have a hunch it would cause them to fold up, which would make me very happy at this particular point. I think if this happens, they can well move their headquarters to Peking or Moscow and get 'em out of this country."

The Goldwater campaign spotlighted Ronald Reagan, who gave a stirring, nationally televised speech, "A Time for Choosing", in support of Goldwater.- The speech prompted Reagan to seek the California Governorship in 1966 and jump-started his political career. Conservative activist Phyllis Schlafly, later well-known for her fight against the Equal Rights Amendment, first became known for writing a pro-Goldwater book, *A Choice, Not an Echo,* attacking the liberal Republican establishment. Senator Prescott Bush a liberal Republican from Connecticut, was a friend of Goldwater's and supported him in the general election campaign. Bush's son, George H.W. Bush then running for the Senate from Texas against Democrat Ralph Yarborough, was also a strong Goldwater supporter in both the nomination and general election campaigns. Future Chief Justice of the Supreme Court and fellow Arizonan William Rehnquist also first came to the attention of national Republicans through his work as a legal adviser to Goldwater's 1964 campaign.

Goldwater was painted as a dangerous figure by the Johnson campaign, which countered Goldwater's slogan "In your heart, you know he's right" with the lines "In your guts, you know he's nuts," and "In your heart, you know he might" that is, might actually use nuclear weapons, as opposed to merely subscribing to deterrence. Johnson himself did not mention Goldwater in his own acceptance speech at the 1964 Democratic National Convention.

Goldwater's provocative advocacy of aggressive tactics to prevent the spread of communism in Asia led to effective counterattacks from Lyndon B. Johnson and his supporters, who claimed that Goldwater's militancy would have dire consequences, possibly even nuclear war. Regarding Vietnam, Goldwater charged that Johnson's policy was devoid of "goal, course, or purpose," leaving "only sudden death in the jungles and the slow strangulation of freedom."- Goldwater's own rhetoric on nuclear war was viewed by many as quite uncompromising, a view buttressed by off-hand comments such as, "Let's lob one into the men's room at the Kremlin."

Although Goldwater was not as important in the American conservative movement as Ronald Reagan after 1965, he shaped and redefined the movement from the late 1950s to 1964. Arizona Senator John McCain summed up Goldwater's legacy thus: "He transformed the Republican Party from an Eastern elitist organization to the breeding ground for the election of Ronald Reagan."- The columnist George Will remarked after the 1980 Presidential election "that it took 16 years to count the votes from 1964 and Goldwater won."

In a speech at the University of Michigan, May 22,1964 President Johnson spoke of a "Great Society." He said, "The Great Society rests on abundance and liberty for all. It demands an end to poverty and racial injustice, to which we are totally committed in our time. But that is just the beginning." The speech set the tone for the fall campaign.

July 2, signed the Civil Rights Act of 1964 in a televised ceremony at the White House. The far reaching law included provisions to protect the right to vote, guarantee access to public accommodations, and withhold federal funds from programs administered in a discriminatory fashion.

On August 2 1964, North Vietnamese torpedo boats attacked the destroyer USS Maddox in the Gulf of Tonkin. August 4, a second North Vietnamese PT boat attack was reported on the USS Maddox and her escort, the USS C. Turner Joy, this time in poor weather.
There would be debate, then and later, over whether the second attack actually occurred.

President Johnson ordered retaliatory air strikes against North Vietnam after being given firm assurance that the attack did occur, and he sought a congressional resolution in support of our Southeast Asia policy.

On August 7, with only two dissenting votes in the Senate and none in the House, Congress passed the Southeast Asia Resolution often called the Gulf of Tonkin Resolution backing him in taking "all necessary measures to repel any armed attack against the forces of the United States and to prevent further aggression." Johnson signed the resolution on August 10.

August 20, in the White House Rose Garden, Johnson signed the Economic Opportunity Act. The act established the Office of Economic Opportunity to direct and coordinate a variety of educational, employment, and training programs which were the foundation of President Johnson's "War on Poverty."

August 26, nominated for President of the United States at the Democratic National Convention in Atlantic City, New Jersey. Hubert Humphrey nominated for Vice President. November 3, elected President of the United States with the greatest percentage of the total popular vote 61% ever attained by a Presidential candidate. Hubert Humphrey was elected Vice President.

The "Great Society" program became the agenda for Congress: aid to education, protection of civil rights including the right to vote, urban renewal, Medicare, conservation, beautification, control and prevention of crime and delinquency, promotion of the arts, and consumer protection. Perhaps the biggest leap to Socialism in our nation's history.

Johnson's foreign policy rested on four principles: deterring and resisting aggression, promoting economic and social progress, encouraging cooperation among nations of the same region and seeking reconciliation with the communist world.

In a ceremony on the front lawn of the former Junction Elementary School, President Johnson sat next to his first schoolteacher, Miss Kathryn Deadrich Loney, and signed the Elementary and Secondary Education Act on April 11 1965.

The act was the first federal general aid to education law and focused on disadvantaged children in city slums and rural areas.

As the situation in South Vietnam deteriorated, President Johnson began enlarging the U. S. commitment in Vietnam. On July 28 1965, he announced that he had ordered U. S. military forces in Vietnam increased from 75,000 men to 125,000. He said he would order further military increases as they were needed, committing the United States to major combat in Vietnam.

July 30 1965, signed the Medicare bill in a ceremony at the Harry S. Truman Library in Independence, Missouri. The act established a medical care program for the aged under the Social Security System. March 31 1968, in order to devote his time to seeking peace in Vietnam and at home, President Johnson announced that he would not be a candidate for another term as President of the United States.

Lyndon Johnson must be the worst excuse for a president the United States ever had. He presided over the Vietnam war and created the Great Society which has cost our nation dearly and it continues to drain our nations wealth and enslaves it's people. He was a horrible man that buried the idea of honesty and then the presidency went downhill again in 1968 with the election of tricky Dickey.

Studies have greatly enriched our understanding of America after the Second World War. But by neglecting the rise of the right they have left us with an incomplete and one-sided view of the 1960s.

That view is about to change. Mary Brennan's Turning Right in the Sixties is the first on what will most likely be a lengthening and important list of detailed studies of the rise of American conservatism.

In recent years a handful of books have been written about the right, but these have tended to be sweeping accounts offering few insights into the nuts and bolts of the conservative movement. Brennan, an assistant professor of history at Southwest Texas State University, chronicles the conservative capture of the Republican Party from 1960 to 1968. In doing so, she not only advances our understanding of the rise of the right; she also offers a more balanced and, ultimately, more accurate view than we have had before of the most tumultuous decade of the century.

Brennan effectively addresses one of the central questions in modern American politics: how conservatism transformed itself from an obscure fringe movement into one of the most powerful political forces in the country. By the late 1950s conservatives had established a strong base of support in the growing Southwest. For much of the century wealthy easterners had controlled the Republican Party, but in the postwar years a growing number of businessmen and political leaders from the Sunbelt, many of whom had prospered in the postwar industrial boom, began playing a greater role in national politics. Stressing individual initiative, free enterprise, and a militant anti communism, conservatives formed a variety of single interest groups to challenge the ideas and programs of the liberal eastern establishment.

In the early 1960s conservatives continued to benefit from large-scale social and demographic changes. In the South the growth of the civil rights movement, industrial expansion, and the rise of an urban middle class revitalized the Republican party. The policies of the Kennedy Administration also helped the conservative cause. As President, Kennedy courted many eastern business leaders, drawing their support away from liberal Republicans. He also undercut much of the appeal of moderate Republicans: his position on civil rights, for example, was virtually indistinguishable from theirs. As conservatives began to develop positions on key issues which increasingly appealed to voters, liberal Republicans had trouble distinguishing themselves from Kennedy-style liberals. At the beginning of the 1960s conservatives were in a better position than at any time since the 1930s to challenge moderate Republicans for control of the party. But large obstacles remained. Not only were conservatives widely viewed as wild-eyed fanatics but they squabbled among themselves, had trouble articulating a positive program of reform, had few grassroots organizations, and lacked the funding to make the movement a serious political force.

The year 1960, though, brought a turning point for the conservative movement. That year Barry Goldwater published The Conscience of a Conservative. Generally dismissed in the national media, the book stands today as one of the most important political tracts in modern American history.

As the historian Robert Alan Goldberg demonstrates in Barry Goldwater, his fine new biography, The Conscience of a Conservative advanced the conservative cause in several ways.

Building on William F. Buckley's path breaking work at National Review, Goldwater adeptly reconciled the differences between traditionalists and libertarians. The expansion of the welfare state, he wrote, was an unfortunate and dangerous development that undermined individual freedom. Suggesting that New Deal liberalism marked the first step on the road to totalitarianism, Goldwater argued that government should be removed from most areas of American life. Yet he was no strict libertarian. Appealing to those on the right who longed to recapture lost certitudes, he argued that the state had a duty to maintain order and promote virtue. "Politics," Goldwater wrote, is "the art of achieving the maximum amount of freedom for individuals that is consistent with the maintenance of social order."

Goldwater also united disparate conservative factions by focusing their attention on the dangers of Soviet communism. He wrote,

And still the awful truth remains: We can establish the domestic conditions for maximizing freedom, along the lines I have indicated, and yet become slaves. We can do this by losing the Cold War to the Soviet Union. Goldwater rejected the containment strategies that had guided U.S. foreign policy since the late 1940s, and called for an aggressive strategy of liberation. Conservatives might disagree about the proper role of government in American life, but surely they could unite to defeat the "Soviet menace."

Goldwater also dispelled the notion that conservatives were a privileged elite out to promote its own economic interests. "Conservatism," he wrote, "is not an economic theory."

Rather, it "puts material things in their proper place" and sees man as "a spiritual creature with spiritual needs and spiritual desires."

According to one right-wing magazine, Goldwater gave conservatives humanitarian reasons for supporting policies usually "associated with a mere lust for gain." But perhaps the greatest achievement of Goldwater's book and the reason for its startling success with the right was that it gave conservatives, for the first time, a blueprint for translating their ideas into political action. In his introduction Goldwater rejected the idea that conservatism was out of date.

The charge is preposterous and we ought boldly to say so. The laws of God, and of nature, have no dateline. The principles on which the Conservative political position is based are derived from the nature of man, and from the truths that God has revealed about His creation. Circumstances do change. So do the problems that are shaped by circumstances. But the principles that govern the solution of the problems do not. To suggest that the Conservative philosophy is out of date is akin to saying that the Golden Rule, or the Ten Commandments or Aristotle's Politics are out of date.

Supporting states' rights, lower taxes, voluntary Social Security, and a strengthened military, Goldwater emphasized the positive in his philosophy and demonstrated "the practical relevance of Conservative principles to the needs of the day."

The Conscience of a Conservative altered the American political landscape, galvanizing the right and turning Goldwater into the most popular conservative in the country. By 1964, just four years after its release, the book had gone through more than twenty printings, and it eventually sold 3.5 million copies. "Was there ever such a politician as this?" one Republican asked in disbelief. The Conscience of a Conservative "was our new testament," Pat Buchanan has said. "It contained the core beliefs of our political faith, it told us why we had failed, what we must do. We read it, memorized it, quoted it.... For those of us wandering in the arid desert of Eisenhower Republicanism, it hit like a rifle shot." The book was especially popular on college campuses. In the early sixties one could find Goldwater badges and clubs at universities across the country.

Expressing the sense of rebellion that Goldwater's book helped inspire, one student conservative explained the phenomenon: "You walk around with your Goldwater button, and you feel that thrill of treason."

Republican Party leaders, however, ignored the Goldwater boomlet. Vice President Richard Nixon, the front-runner for the 1960 Republican nomination, believed that the greatest threat to the party came not from the right but from the left. In July, Nixon met with Nelson Rockefeller, the governor of New York, and agreed to change the party platform to win moderate-Republican support. Conservatives were outraged, referring to the pact, in Goldwater's words, as the "Munich of the Republican Party."

A few days later, at the Republican National Convention, an angry Goldwater called on conservatives to grow up and take control of the party. And that, according to Brennan, is exactly what they set out to do. At a time when "liberal and moderate Republicans, like the rest of the country at that time and like historians ever since, continued to view conservatives in a one dimensional mode," conservatives believed that Goldwater's popularity, the rise of a conservative press, and the growing strength of conservative youth groups boded well for the future.

Increasingly disillusioned with Republican moderates and with the whole tenor of American political debate, the right began to see organization as the key to political power. In the midst of the 1960 presidential campaign, for example, William Buckley, the conservative fundraiser Marvin Liebman, and almost a hundred student activists met at Buckley's estate in Sharon, Connecticut, and formed Young Americans for Freedom. Within six months the organization could claim more than a hundred campus and precinct-level political-action groups and at least 21,000 dues-paying members. Using newsletters, radio broadcasts, and frequent rallies, YAF had almost overnight become a powerful nationwide movement.

Had Young Americans for Freedom and other grassroots organizations remained isolated from one another, their impact would have been weak.

But in 1961 the political activist F. Clifton White organized a movement to nominate a conservative for President. Traveling around the country, White exhorted conservatives to seize control of their local party organizations and elect conservative delegates to the national convention.

The movement orchestrated by White gave conservatives control over the Republican Party and helped to persuade Goldwater to run for President.

Capturing the presidential nomination was one thing; winning the presidency proved much more difficult. In the early 1960s conservatives tried to distance themselves from the radical right. No group troubled conservatives more than the John Birch Society. With organizations in all fifty states, thousands of members who, according to Brennan, were "zealous letter writers, demonstrators, and voters", and a full-time staff, the society wielded significant influence.

But Birchers, many of whom believed that Dwight Eisenhower and other government officials were Communist agents, tarnished the reputations of more rational conservatives.

Buckley understood the problem: conservatism, he explained, had to bring "into our ranks those people who are, at the moment, on our immediate left--the moderate, wishy-washy conservatives. ... I am talking ... about 20 to 30 million people.... If they are being asked to join a movement whose leadership believes the drivel of Robert Welch [the founder of the John Birch Society, they will pass by crackpot alley, and will not pause until they feel the warm embrace of those way over on the other side, the Liberals."

But in 1964 Goldwater could not escape the taint of extremism. Brennan points out that despite their sporadic attacks on the radical right, conservatives were still political neophytes. Goldwater and his supporters believed that all they had to do was expose Americans to conservative ideas.

But Goldwater had no positive program, and spent much of the campaign railing against Social Security and threatening to roll back the Communist tide. Moderate Republicans labeled him a racist and a warmonger, and Goldwater seemed to confirm such charges when he threatened to "lob" missiles "into the men's room at the Kremlin." Perhaps most damaging, the media condemned him as a kook who sounded more like Adolf Hitler than like a Republican presidential candidate. Norman Mailer, writing in Esquire, compared the Republican National Convention to a Nazi rally.

The columnist Drew Pearson described the "smell of fascism" in the air. Roy Wilkins, of the NAACP, told readers of The New York Times that "a man came out of the beer halls of Munich, and rallied the forces of Rightist in Germany" and that "all the same elements are there in San Francisco now." When Democrats mocked Goldwater's campaign slogan, "In your heart, you know he's right," by adding, "Yes, extreme Right," Goldwater's candidacy was doomed. In fact it was the statist liberal administrations of the past 30 plus years that were helping us fall under a quasi totalitarian state.

Poor campaign management, Goldwater's image, and the lack of unity in the Republican Party contributed to the Democratic landslide in November of 1964.
But whereas liberals saw the election results as the final repudiation of the American right, conservatives took solace in Goldwater's 27 million votes and vowed not to repeat their mistakes. What appeared to be a defeat for conservatives was actually a dramatic success: Goldwater had paved the way for a generation of Republicans by appealing to the forgotten and silent Americans "who quietly go about the business of paying and praying,

working and saving." He had also raised new social and moral issues that would prove vital to future conservative successes.

As early as 1962 he lamented the moral crisis afflicting America, the "meaningless violence and meaningless sex" on TV, and the barbaric quality of modern art. As Robert Alan Goldberg astutely puts it in his biography, "It was only a beginning, but Goldwater had begun to validate the concerns of social conservatives, and in time they would grow bolder in shaping the movement's agenda." Cliff White, meanwhile, had taught conservatives the value of grassroots organization and had given thousands of people their first taste of political action. Out of the ruins of the 1964 campaign emerged a well-organized, experienced movement that was more determined than ever to win political power.

In the mid-1960s movement activists severed almost all ties to more-radical groups, organized a tremendous direct-mail fundraising drive, and created a more positive platform that emphasized the benefits of local power. And, as Brennan argues, conservatives put themselves in a position to take advantage of the growing disillusionment over civil rights, student protests, and Vietnam. By 1968 conservatives dominated the Republican Party. In 1960 Nixon had wooed those on his left; eight years later he employed the conservative speechwriter Pat Buchanan, chose the fiery Spiro Agnew as his running mate, and trumpeted his anti-Communist credentials and his opposition to busing to win southern delegates. Nixon was not an ideological conservative, but to gain the nomination he had to appeal to the party's new conservative majority.

With so much attention currently being focused on the Contract With America, the Republican presidential nomination, and right-wing militias, Turning Right in the Sixties will appeal to anyone interested in a thoughtful, serious discussion of the origins of modern American conservatism.

Brennan is less successful in her treatment of the larger events of the decade. Her writing is often dry, and one finds missing much of the drama of the sixties. Brennan also fails to explain why so many middle- and lower-middle-class Americans were drawn to conservative causes in the 1960s. Grassroots activism, she makes clear, was instrumental in the rise of the right. But what motivated so many people to contribute money and volunteer time to the conservative movement?

Many observers have cited a white backlash to civil rights. Surely this played an important role, but conservatism seemed to benefit from a complex convergence of forces, only some of which had to do with race. Unprecedented prosperity, for example, gave rise to a new middle class that was hostile to high taxes and to many of the social programs they financed. Social unrest--most notably urban riots, violent crime, and student protests--also pushed many Americans toward conservative candidates who promised to restore law and order.

But perhaps most important was a growing disillusionment with the federal government. Vietnam, deteriorating conditions in the cities, and forced busing affected the lives of working- and middle-class Americans in profound and often unsettling ways, and led them to believe that government no longer served their interests.

Although Brennan's book does not sufficiently address these issues, it is valuable, shedding much-needed light on a key aspect of the conservative revival and giving us a deeper understanding of why conservatism continues to be the most powerful political force in American life. The front-runner for the Republican nomination in 1968 was former Vice President Richard M. Nixon, and to a great extent the story of the Republican primary campaign and nomination is the story of one Nixon opponent after another entering the race and then dropping out.

Nixon's first challenger was Michigan Governor George W. Romney. A Gallup poll in mid-1967 showed Nixon with 39%, followed by Romney with 25%. However, in a slip of the tongue, Romney told a news reporter that he had been "brainwashed" by the military and the diplomatic corps into supporting the Vietnam War; the remark led to weeks of ridicule in the national news media. As the year 1968 opened, Romney was opposed to further American intervention in Vietnam and had decided to run as the Republican version of Eugene McCarthy (New York Times 2/18/1968). Romney's support faded slowly, and he withdrew from the race on February 28, 1968.

Nixon won a resounding victory in the important New Hampshire primary on March 12, winning 78% of the vote. Antiwar Republicans wrote in the name of New York Governor Nelson Rockefeller, the leader of the GOP's liberal wing, who received 11% of the vote and became Nixon's new challenger. Nixon led Rockefeller in the polls throughout the primary campaign. Rockefeller defeated Nixon in the Massachusetts primary on April 30 but otherwise fared poorly in the state primaries and conventions.

By early spring, California Governor Ronald Reagan, the leader of the GOP's conservative wing, had become Nixon's chief rival. In the Nebraska primary on May 14, Nixon won with 70% of the vote to 21% for Reagan and 5% for Rockefeller. While this was a wide margin for Nixon, Reagan remained Nixon's leading challenger. Nixon won the next primary of importance, Oregon, on May 15 with 65% of the vote and won all the following primaries except for California (June 4), where only Reagan appeared on the ballot. Reagan's margin in California gave him a plurality of the nationwide primary vote, but when the Republican National Convention assembled, Nixon had 656 delegates according to a UPI poll with 667 needed for the nomination.

At the 1968 Republican National Convention in Miami Beach, Florida, Reagan and Rockefeller planned to unite their forces in a stop-Nixon movement, but the strategy fell apart when neither man agreed to support the other for the nomination. Nixon won the nomination on the first ballot.

Despite the growing opposition to Johnson's policies in Vietnam, no prominent Democratic candidate was prepared to run against a sitting President of his own party. Even Senator Robert F. Kennedy of New York, an outspoken critic of Johnson's policies with a large base of support, refused to run against Johnson in the primaries. Only Senator Eugene McCarthy of Minnesota proved willing to openly challenge Johnson. Running as an anti-war candidate in the New Hampshire primary, McCarthy hoped to pressure the Democrats into publicly opposing the Vietnam War. Normally, an incumbent president faces little formidable opposition within his own party.

However, McCarthy, although he was trailing badly in the national polls, decided to pour most of his resources into New Hampshire, the first state to hold a primary election. He was boosted by thousands of young college students, who shaved their beards and cut their hair to be "Clean for Gene". These students rang doorbells and worked hard in New Hampshire for McCarthy. On March 12, McCarthy won 42% of the primary vote to Johnson's 49%, an amazingly strong showing for such a challenger, and one which gave McCarthy's campaign legitimacy and momentum.

The momentum ended, however, when Senator Kennedy announced his candidacy four days later, on March 16, as McCarthy supporters cried betrayal and vowed to defeat Kennedy. Thereafter McCarthy and Kennedy would engage in an increasingly bitter series of state primaries; although Kennedy won most of the primaries, he could never shake McCarthy and his devoted following of anti-war activists, which included many Hollywood celebrities. On March 31, 1968, following the New Hampshire primaries and Kennedy's entry into the election, the President startled the nation by announcing he would not seek re-election. With Johnson's withdrawal, the Democratic Party quickly split into four factions, each of which distrusted the other three.

The first faction comprised labor unions and big-city party bosses led by Mayor Richard J. Daley. This group had traditionally controlled the Democratic Party since the days of President Franklin D. Roosevelt, and they feared their loss of control over the party.

After Johnson's withdrawal this group rallied to support Hubert H. Humphrey, Johnson's Vice-President; it was also believed that President Johnson himself was covertly supporting Humphrey, despite his public claims of neutrality.

The second faction, which rallied behind Senator McCarthy, was composed of students and intellectuals who had been the early activists against the war in Vietnam; they perceived themselves as the future of the Democratic Party.

The third group was primarily composed of Catholics, African-Americans, and other racial and ethnic minorities; these groups rallied behind Senator Robert Kennedy. The fourth group consisted of conservative white Southern Democrats, or "Dixiecrats." Some members of this group probably older ones remembering the New Deal's positive impact upon rural areas supported Vice-President Humphrey, but most of them would rally behind George C. Wallace and the Alabama governor's third party campaign in the general election.

Since the Vietnam War had become the major issue that was dividing the Democratic Party, and Johnson had come to symbolize the war for many liberal Democrats, Johnson believed that he could not win the nomination without a major struggle, and that he would probably lose the election in November to the Republicans. However, by withdrawing from the race he could avoid the stigma of defeat, and he could keep control of the party machinery by giving the nomination to Humphrey, who had been a loyal Vice-President.

As the year developed, it also became clear that Johnson believed he could secure his place in the history books by ending the war before the election in November, thus giving Humphrey the boost he would need to win.

After Johnson's withdrawal, Vice President Hubert Humphrey announced his candidacy. Kennedy was successful in four primaries and McCarthy five; however, in primaries where they campaigned directly against one another, Kennedy won three primaries and McCarthy one. Humphrey did not compete in the primaries, leaving that job to favorite sons who were his surrogates, notably Senator George A. Smathers from Florida, Senator Stephen M. Young from Ohio, and Governor Roger D. Branigin of Indiana. Instead, Humphrey concentrated on winning the delegates in non-primary states, where party leaders such as Chicago Mayor Richard J. Daley controlled the delegate votes in their states.

Kennedy defeated Branigin and McCarthy in the Indiana primary, and then defeated McCarthy in the Nebraska primary. However, McCarthy upset Kennedy in the Oregon primary. After Kennedy's defeat in Oregon, the California primary was seen as crucial to both Kennedy and McCarthy. McCarthy stumped the state's many colleges and universities, where he was treated as a hero for being the first presidential candidate to oppose the war. Kennedy campaigned in the ghettos and barrios of the state's larger cities, where he was mobbed by enthusiastic supporters. Kennedy and McCarthy engaged in a television debate a few days before the election, it was generally considered a draw. On June 4 Kennedy narrowly defeated McCarthy in California, 46% - 42%.

However, McCarthy refused to withdraw from the Presidential race and made it clear that he would contest Kennedy in the upcoming New York primary, where McCarthy had much support from antiwar activists in New York City. The New York primary quickly became a moot point, however, for on the early morning of June 5, Kennedy was shot shortly after his victories in the California and South Dakota primaries; he died twenty-six hours later. Kennedy had just given his victory speech in a crowded ballroom of the Ambassador Hotel in Los Angeles; he and his aides squeezed into a kitchen on their way to another ballroom to celebrate their victory.

In the kitchen's pantry, Kennedy and five other people were shot. Sirhan Sirhan, a young Palestinian militant who disliked Kennedy for his support of the state of Israel, was arrested, tried and convicted. Robert Kennedy's death altered the dynamics of the race, and threw the Democratic Party into disarray. Although Humphrey appeared the prohibitive favorite for the nomination, thanks to his support from the traditional power blocs of the party, he was an unpopular choice with many of the anti-war elements within the party, who identified him with Johnson's controversial position on the Vietnam War.

However, Kennedy's delegates failed to unite behind a single candidate who could have prevented Humphrey from getting the nomination. Some of Kennedy's support went to McCarthy, but many of Kennedy's delegates, remembering their bitter primary battles with McCarthy, refused to vote for him. Instead, these delegates rallied around the late-starting candidacy of Senator George McGovern of South Dakota, a Kennedy supporter in the spring primaries, and who had presidential ambitions.

However, by dividing the antiwar votes at the Democratic Convention, it made it easier for Humphrey to gather the delegates he needed to win the nomination.

When the 1968 Democratic National Convention opened in Chicago, thousands of young antiwar activists from around the nation gathered in the city to protest the Vietnam War. In a clash which was covered on live television, Americans were shocked to see Chicago police brutally beating anti-war protesters in the streets of Chicago. While the protesters chanted "the whole world is watching", the police used clubs and tear gas to beat back the protesters, leaving many of them bloody and dazed.

The tear gas even wafted into numerous hotel suites; in one of them Vice-President Humphrey was watching the proceedings on television. Meanwhile, the convention itself was marred by the strong arm tactics of Chicago's mayor Richard J. Daley who was seen on television angrily cursing Senator Abraham Ribicoff of Connecticut, who made a speech at the convention denouncing the excesses of the Chicago police in the riots. In the end, the nomination itself was anticlimactic, with Vice President Humphrey handily beating McCarthy and McGovern on the first ballot. The convention then chose Senator Edmund Muskie of Maine as Humphrey's running mate. However, the tragedy of the antiwar riots crippled Humphrey's campaign from the start, and it never fully recovered.

In the election of 1964, after serving the 14 remaining months after President John F. Kennedy's assassination, Democrat Lyndon Johnson had won the largest popular vote landslide in US Presidential election history over Republican Barry Goldwater. During his term, Johnson had seen many political successes, including the passage of his sweeping Great Society domestic programs also known as the "War on Poverty", landmark civil rights legislation, and the continued exploration of space. At the same time, however, the country had experienced large-scale race riots in the streets of its larger cities, along with a generational revolt of young people and violent debates over foreign policy.

The emergence of the hippie counterculture, the rise of New Left activism, and the emergence of the Black Power movement exacerbated social and cultural clashes between classes, generations and races. Every summer during Johnson's post-election administration, known thereafter as the long, hot summers, major U.S. cities erupted in massive race riots that left hundreds dead or injured and destroyed hundreds of millions of dollars in property. Adding to the national tension, on April 4, 1968, civil rights leader Rev. Martin Luther King, Jr. was assassinated in Memphis, Tennessee sparking further mass rioting and chaos, including Washington, where rioting came within just a few blocks of the White House.

A major factor in the precipitous decline of President Johnson's popularity was the Vietnam War, which he greatly escalated during his time in office. By late 1967 over 500,000 American soldiers were fighting in Vietnam and suffering thousands of casualties every month.

Johnson was especially hurt when, despite his repeated assurances that the war was being won, the American news media began to show just the opposite. The Tet Offensive of February 1968, in which Communist Vietcong forces launched major attacks on several large cities in South Vietnam, led to increased criticism from antiwar activists that the war was unwinnable. The Johnson Administration was particularly damaged during the Tet Offensive when Vietcong forces managed to penetrate the US Embassy, Saigon, the South Vietnamese capital, before being killed by U.S. troops in a fierce struggle captured on national television.

In response to the Tet Offensive, the U.S. military claimed that the war could only be won by adding several hundred thousand more soldiers to the American forces already in South Vietnam. In the months following Tet, Johnson's approval ratings fell below 35%, and the Secret Service refused to let the President make public appearances on the campuses of American colleges and universities, due to his extreme unpopularity among college students. The Secret Service also prevented Johnson from appearing at the 1968 Democratic National Convention in Chicago, because of their fear that his appearance might cause riots.

The United States presidential election of 1968 was the 46th United States presidential election. It was a wrenching national experience, conducted against a backdrop that included the assassination of civil rights leader Martin Luther King, Jr. and subsequent race riots across the nation, the assassination of presidential candidate Robert F. Kennedy, widespread demonstrations against the Vietnam War across American university and college campuses, and violent confrontations between police and anti-war protesters at the 1968 Democratic National Convention.

On November 5, 1968, the Republican nominee, former Vice President Richard Nixon won the election over the Democratic nominee, Vice President Hubert Humphrey. Nixon ran on a campaign that promised to restore "law and order". Some consider the election of 1968 a re-aligning election that permanently disrupted the New Deal Coalition that had dominated presidential politics for 36 years. It was also the last election in which two opposing candidates were vice-presidents.

The election also featured a strong third party effort by former Alabama Governor George Wallace. Because Wallace's campaign promoted segregation, he proved to be a formidable candidate in the South; no third-party candidate has won an entire state's electoral votes since. So when the smoke cleared Richard M. Nixon was president and was right leaning, but Nixon was crafty and clever. In 1960 he needed to appear Liberal so he did. In 1968 he was Conservative so he did. Ronald Reagan's attempt at Presidential office lacked maturity so Nixon would lead.
The cultural revolution of the 1960's had many victims on both the right and the left, perhaps the greatest victim was America which had lost itself. Fortunately the birth of a new Conservative revolution was taking place.

William Buckley's column *On The Right* was syndicated by Universal Press Syndicate beginning in 1962. From the early 1970s, his twice-weekly column was distributed to more than 320 newspapers across the country.

In the early 1960s, at Sharon, Connecticut, Buckley founded the conservative political youth group, "Young Americans for Freedom" (YAF). Young Americans for Freedom was guided by principles Buckley called, "The Sharon Statement". The successful campaign of his elder brother Jim Buckley's to capture the U.S. Senate seat from New York State held by incumbent Republican Charles Goodell on the Conservative Party ticket in 1970 was due, in large part, to the activist support of the New York State chapter of Y.A.F.

A Congressman representing New York's old 43rd Congressional District, Goodell had been appointed to the Senate by Barry Goldwater's arch-nemesis Nelson Rockefeller, the liberal Republican Governor of New York, to fill the seat vacated by the assassination of Robert F. Kennedy, a Democrat. In the Senate, Goodell had moved to the left and thus incurred the enmity of conservatives in the New York State Republican Party, who threw in their lot with Jim Buckley. Buckley served one term in the Senate, then was defeated by Democrat Daniel Patrick Moynihan in 1976.

For many Americans, Buckley's erudition on his weekly PBS show *Firing Line* (1966–1999) was their primary exposure to him. In it he displayed a scholarly, and humorous conservatism and was known for his facial expressions, gestures and probing questions of his guests. Buckley appeared in a series of televised debates with Gore Vidal during the 1968 Democratic National Convention in Chicago. In their penultimate debate on August 28 of that year, the two disagreed over the actions of the city police and the protesters at the ongoing convention.

After Buckley responded to Vidal's argument by stating that Vidal's position was "so naive" and saying of the protesters "some people were pro-Nazi", Vidal called Buckley a "crypto-Nazi", to which Buckley replied, "Now listen, you queer, stop calling me a crypto-Nazi or I will sock you in your goddamn face, and you will stay plastered."

Buckley's essay "On Experiencing Gore Vidal", was published in the August 1969 issue, and led Vidal to sue for libel. The court threw out Vidal's case.- Vidal's September essay in reply-, "A Distasteful Encounter with William F. Buckley", was similarly litigated by Buckley. In it Vidal strongly implied that, in 1944, Buckley and unnamed siblings had vandalized a Protestant church in their Sharon, Connecticut, hometown after the pastor's wife had sold a house to a Jewish family. Buckley sued Vidal and *Esquire* for libel; Vidal counter-claimed for libel against Buckley, citing Buckley's characterization of Vidal's novel *Myra Breckenridge* as pornography. Both cases were dropped, with Buckley settling for court costs paid by Vidal, while Vidal absorbed his own court costs. Buckley also received an editorial apology in the pages of *Esquire* as part of the settlement.

When Nixon took office, 300 American soldiers were dying per week in Vietnam. The Johnson administration had negotiated a deal in which the U.S. would suspend bombing in North Vietnam in exchange for unconditional negotiations, but this faltered. Nixon faced the choice of devising a new policy to chance securing South Vietnam as a non-communist state, or withdrawing American forces completely.

Amid protests at home, he implemented what became known as the Nixon Doctrine, a strategy of replacing American troops with Vietnamese troops, also called "Vietnamization". He soon enacted phased U.S. troop withdrawals- but authorized incursions into Laos, in part to interrupt the Ho Chi Minh trail that passed through Laos and Cambodia.

Nixon's 1968 campaign promise to curb the war and his subsequent Laos bombing raised questions in the press about a credibility gap, similar to that encountered earlier in the war by Lyndon B. Johnson.- In a televised speech on April 30, 1970, Nixon announced the incursion of U.S. troops into Cambodia to disrupt so-called North Vietnamese sanctuaries. This led to protest and student strikes that temporarily closed 536 universities, colleges, and high schools.

The Gates Commission issued its report in February 1970, describing how adequate military strength could be maintained without conscription.- The draft was extended to June 1973,- and then ended. Military pay was increased as an incentive to attract volunteers, and television advertising for the United States Army began for the first time.

Other parts of the Nixon plan included the reimposition of a 10% investment tax credit, assistance to the automobile industry in the form of removal of excise taxes provided the savings were passed directly to the consumer, an end to fixed exchange rates, devaluation of the dollar on the free market, and a 10% tax on all imports into the U.S.-Income per family rose, and unionization declined. Nixon wanted to lift the spirits of the country as polls showed increasing concern about the economy.

His program was viewed by nearly everyone as exceptionally bold, and astounded the Democrats. Nixon soon experienced a bounce in the polls. His economic program was determined to be a clear success by December 1971.- One of Nixon's economic advisers, Herbert Stein, wrote: "Probably more new regulation was imposed on the economy during the Nixon administration than in any other presidency since the New Deal." Nixon believed in using government wisely to benefit all and supported the idea of practical liberalism. Nixon initiated the Environmental Decade by signing the National Environmental Policy Act, the Clean Air Act of 1970 and the Federal Water Pollution Control Act amendments of 1972, as well as establishing many government agencies.

He was a usurper a chameleon who would say or do whatever he had to do to win and be popular not what was right or correct.
These included the Environmental Protection Agency (EPA), the Occupational Safety and Health Administration (OSHA),- and the Council on Environmental Quality. The Clean Air Act was noted as one of the most significant pieces of environmental legislation ever signed. Frustrated by the lack of progress on social and political issues and reacting to the turmoil that had spread across the land, a number of groups began to advocate radical measures to achieve their goals of justice and equality. Four of the most prominent and successful of these organizations were the Black Panther Party, the Students for a Democratic Society, the Weather Underground Organization, and the Youth International Party, or the Yippies.

The Black Panther Party was founded in 1966 in Oakland, California, by Bobby Seale and Huey Newton. They demanded the right to control the schools, medical centers, welfare programs, and police system in poor black areas, exemption from military service and the right to bear arms for self-protection. They organized chapters throughout the country, initiating 'liberation' schools, breakfast programs for children, and medical clinics in poor areas. The Black Panthers had many confrontations with the police that led to shootings and arrests.

The SDS was founded in Chicago in 1962 and was active throughout the sixties on college campuses across the land. In the mid-sixties, they were active mainly in civil rights causes, but later they became more concerned with ending the United States' involvement in Vietnam. The SDS often coordinated activities with the Black Panthers and espoused radical, though at first, Marxist, means of protest. A splinter group known as the Weathermen believed in violent revolution and acts of terrorism to achieve their goals. This group was implicated in a number of bombings at colleges and federal institutions. Under our current President some of these are friends of our current administration.

The Youth International Party (the Yippies), was the brain child of sixties activists Abbie Hoffman and Jerry Rubin. They staged guerrilla street theater designed mainly to attract media attention to their causes.

They were most successful at the 1968 Democratic Convention in Chicago where they promoted the Yippie candidate for president pig named Pigasus.

After the ensuing riots that rocked Chicago for days, Hoffman, Rubin, Black Panther Bobby Seale and four others were arrested for conspiring to incite violence and crossing state lines with the intent to riot. The group became known as the Chicago Seven. After a protracted trial, all charges were dismissed.

CHAPTER TWELVE - Vietnam, Watergate, The Aftermath.

The priorities of the Nixon presidency lay not in domestic social or economic policies which were simply the means to the end but in reelection through creation of a majority coalition. What really interested Nixon was statecraft, the application of American power and diplomatic influence to regional and global problems. The key problem for his presidency clearly would be the Vietnam War.

Nixon, his national security adviser Henry Kissinger, and Secretary of Defense Melvin Laird settled on an approach with several elements. First, the Laird policy for "Vietnamization" was adopted. Responsibility for fighting would be turned over to the Vietnamese, in order to reduce American casualties. Gradually American forces would be withdrawn. This would buy time on the home front. Second, a variant of the "madman" approach in international relations would be adopted. The administration would warn the North Vietnamese that unless they settled soon they would be subjected to carpet bombing of cities, mining of harbors, and even the spread of radioactive debris to halt infiltration of the South. Irrigation dikes would be destroyed and forests defoliated. Third, Nixon and Kissinger would apply the principle of linkage in dealing with the Soviet Union: the arms and trade agreements to be proposed to the Soviets would require a quid pro quo Moscow would have to pressure Hanoi to agree to a settlement.

The Vietnam policy failed. Nixon announced the with-drawal of a half million troops, and by May 1972 no American forces were on combat missions. By January 1973, only twenty-five thousand American troops re-mained in Vietnam. The level of fatalities and injuries dropped. But the combat effectiveness of the South Viet-namese did not improve. The invasion of Laos by South Vietnamese forces not only was ineffective but turned into a rout, leaving little doubt that they would be no match for the North Vietnamese.

Congress had imposed restrictions on presidential war-making powers in Southeast Asia, beginning in 1970 with the Cooper Amendment, which provided that no combat troops could be sent to Laos or Thailand, followed by the Cooper-Church Amendment 1970, which prohibited the reintroduction of ground forces into Cambodia, and cul-minating with passage of the Eagleton Amendment, which called for a halt in all American land, sea, and air military operations in Laos, Cambodia, and Vietnam after 15 August 1973.

Any attempt by Nixon or his successors to use American armed forces to guarantee the survival of the Saigon re-gime would be illegal. Moreover, the War Powers Reso-lution, passed by Congress over Nixon's veto in 1973, required any American president to obtain congressional approval within sixty days for any military action; this pre-sented yet another problem in shoring up the South Viet-namese government. The Nixon commitments to Thieu were therefore not honored by the Ford administration in 1975, which resulted in the reunification of North and South Vietnam under Communist rule.

Vietnam was a horrible mistake started by the Johnson administration and ended without honor by the Nixon administration. This war would have made Woodrow Wilson proud, the US was interfering in a struggle thousands of miles away in a civil war that had no impact on our nation's trade with other nations.

Nixon entered his name on the New Hampshire primary ballot on January 5, 1972, effectively announcing his candidacy for reelection.- Largely assured the Republican nomination, the President had expected his Democratic opponent to be Senator Ted Kennedy, but Senator Edmund Muskie instead became the front runner, with Senator George McGovern in a close second place. Though Muskie defeated McGovern in the New Hampshire primary, his showings were poorer in Florida and he soon ended his campaign.- Alabama Governor George Wallace entered the race as an Independent; popular in Florida, he would create havoc among the Democrats and boost Nixon's campaign.

Prominent issues of the early campaign included school busing and heated relations between the three branches of the government. Nixon addressed the nation on March 16 about the school busing issue, reiterating that it was wrong to force a child onto a school bus and that busing lowered the quality of education.-He announced the Equal Education Opportunities bill that would seek a moratorium on local school busing;- the bill later passed. Vietnam was still ongoing, though Nixon had reduced troop levels dramatically.

On June 10, McGovern won the California primary and secured the Democratic nomination. Nixon's victory made him the first former Vice President since Thomas Jefferson to win two terms as President. Nixon and Franklin Roosevelt are the only candidates in U.S. history to appear on five presidential tickets for a major party.

On October 10, 1973, Vice President Agnew resigned, amid charges of bribery, tax evasion and money laundering from his tenure as Maryland's governor. Nixon chose Representative Gerald Ford, Republican Minority Leader of the House of Representatives, to replace Agnew.

The price controls became unpopular with the public and businesspeople, who saw powerful labor unions as preferable to the price board bureaucracy.-Business owners, however, now saw the controls as permanent rather than temporary, and voluntary compliance decreased.- The controls produced food shortages, as meat disappeared from grocery stores and farmers drowned chickens rather than sell them at a loss.- The controls were slowly ended, and by April 30, 1974, the control authority from Congress had lapsed.- However, the controls on oil and natural gas prices persisted for several years.-Nixon also dramatically increased spending on federal employees' salaries while the economy was plagued by the 1973–1974 stock market crash.

The Nixon administration supported Israel, a powerful American ally in the Middle East, during the Yom Kippur War. When an Arab coalition led by Egypt and Syria attacked in October 1973, Israel suffered initial losses and pressed European powers for help, but the exception of the Netherlands the Europeans responded with inaction.

Nixon cut through inter-departmental squabbles and bureaucracy to initiate an airlift of American arms. By the time the U.S. and the Soviet Union negotiated a truce, Israel had penetrated deep into enemy territory. A long-term effect was the movement of Egypt away from the Soviets toward the U.S. But Israel's victory came at the cost to the U.S. of the 1973 oil crisis; the members of OPEC decided to raise oil prices in response to the American support of Israel.

After Nixon chose to go off the gold standard, foreign countries increased their currency reserves in anticipation of currency fluctuation, which caused deflation of the dollar and other world currencies. Since oil was paid for in dollars, OPEC was receiving less value for their product. They cut production and announced price hikes as well as an embargo targeted against the United States and the Netherlands, specifically blaming U.S. support for Israel in the Yom Kippur War for the actions.

A break-in occurred on the night of June 17, 1972, as five burglars entered the Democratic National Committee offices inside the Watergate office complex in Washington. Discovered by 24-year-old night watchman Frank Wills, they were arrested at the scene by police at 2:30 a.m.

Investigations soon revealed the Watergate burglars were employed by the Committee to Re-elect President Nixon. However, a White House spokesman dismissed the incident as a "third-rate burglary attempt."
In August of 1972, President Nixon told reporters, "no one in the White House staff, no one in this administration, presently employed, was involved in this very bizarre incident."

The arrest of the Watergate burglars marked the beginning of a long chain of events in which President Nixon and his top aides became deeply involved in an extensive coverup of the break-in and other White House sanctioned illegal activities.

In 1972, as part of Nixon's re-election effort, a massive campaign of political spying and 'dirty tricks' was initiated against Democrats, leading to the Watergate break-in to plant bugs inside the offices of the Democratic National Committee.

Two young reporters from the *Washington Post*, Bob Woodward and Carl Bernstein, then began a dogged pursuit of the facts surrounding the break-in. Among the many items revealed by them one of the Watergate burglars, retired CIA employee James W. McCord, was actually the security coordinator for Nixon's re-election committee a $25,000 cashier's check for Nixon's re-election campaign had been diverted to the bank account of one of the burglars. Attorney General John Mitchell had controlled a secret fund which financed political spying and dirty tricks targeting Democratic presidential candidates.

Perhaps the most notorious dirty trick was a letter planted in a New Hampshire newspaper alleging that leading Democratic presidential candidate, Senator Edmund Muskie of Maine, had referred to Americans of French-Canadian descent as "Canucks."

On a snowy New Hampshire day, standing outside the offices of the newspaper, Musky gave a rambling, tearful denial.

His emotional conduct, replayed on television, caused him to drop in the New Hampshire polls shortly before the presidential primary. George McGovern, considered a weaker candidate by Nixon political strategists, eventually won the 1972 Democratic nomination and lost the general election to Nixon in a landslide.

In February of 1973, the U.S. Senate established a Select Committee on Presidential Campaign Activities, chaired by Sen. Sam Ervin, to investigate all of the events surrounding Watergate and other allegations of political spying and sabotage conducted on behalf of Nixon's re-election.

March and April of 1973 saw the start of the unraveling of the coverup. On March 23, one of the five burglars convicted after the Watergate break-in, James W. McCord, informed U.S. District Judge John J. Sirica that he was being pressured to remain silent. On April 20, acting FBI Director L. Patrick Gray resigned after admitting he had destroyed Watergate evidence under pressure from Nixon aides. Ten days later, four of Nixon's top officials resigned: Chief of Staff H.R. Haldeman; Domestic Affairs Assistant John Ehrlichman; Attorney General Richard Kleindienst; and Presidential Counsel John Dean.

The Senate Select Committee began televised hearings on May 17. A month later, former Presidential Counsel John Dean testified there was an ongoing White House coverup and that Nixon had been personally involved in the payment of hush money to the five burglars and two other operatives involved in planning the Watergate break-in.

Three weeks later, another Nixon aide revealed the President had ordered hidden microphones installed in the Oval Office in the spring of 1971 and had recorded most conversations since then on audio tape.

The tapes then became the focus of an intensive year-long legal battle between all three branches of the U.S. government. In October of 1973, Watergate Special Prosecutor Archibald Cox, who had been appointed by the Nixon administration, publicly vowed to obtain the tapes despite Nixon's strong objections.

Nixon responded to public outrage by initially agreeing to turn over some of the tapes. However, the White House then revealed that two of the tapes no longer existed and later revealed there was an 18 minute blank gap on a crucial recording of the President and H.R. Haldeman taped three days after the Watergate break-in.

Nixon's new Chief of Staff Alexander M. Haig Jr. suggested the possibility that some sinister force had erased portions of the subpoenaed tape. President Nixon's personal secretary Rose Mary Woods was eventually blamed as having caused the erasure supposedly after she had been asked to prepare a summary of taped conversations for the President.

In November of 1973, amid all of the controversy, Nixon made a scheduled appearance before 400 Associated Press managing editors in Florida. During a feisty question and answer period he maintained his innocence, stating, "... in all of my years in public life I have never obstructed justice...People have got to know whether or not their President is a crook. Well, I'm not a crook."

The new Special Prosecutor, Leon Jaworski, who had been appointed by the Justice Department, pursued Nixon's tapes all the way to the U.S. Supreme Court. On July 24, 1974, the Court unanimously ruled that Nixon had to surrender the tapes.

On Saturday, July 27,1974 the House Judiciary Committee approved its first article of impeachment charging President Nixon with obstruction of justice. Six of the Committee's 17 Republicans joined all 21 Democrats in voting for the article. The following Monday the Committee approved its second article charging Nixon with abuse of power. The next day, the third and final article, contempt of Congress, was approved.

On Friday, August 9, Nixon resigned the presidency and avoided the likely prospect of losing the impeachment vote in the full House and a subsequent trial in the Senate. He thus became the only U.S. President ever to resign. Vice President Gerald R. Ford succeeded him and a month later granted Nixon a full pardon for any crimes he might have committed while President.

Richard Nixon had served a total of 2,026 days as the 37th President of the United States. He left office with 2 1/2 years of his second term remaining. Richard Nixon the Chameleon president had done more damage to the office than anyone including Wilson and Jackson. Now Gerald Ford would assume the reigns of the presidency.

After becoming part of the Republican leadership in Congress in the mid-1960s, Ford fought against President Lyndon B. Johnson's social welfare legislation and opposed the gradual escalation of American military involvement in Vietnam.

In late 1973, Ford was named to replace scandal plagued Vice President Spiro T. Agnew. President Richard M. Nixon and other high-ranking officials said publicly that Ford was selected for his reputation of integrity and trustworthiness in Congress, while off-the-record some suggested he was chosen more because his blandness made him acceptable to both left and right. He had been friends with Nixon since the mid-1950s. Ford served as Nixon's Vice President for just eight months, until the Watergate cover-up led to Nixon's resignation. Ford was sworn in as President on 9 August 1974.

Only a month later, Ford issued an unprecedented pre-emptive pardon to Nixon "for any crimes he may have committed" while President. To most Americans who had endured the Nixon and Agnew scandals, the pardon reeked of a cynical, pre-arranged deal, though Ford has always denied any *quid pro quo* arrangement. The pardon was greeted with widespread outrage, and became the defining moment of Ford's Presidency.

As President, Ford named Nelson Rockefeller to be his Vice President, but most of their administration's initiatives were stifled by a Democratic controlled Congress. Ford can be credited with bills involving energy decontrol, tax cuts, deregulation of the securities industries, and antitrust law reform. Ford sought to combat high inflation by having large quantities of buttons printed and distributed nationwide, with only the word "WIN" on the button's face an acronym for "Whip Inflation Now." Not surprisingly, the buttons did little to curb inflation.

When he sought election to his office in 1976, Ford snubbed Rockefeller and instead selected Senator Bob Dole as his running mate to try an appeal to the Conservative faction of the party. During a campaign debate against former Georgia Governor Jimmy Carter, Ford incorrectly stated that Poland was independent and autonomous from the Soviet Union, though at the time the Soviet Union dominated Poland and much of Eastern Europe. When pressed, instead of reconsidering, Ford responded more firmly that "There is no Soviet domination of Eastern Europe, and there never will be under a Ford administration". Ford's misstatements were considered a major factor in his loss to Carter, and are cited again every four years as among the worst gaffes made in any televised political debate.

During his Presidency, two crazed women made separate attempts to assassinate Ford. In Sacramento on 5 September 1975, Lynnette 'Squeaky' Fromme, a member of Charles Manson's "family", raised a .45 caliber handgun in Ford's direction.

She was wrestled to the ground by Secret Servicemen, but there was no bullet in the chamber of her gun. Two and a half weeks later, on 22 September 1975, an accountant named Sara Jane Moore took a shot at Ford in San Francisco. She missed when a bystander, former Marine Oliver Sipple, saw the gun and grabbed Moore's arm, ruining her aim. Though Ford was not hit, the White House waited three days before publicly thanking Sipple, while staff debated an appropriate response after learning that the heroic Sipple was gay.

Both Moore and Fromme were given life sentences, and both later escaped from the same West Virginia prison. Fromme escaped in 1979, and was captured again several hours later about 25 miles away. Moore escaped in 1989, and turned herself in two days later. Both women were transferred to other prisons, and both remain imprisoned.

As President, Ford signed the Helsinki Accords, marking a move toward détente in the Cold War. With the conquest of South Vietnam by North Vietnam nine months into his presidency, US involvement in Vietnam essentially ended. Domestically, Ford presided over what was then the worst economy since the Great Depression, with growing inflation and a recession during his tenure. Ford had appeal to both left and some on the right. Wishy washy as a victim of Watergate himself he led mostly from the center.

During Ford's incumbency, foreign policy was characterized in procedural terms by the increased role Congress began to play, and by the corresponding curb on the powers of the President.

Ford reluctantly agreed to run for office in 1976, but first he had to counter a challenge for the Republican party nomination. Then-former Governor of California Ronald Reagan and the party's conservative wing faulted Ford for failing to do more in South Vietnam, for signing the Helsinki Accords and for negotiating to cede the Panama Canal negotiations for the canal continued under President Carter, who eventually signed the Torrijos-Carter Treaties.

Reagan launched his campaign in autumn of 1975 and won several primaries before withdrawing from the race at the Republican Convention in Kansas City, Missouri.

On July 7, 1976, the President and First Lady served as hosts at a White House state dinner for Queen Elizabeth II and Prince Philip of the United Kingdom, which was televised on the Public Broadcasting Service network. The 200th anniversary of the Battles of Lexington and Concord in Massachusetts gave Ford the opportunity to deliver a speech to 110,000 in Concord acknowledging the need for a strong national defense tempered with a plea for "reconciliation, not recrimination" and "reconstruction, not rancor" between the United States and those who would pose "threats to peace".

James Earl "Jimmy" Carter, Jr. served as the 39th President of the United States from 1977 to 1981. Before he became President, Carter served two terms as a Georgia State Senator and one as Governor of Georgia, from 1971 to 1975, and was a peanut farmer and naval officer. As president, Carter created two new cabinet-level departments: the Department of Energy and the Department of Education. He established a national energy policy that included conservation, price control, and new technology. In foreign affairs, Carter pursued the Camp David Accords, the Panama Canal Treaties, the second round of Strategic Arms Limitation Talks (SALT II), and returned the Panama Canal Zone to Panama.

Throughout his career, Carter strongly emphasized human rights. He took office during a period of stagflation, which persisted throughout his term.

The final year of his presidential tenure was marked by the 1979 takeover of the American embassy in Iran and holding of hostages by Iranian students, an unsuccessful rescue attempt of the hostages, fuel shortages, and the Soviet invasion of Afghanistan.

When Carter entered the Democratic Party presidential primaries in 1976, he was considered to have little chance against nationally better-known politicians. He had a name recognition of only two percent. When he told his family of his intention to run for President, his mother asked, "President of what?" However, the Watergate scandal was still fresh in the voters' minds, and so his position as an outsider, distant from Washington, D.C., became an asset. The centerpiece of his campaign platform was government reorganization.

Carter began the race with a sizable lead over Ford, who was able to narrow the gap over the course of the campaign, but was unable to prevent Carter from narrowly defeating him on November 2, 1976. Carter won the popular vote by 50.1 percent to 48.0 percent for Ford and received 297 electoral votes to Ford's 240. He became the first contender from the Deep South to be elected President since the 1848 election.

Carter was elected over Gerald Ford in 1976. His tenure was a time of continuing inflation and recession, as well as an energy crisis. On January 7, 1980, Carter signed Law H.R. 5860 known as *The Chrysler Corporation Loan Guarantee Act of 1979* bailing out Chrysler Corporation. He led the plan to deregulate the airline industry. He canceled military pay raises during a time of high inflation and government deficits. He declared amnesty to Vietnam draft dodgers.

He encouraged energy conservation, installed solar panels on the White House,- and wore sweaters while turning down the heat. While attempting to calm various conflicts around the World, most visibly in the Middle East resulting in the signing of the Camp David Accords, giving back the Panama Canal and signing the SALT II nuclear arms reduction treaty with the USSR, the final year of his administration was marred by the Iran hostage crisis.

He wore a sweater on April 17, 1977 and delivered a fireside chat where he famously declared that the energy situation was the moral equivalent of war while clenching his fist. One of Carter's most bitterly controversial decisions was his boycott of the 1980 Summer Olympics in Moscow in response to the 1979 Soviet invasion of Afghanistan. This marks the only time since the founding of the modern Olympics in 1896 that the United States has ever failed to participate in a Summer or Winter Olympics. The Soviet Union retaliated by boycotting the 1984 Summer Olympics in Los Angeles and did not withdraw troops from Afghanistan until 1989 eight years after Carter left office.

Carter wrote that the most intense and mounting opposition to his policies came from the liberal wing of the Democratic Party, which he attributed to Ted Kennedy's ambition to replace him as president.

Jimmy Carter ran as an outsider and was such an outsider that he was ill equipped to be president. He was inexperienced and well over his head in the oval office. In fact, his presidency was a miserable failure. America was in the doldrums with Nixon, Ford and now Carter.

When he first left office, Carter's presidency was viewed by most as a failure. *The Independent* reported, "Carter is widely considered a better man than he was a president." While he began his term with a 66% approval rating, this dropped to 34% approval by the time he left office, with 55% disapproving.

Ultimately, the combination of the economic problems, Iran hostage crisis, and lack of Washington cooperation made it easy for many to portray him as an ineffectual leader.

The Iran hostage crisis was a diplomatic crisis between Iran and the United States. 52 Americans were held hostage for 444 days from November 4, 1979 to January 20, 1981, after a group of Islamist students and militants took over the American Embassy in support of the Iranian Revolution.

Sixty six Americans were taken captive when Iranian militants seized the U.S. Embassy in Tehran on Nov. 4, 1979, including three who were at the Iranian Foreign Ministry. Six more Americans escaped and of the 66 who were taken hostage, 13 were released on Nov. 19 and 20, 1979; one was released on July 11, 1980, and the remaining 52 were released on Jan. 20, 1981.

The episode reached a climax when, after failed attempts to negotiate a release, the United States military attempted a rescue operation, Operation Eagle Claw, on April 24, 1980, which resulted in a failed mission, the destruction of two aircraft and the deaths of eight American servicemen and one Iranian civilian. It ended with the signing of the Algiers Accords on January 19, 1981.

The hostages were formally released into United States custody the following day, just minutes after the new American president Ronald Reagan was sworn in.

The crisis has been described as an entanglement of vengeance and mutual incomprehension. In Iran, despite freezing of all Iranian assets held in the United States, the hostage taking was widely seen as a blow against the U.S, and its influence in Iran, its perceived attempts to undermine the Iranian Revolution, and its long-standing support of the recently overthrown government of the Shah of Iran, Mohammad Reza Pahlavi.

In the United States, the hostage-taking was seen as an outrage violating a centuries old principle of international law granting diplomats immunity from arrest and diplomatic compounds sovereignty in their embassies.
The crisis has also been described as the pivotal episode in the history of Iran United States relations.- In the U.S., some political analysts believe the crisis was a major reason for U.S. President Jimmy Carter's defeat in the November 1980 presidential election. In Iran, the crisis strengthened the prestige of the Ayatollah Khomeini and the political power of those who supported theocracy and opposed any normalization of relations with the West.- The crisis also marked the beginning of U.S. legal action, or economic sanctions against Iran, that further weakened economic ties between Iran and the United States.

Shortly before the revolution on New Year's Day 1979, American president Jimmy Carter further angered anti-Shah Iranians with a televised toast to the Shah, declaring how beloved the Shah was by his people.

After the revolution in February, the embassy had been occupied and staff held hostage briefly. Rocks and bullets had broken enough of the embassy front-facing windows for them to be replaced with bullet-proof glass. Its staff was reduced to just over 60 from a high of nearly 1000 earlier in the decade.

The Carter administration attempted to mitigate the anti-American feeling by finding a new relationship with the *de facto* Iranian government and by continuing military cooperation in hopes that the situation would stabilize. However, on October 22, 1979 the U.S. permitted the Shah who was ill with cancer to attend the Mayo Clinic for medical treatment. The Shah's admission to the US intensified Iranian revolutionaries anti-Americanism and spawned rumors of another U.S.-backed coup and re-installation of the Shah. Revolutionary leader Ayatollah Khomeini who had been exiled by the Shah for 15 years heightened rhetoric against the "Great Satan", the United States, talking of what he called "evidence of American plotting."

In the United States, the hostage-taking is said to have created a surge of patriotism and left the American people more united than they have been on any issue in two decades.

The action was seen not just as a diplomatic affront, but as a declaration of war on diplomacy itself.- Television news gave daily updates.- President Carter applied economic and diplomatic pressure on Iran: oil imports from Iran were ended on November 12, 1979, and through the issuance of Executive Order 12170, around $8 billion of Iranian assets in the U.S. were frozen by the Office of Foreign Assets Control on November 14.

Rumors of a release leaked to the American public and on February 19, 1980, the American Vice President Walter Mondale told an interviewer that "the crisis was nearing an end." The plan fell apart however after Ayatollah Khomeini gave a speech praising the embassy occupation as "a crushing blow to the world-devouring USA" and announced the fate of the hostages would be decided by the parliament (Majlis), which had yet to be seated or even elected. When the six-man international UN commission came to Iran they were not allowed to see the hostages.

The next unsuccessful attempt occurred in April and called first for the American president Carter to publicly promise not to impose additional sanctions on Iran. In exchange custody of the hostages would be transferred to the government of Iran, which after a short period would release the hostages the Iranian president and foreign minister both opposing the continued holding of the hostages.

To the American's surprise and disappointment, after Carter made his promise, President Bani-Sadr added additional demands: official American approval of resolution of the hostage question by Iran's parliament which would leave the hostages in Tehran for another month or two, and a promise by Carter to refrain from making `hostile statements.` Carter also agreed to these demands, but again Khomeini vetoed the plan. At this point Bani-Sadr announced he was `washing his hands` of the hostage mess."

The death of the Shah on July 27 and the invasion of Iran by Iraq in September 1980 may have made Iran more receptive to the idea of resolving the hostage crisis. On November 2, the Iranian parliament finally set forth formal conditions for the hostages' release and eight days later Deputy Secretary of State Warren Christopher arrived in Algiers with the first US reply setting off a slow motion diplomatic shuffle between Washington, Algiers and Tehran. Algerian diplomat Abdulkarim Ghuraib's negotiations between the U.S. and Iran resulted in the "Algiers Accords"- of January 19, 1981. The Algiers Accords called for Iran's immediate freeing of the hostages, the unfreezing of $7.9 billion of Iranian assets and immunity from lawsuits Iran might have faced in America, and a pledge by the United States that "it is and from now on will be the policy of the United States not to intervene, directly or indirectly, politically or militarily, in Iran's internal affairs."

The release of the hostages came a day after President Carter's term ended. While Carter had an "obsession" with finishing the matter before stepping down, the hostage takers are thought to have wanted the release delayed as punishment for his perceived support for the Shah.- Iranians insisted on payment in gold rather than US dollars so the U.S. government transferred 50 tons of gold to Iran while simultaneously taking ownership of an equivalent quantity of Iranian gold that had been frozen at the New York Federal Reserve Bank.

CHAPTER THIRTEEN - The Reagan Revolution

Through the 1970s, the United States underwent a wrenching period of low economic growth, high inflation and interest rates, and intermittent energy crises. Added to this was a sense of malaise that in both foreign and domestic affairs, certain people perceived that the nation was headed downward. By the beginning of the election season, the prolonged Iran hostage crisis had sharpened public perceptions of a national crisis.

Jimmy Carter was blamed for the Iran hostage crisis, in which the followers of the Ayatollah Khomeni burned American flags and chanted anti-American slogans, parading the captured American hostages in public, and burning effigies of Carter. Carter's critics saw him as an inept leader who had failed to solve the worsening economic problems at home. His supporters defended the president as a decent, well-intentioned man being attacked for problems that had been building for years. Having defeated Senator Edward M. Kennedy of Massachusetts in 24 of 34 primaries, President Carter entered the party's convention in New York in August 1980 with 60 percent of the delegates pledged to him on the first ballot. Despite this, Kennedy refused to drop out, and the 1980 Democratic National Convention was one of the nastiest on record.

There was a short-lived "Draft Muskie" movement in the summer of 1980 that was seen as a favorable alternative to a deadlocked convention.

One poll showed that Secretary of State Edmund Muskie would be a more popular alternative to Carter than Kennedy, implying that the attraction was not so much to Kennedy as to the fact that he was not Carter. Muskie was polling even with Ronald Reagan at the time, while Carter was seven points down.- Although the underground Draft Muskie campaign failed, it became a political legend.

After a futile last-ditch attempt by Kennedy to alter the rules to free delegates from the first-ballot pledge, Carter was renominated with 2,129 votes to 1,146 for Kennedy. Vice President Walter Mondale was also renominated. In his acceptance speech, Carter warned that Reagan's conservatism posed a threat to world peace and progressive social welfare programs from the New Deal to the Great Society.

Kennedy was at that time, attempting to come out of the shadow of his big brothers, and trying to overcome the taint of Chappaquiddick. He was now the de facto leader of the liberals in the Senate, and the most outspoken critic of Carter of all the Democrats in either house of Congress. His decision to run against him was motivated partly out of desperation to prove he was his own person, partly because as a Kennedy, it was expected of him and partly to consolidate his senatorial base in opposition to Carter and most of his policies. He felt Carter was too moderate despite the fact that Carter was a pro-civil rights southern Democrat, which made him liberal in ways Kennedy failed to understand at the time. Still, incumbency is a powerful tool, and Kennedy found out not only that, but that the liberal wing of the party was not destined to be its majority in Congress.

His defining moment in that ill conceived run was when a TV news guy I don't remember which one asked Ted why he wanted to be President, and Ted sat there, mute and blank. He had no answer. That was where it ended for him.

Former Governor Ronald Reagan was the odds-on favorite to win his party's nomination for president after nearly beating incumbent President Gerald Ford just four years earlier. He won the nomination on the first round at the 1980 Republican National Convention in Detroit, Michigan, in July, then chose George H. W. Bush, his top rival, as his running mate.

John Bayard Anderson, after being defeated in the Republican primaries, entered the general election as an independent candidate, campaigning as a moderate Republican alternative to Reagan's conservatism. His support progressively evaporated through the campaign season as his supporters were pulled away by Carter and Reagan. His running mate was Patrick Lucey, a Democratic former Governor of Wisconsin and then Ambassador to Mexico, appointed by President Carter.

The 1980 election is considered by some to be a realigning election. Reagan's supporters praise him for running a campaign of upbeat optimism. Carter ran a campaign based on despair and pessimism which cost him the election. Carter emphasized his record as a peacemaker, and said Reagan's election would threaten civil rights and social programs that stretched back to the New Deal. Reagan's platform also emphasized the importance of peace, as well as a prepared self-defense.

Immediately after the conclusion of the primaries, a Gallup poll held that Reagan was ahead, with 58% of voters upset by Carter's handling of the Presidency.· The campaign was largely negative, with many voters disliking Carter's handling of the economy. The election of 1980 was a key turning point in American politics. It signaled the new electoral power of the suburbs and the Sun Belt. Reagan's success as a conservative would initiate a realigning of the parties, as liberal Republicans and conservative Democrats would either leave politics or change party affiliations through the 1980s and 1990s to leave the parties much more ideologically polarized. While during Barry Goldwater's 1964 campaign, many voters saw his warnings about a too powerful government as hyperbolic and only 30% of the electorate agreed that government was too powerful, by 1980 a majority of Americans believed that government held too much power.

In September 1980, former Watergate scandal prosecutor Leon Jaworski accepted a position as honorary chairman of Democrats for Reagan. Five months earlier, Jaworski had harshly criticized Reagan as an extremist; he said after accepting the chairmanship, "I would rather have a competent extremist than an incompetent moderate."

The election was held on November 4, 1980. Ronald Reagan with running mate George H.W. Bush beat Carter by almost 10 percentage points in the popular vote. Republicans also gained control of the Senate for the first time in twenty-five years on Reagan's coattails. The electoral college vote was a landslide, with 489 votes representing 44 states for Reagan and 49 votes for Carter representing 6 states and the District of Columbia.

Carter's loss was the worst defeat for an incumbent President since Herbert Hoover lost to Franklin D. Roosevelt in 1932 by a margin of 18%. Carter's defeat is the most lopsided defeat for any incumbent president in an election where only two candidates won electoral votes. As president, Reagan implemented sweeping new political and economic initiatives. His supply-side economic policies, dubbed "Reaganomics", advocated controlling the money supply to reduce inflation, and spurring economic growth by reducing tax rates, government regulation of the economy, and certain types of government spending. In his first term he survived an assassination attempt, took a hard line against labor unions, and ordered military actions in Grenada. He was reelected in a landslide in 1984, proclaiming it was "Morning in America". His second term was primarily marked by foreign matters, such as the ending of the Cold War, the bombing of Libya, and the revelation of the Iran-Contra affair.

Publicly describing the Soviet Union as an "evil empire", he supported anti-Communist movements worldwide and spent his first term forgoing the strategy of détente by ordering a massive military buildup in an arms race with the USSR. Reagan negotiated with Soviet General Secretary Mikhail Gorbachev, culminating in the INF Treaty and the decrease of both countries' nuclear arsenals. By campaigning on a platform of sending "the welfare bums back to work," he spoke out against the idea of the welfare state. He also strongly advocated the Republican ideal of less government regulation of the economy, including that of undue federal taxation.

To date, Reagan is the oldest man elected to the office of the presidency at age 69. In his first inaugural address on January 20, 1981, which Reagan himself wrote,- he addressed the country's economic malaise arguing: "In this present crisis, government is not the solution to our problems; government is the problem."

The Reagan Presidency began in a dramatic manner; as Reagan was giving his inaugural address, 52 U.S. hostages, held by Iran for 444 days were set free.

On March 30, 1981, Reagan, along with his press secretary James Brady and two others, were shot by a would-be assassin, John Hinckley, Jr., outside of the Hilton Washington hotel. Missing Reagan's heart by less than one inch,- the bullet instead pierced his left lung. In the operating room, Reagan joked to the surgeons, "I hope you're all Republicans!"- Though they were not, Joseph Giordano (a Democrat) replied, "Today, Mr. President, we're all Republicans."

 The president was released from the hospital on April 11 and recovered relatively quickly,- becoming the first serving U.S. President to survive being shot in an assassination attempt.- The attempt had great influence on Reagan's popularity; polls indicated his approval rating to be around 73%.- Reagan believed that God had spared his life so that he might go on to fulfill a greater purpose. Only a short time into his administration, federal air traffic controllers went on strike, violating a regulation prohibiting government unions from striking.

Declaring the situation an emergency as described in the 1947 Taft Hartley Act, Reagan held a press conference in the White House Rose Garden, where he stated that if the air traffic controllers "do not report for work within 48 hours, they have forfeited their jobs and will be terminated." Despite fear from some members of his cabinet over a potential political backlash, on August 5, Reagan fired 11,345 striking air traffic controllers who had ignored his order to return to work, busting the union.

According to Charles Craver, a labor law professor at George Washington University Law School, the move gave Americans a new view of Reagan, who "sent a message to the private employer community that it would be all right to go up against the unions".

Reagan implemented policies based on supply-side economics and advocated a classical liberal and *laissez-faire* philosophy,- seeking to stimulate the economy with large, across-the-board tax cuts ̇ Citing the economic theories of Arthur Laffer, Reagan promoted the proposed tax cuts as potentially stimulating the economy enough to expand the tax base, offsetting the revenue loss due to reduced rates of taxation, a theory that entered political discussion as the Laffer curve. Reaganomics was the subject of debate with supporters pointing to improvements in certain key economic indicators as evidence of success, and critics pointing to large increases in federal budget deficits and the national debt. His policy of "peace through strength" also described as firm but fair resulted in a record peacetime defense buildup including a 40% real increase in defense spending between 1981 and 1985.

During Reagan's presidency, federal income tax rates were lowered significantly with the signing of the bipartisan Economic Recovery Tax Act of 1981. The top tier tax bracket rates were lowered from 70% to 28%. Conversely, Congress raised some taxes in every year from 1981 to 1987 to continue funding such government programs as TEFRA, Social Security, and the Deficit Reduction Act of 1984. Despite the fact that TEFRA was the "largest peacetime tax increase in American history," Reagan is better known for his tax cuts and lower taxes philosophy. Real gross domestic product (GDP) growth recovered strongly after the 1982 recession and grew during his eight years in office at an annual rate of 3.85% per year. Unemployment peaked at 10.8% percent in December 1982 higher than any time since the Great Depression then dropped during the rest of Reagan's presidency. Eighteen million new jobs were created, while inflation significantly decreased. The net effect of all Reagan era tax bills was a 1% decrease in government revenues when compared to Treasury Department revenue estimates from the Administration's first post enactment January budgets. However, federal Income Tax receipts almost doubled from 1980 to 1989, rising from $308.7Bn to $549.0Bn.

During the Reagan Administration, federal receipts grew at an average rate of 8.2% (2.5% attributed to higher Social Security receipts), and federal outlays grew at an annual rate of 7.1%. Reagan also revised the tax code with the bipartisan Tax Reform Act of 1986.

He reappointed Paul Volcker as Chairman of the Federal Reserve, and in 1987 he appointed monetarist Alan Greenspan to succeed him.

Reagan ended the price controls on domestic oil which had contributed to energy crises in the 1970s.- The price of oil subsequently dropped, and the 1980s did not see the fuel shortages that the 1970s had.-Reagan also fulfilled a 1980 campaign promise to repeal the Windfall profit tax in 1988, which had previously increased dependence on foreign oil-- Some economists, such as Nobel Prize winners Milton Friedman and Robert A. Mundell, argue that Reagan's tax policies invigorated America's economy and contributed to the economic boom of the 1990s. Unlike any president perhaps in history, Reagan's tax policy gave us an economic boom that lasted nearly into the twenty first century. Reagan escalated the Cold War, accelerating a reversal from the policy of détente which began in 1979 following the Soviet invasion of Afghanistan.- Reagan ordered a massive buildup of the United States Military- and implemented new policies towards the Soviet Union: reviving the B-1 bomber program that had been canceled by the Carter administration, and producing the MX "Peacekeeper" missile. In response to Soviet deployment of the SS-20, Reagan oversaw NATO's deployment of the Pershing II missile in West Germany.

Together with Britain's prime minister Margaret Thatcher, Reagan denounced the Soviet Union in ideological terms.- In a famous address on June 8, 1982 to the British Parliament in the Royal Gallery of the Palace of Westminster, Reagan said, "the forward march of freedom and democracy will leave Marxism-Leninism on the ash-heap of history."-On March 3, 1983, he predicted that communism would collapse, stating, "Communism is another sad, bizarre chapter in human history whose last pages even now are being written."

Under a policy that came to be known as the Reagan Doctrine, Reagan and his administration also provided overt and covert aid to anti-communist resistance movements in an effort to rollback Soviet backed communist governments in Africa, Asia and Latin America.- Reagan deployed the CIA's Special Activities Division to Afghanistan and Pakistan. They were instrumental in training, equipping and leading Mujaheddin forces against the Soviet Red Army. President Reagan's Covert Action program has been given credit for assisting in ending the Soviet occupation of Afghanistan.

Reagan accepted the Republican nomination in Dallas, Texas, on a wave of positive feeling. He proclaimed that it was "morning again in America", regarding the recovering economy and the dominating performance by the U.S. athletes at the Los Angeles Olympics that summer, among other things. He became the first American president to open an Olympic Games held in the United States.

Reagan's opponent in the 1984 presidential election was former Vice President Walter Mondale. With questions about Reagan's age, and a weak performance in the first presidential debate, it was questioned whether he was capable to be president for another term. Reagan rebounded in the second debate, and confronted questions about his age, quipping, "I will not make age an issue of this campaign. I am not going to exploit, for political purposes, my opponent's youth and inexperience", which generated applause and laughter.

That November, Reagan was re-elected, winning 49 of 50 states. The president's landslide victory saw Mondale carry only his home state of Minnesota (by 3800 votes) and the District of Columbia. Reagan won a record 525 electoral votes, the most of any candidate in United States history, and received 58.8% of the popular vote to Mondale's 40.6%.

Many conservative and liberal scholars agree that Reagan has been the most influential president since Franklin D. Roosevelt, leaving his imprint on American politics, diplomacy, culture, and economics.

The first generation of writing about Reagan comprised studies on the right that approached hagiography, and on the left a devil theory, all relying on popular journalism for their facts.

A second generation has emerged, based on newly available documents from the archives, that provides a much more sophisticated and complex view. The schol- ars of the second generation have reached a consensus, as summarized by British historian M. J. Heale, who finds that scholars now concur that Reagan rehabilitated conservatism, turned the nation to the right, practiced a pragmatic conservatism that balanced ideology and the constraints of politics, revived faith in the presidency and in American self respect, and contributed to victory in the Cold War.

Reagan's ability to connect with the American people earned him the laudatory moniker "The Great Communi- cator". Of it, Reagan said, "I won the nickname the great communicator.

But I never thought it was my style that made a difference it was the content. I wasn't a great communicator, but I communicated great things." His age and soft-spoken speech gave him a warm grandfatherly image.

The combination of Reagan's speaking style, unabashed patriotism, negotiation skills, as well as his savvy use of the media, played an important role in defining the 1980s and his future legacy. Reagan left office in 1989. In 1994, the former president disclosed that he had been diagnosed with Alzheimer's disease earlier in the year; he died ten years later at the age of 93. Although his Presidency was controversial to contemporaries, his reputation has grown over time and he is now often rated as one of the greatest U.S. Presidents.

George Bush brought to the White House a dedication to traditional American values and a determination to direct them toward making the United States "a kinder and gentler nation." In his Inaugural Address he pledged in "a moment rich with promise" to use American strength as "a force for good."

Like his father, Prescott Bush, who was elected a Senator from Connecticut in 1952, George became interested in public service and politics. He served two terms as a Representative to Congress from Texas. Twice he ran unsuccessfully for the Senate. Then he was appointed to a series of high-level positions: Ambassador to the United Nations, Chairman of the Republican National Committee, Chief of the U. S. Liaison Office in the People's Republic of China, and Director of the Central Intelligence Agency.

In 1980 Bush campaigned for the Republican nomination for President. He lost, but was chosen as a running mate by Ronald Reagan. As Vice President, Bush had responsibility in several domestic areas, including Federal deregulation and anti-drug programs, and visited scores of foreign countries. In 1988 Bush won the Republican nomination for President and, with Senator Dan Quayle of Indiana as his running mate, he defeated Massachusetts Governor Michael Dukakis in the general election.

Bush faced a dramatically changing world, as the Cold War ended after 40 bitter years, the Communist empire broke up, and the Berlin Wall fell. The Soviet Union ceased to exist; and reformist President Mikhail Gorbachev, whom Bush had supported, resigned. While Bush hailed the march of democracy, he insisted on restraint in U. S. policy toward the group of new nations.

In other areas of foreign policy, President Bush sent American troops into Panama to overthrow the corrupt regime of General Manuel Noriega, who was threatening the security of the canal and the Americans living there. Noriega was brought to the United States for trial as a drug trafficker.

Bush's greatest test came when Iraqi President Saddam Hussein invaded Kuwait, then threatened to move into Saudi Arabia. Vowing to free Kuwait, Bush rallied the United Nations, the U. S. people, and Congress and sent 425,000 American troops. They were joined by 118,000 troops from allied nations. After weeks of air and missile bombardment, the 100-hour land battle dubbed Desert Storm routed Iraq's million-man army.

In the wake of a struggle with Congress, Bush was forced by the Democratic majority to raise tax revenues; as a result, many Republicans felt betrayed because Bush had promised "no new taxes" in his 1988 campaign. Perceiving a means of revenge, Republican congressmen defeated Bush's proposal which would enact spending cuts and tax increases that would reduce the deficit by $500 billion over five years. Scrambling, Bush accepted the Democrats' demands for higher taxes and more spending, which alienated him from Republicans and gave way to a sharp decrease in popularity. Bush would later say that he wished he had never signed the bill.

Near the end of the 101st Congress, the president and congressional members reached a compromise on a budget package that increased the marginal tax rate and phased out exemptions for high-income taxpayers. Despite demands for a reduction in the capital gains tax, Bush relented on this issue as well. This agreement with the Democratic leadership in Congress proved to be a turning point in the Bush presidency; his popularity among Republicans never fully recovered. But the nifty thing about Reagan's legacy is that every segment of the GOP coalition can claim a piece of it.

Libertarians can cite his small government rhetoric. Supply-siders can emphasize his tax cuts. Defense hawks can highlight his arms buildup, his willingness to use military force in Grenada and Libya, and his "evil empire" talk.

Social conservatives can point to his 1983 pro-life tract, "Abortion and the Conscience of the Nation," and his promulgation of the so-called Mexico City Policy which bans U.S. funding of foreign NGOs that promote or perform abortions. Moderate Republicans can stress his sunny disposition and big tent philosophy. All these groups can celebrate his anti-Communism.

Of course, Reagan's White House record was far more varied than many conservatives now care to admit. An artificial "Reagan reverence" may make for good primary politics, but it also threatens to constrict Republicans. As David Brooks writes, "Conservatives have allowed a simplistic view of Ronald Reagan to define the sacred parameters of thought. Reagan himself was flexible, unorthodox, and creative. But conservatives have created a mythical, rigid Reagan, and any deviation from that is considered unholy."

In big-picture terms, Reagan was a very conservative and very successful chief executive, who dragged the entire political spectrum rightward. But the received wisdom about Reagan tends to be somewhat one dimensional. Had he truly been as doctrinaire and unwavering as many now seem to imagine he was, chances are he would have been less popular.

Other contemporaries of Reagan's ideals in the 80's and 90's would not always agree with him, but few could argue with his success. William F Buckley participated in a live and very heated debate with scientist Carl Sagan on ABC, following the airing of *The Day After*, a 1983 made-for-television film about the effects of nuclear war.

Sagan argued against nuclear proliferation, while Buckley, a staunch anti-communist, promoted the concept of nuclear deterrence.

During the debate, Sagan discussed the concept of nuclear winter and made his famous analogy, equating the arms race to "two sworn enemies standing waist-deep in gasoline, one with three matches, the other with five".
In 1988 Buckley was instrumental in the defeat of liberal Republican Senator Lowell Weicker. Buckley organized a committee to campaign against Weicker and endorsed his Democratic opponent, Connecticut Attorney General Joseph Lieberman.- Lieberman defeated Weicker.

In 1991, Buckley received the Presidential Medal of Freedom from President George H. W. Bush. Buckley retired as active editor of *National Review* in 1990.
On February 4 and 5, 1999 the Ronald Reagan Presidential Foundation and Center for Public Affairs sponsored a two-day symposium at the Ronald Reagan Library and Museum in Simi Valley, California. The theme of the event was "Eight Years that Changed the World: The Reagan Legacy in the New Century." The keynote speaker was none other than Buckley.

This being a convocation of friends and admirers, in celebration of his birthday, I propose as keynoter to dwell a while on a longtime friendship. It began in the spring of 1960.

Ronald and Nancy Reagan, whom I hadn't met, were seated at one end of the restaurant, I and my sister-in-law at the other end. We were out of sight of one another. Both parties were headed, after dinner, across the street to an auditorium in a public high school.

There I would be introduced, as the evening's speaker addressing an assembly of doctors and their wives, by Ronald Reagan, a well-known actor and currently the host of a television series sponsored by General Electric; moreover, a public figure who had taken an interest in conservatives and conservative writings.

We bumped into each other going out the door. Ronald Reagan introduced himself and Nancy, and said he had just finished reading my book, Up From Liberalism. He quoted a crack from it, done at the expense of Mrs. Roosevelt, which he relished. I requited his courtesy by relishing him and Nancy for life.

He distinguished himself that night and dismayed Mrs. Reagan by what he proceeded to do after discovering that the microphone hadn't been turned on. He had tried, raising his voice, to tell a few stories. But the audience was progressively impatient. Waiting in vain for the superintendent to unlock the door to the tight little office at the other end of the hall in which the control box lay, he sized up the problem and, having surveyed all possible avenues of approach, climbed out of the window at stage level and, one story above the busy traffic below, catwalked, Cary Grant style, twenty or thirty yards to the remote office window of the control room. This he penetrated by breaking the glass window with a thrust of his elbow, climbing in, turning on the light, flipping on the microphone, unlocking the office door, and emerging with that competent, relaxed smile of his, which we came to know after Grenada, Libya, Reykjavik, and Moscow; proceeding with the introduction of the speaker. And all that was thirty years before bringing peace to our time!

In later years I thought his movements that night a nifty allegory of his approach to foreign policy, the calm appraisal of a situation, the willingness to take risks, and then the decisive moment: leading to lights and sound and music, the music of the spheres. We stayed friends. Twenty years later he was running for President of the United States. Early that winter the Soviet military had charged into Afghanistan, beginning a long, costly, brutal exercise. A week or two after he was nominated in Detroit, I wrote him. I told him I thought he would be elected. And told him then that, on the assumption that on reaching the White House he might wish to tender me an office, I wished him to know that I aspired to no government job of any kind. He wrote back that he was disappointed. "I had in mind," he said, "to appoint you ambassador to Afghanistan." Over the next eight years, in all my communications with him, I would report fleetingly on my secret mission in Kabul, the capital of Afghanistan where, in our fiction, I lived and worked. In his letters to me he would always address me as Mr. Ambassador. The show must go on, where Ronald Reagan was involved.

Soon after his election I was asked by the Philadelphia Society to speak on the theme, "Is President Reagan doing all that can be done?" It was a coincidence that my wife Pat and I had spent the weekend before the speech as guests of the President and Mrs. Reagan in Barbados. I recalled with delight an exchange I had with my host on the presidential helicopter. We were flying to our villa the first evening, before the two days on Easter weekend reserved for bacchanalian sunning and swimming on the beach in front of Claudette Colbert's house.

I leaned over and told him I had heard the rumor that the Secret Service was going to deny him permission to swim on that beach on the grounds that it was insufficiently secure. I asked him whether that were so, that he wouldn't be allowed in the water.

Helicopters, even Marine One helicopters, are pretty noisy, but I was able to make out what he said. It was, "Well, Bill, Nancy here tells me I'm the most powerful man in the Free World. If she's right, then I will swim tomorrow with you." Which indeed he did.

I recall also that during one of those swims I said to him, "Mr. President, would you like to earn the National Review Medal of Freedom?" He confessed to being curious as to how he would qualify to do this. I explained, "I will proceed to almost drown, and you will rescue me." We went through the motions, and that evening I conferred that medal on him, in pectore.

I remember telling the Philadelphia Society that the most powerful man in the Free World is not powerful enough to do everything that needs to be done. Retrospectively, I have speculated on what I continue to believe was the conclusive factor in the matter of American security against any threat of Soviet aggression. It was the character of the occupant of the White House; the character of Ronald Reagan. The reason this is so, I have argued, is that the Soviet Union, for all that from time to time it miscalculated tactically, never miscalculated in respect of matters apocalyptic in dimension. And the policymakers of the Soviet Union knew that the ambiguists with whom they so dearly loved to deal were not in power during those critical years.

So that if ever the Soviet leaders were tempted to such suicidal foolishness as to launch a strike against us, suicidal is exactly what it would prove to have been. The primary obstacle to the ultimate act of Soviet imperialism was the resolute U.S. determination to value what we have, over against what they, under Soviet dominion, did not have; value it sufficiently to defend it with all our resources.

Ronald Reagan, in my judgment, animated his foreign policy by his occasional diplomatic indiscretions: because of course it was a diplomatic indiscretion to label the Soviet Union an "evil empire." But then, quite correctly, he would switch gears when wearing diplomatic top hat and tails.

He did not on those occasions talk the language of John Wayne or of Thomas Aquinas. But how reassuring it was for us, you remember, every now and then "Mr. Gorbachev, tear down that wall!", to vibrate to the music of the very heartstrings of the leader of the Free World who, to qualify convincingly as such, had after all to feel a total commitment to the free world.

When in formal circumstances the President ventured out to exercise conviviality with the leaders of the Soviet Union, the scene was by its nature wonderful, piquant: What would he say that was agreeable, congenial, to the head of the evil empire? The summit conferences brought to mind the Russian who, on discovering that his pet parrot was missing, rushed out to the KGB office to report that his parrot's political opinions were entirely unrelated to his own.

The ensuing chapter in the life of Russia presents its own problems. They are internal problems, with a surly outer face. You can hear the words framed on the mouth of the few remaining statues of Lenin. His lips are saying, So much for your capitalism! Russia poses no strategic threat to the Free World, to which Russia, de jure, belongs. But the contemporary experience of Russia is a devastating rebuke to facile, universalist ideas about what it is that needs to be done to nurture advances towards prosperity.

One key, of course, an indispensable key, is human freedom. When West Germany was liberated from fascist tyranny, and Japan from imperialist militarism, well-wishers of freedom cheered the results as life began its dramatic turn toward self-rule and a market economy. But in Russia the old brew didn't mix, did it? It isn't hard to compile a list of the missing elements. We know now about the profound corruption, and know how corruption conjoined with industrial satrapies can defy the benevolent ministrations of a free market. The causes of the wealth of nations heralded by Adam Smith cannot make their way in the absence of a reasoned mobility of a nation's resources and a receptive theater for the entrepreneurial energies of its people.

There will be many books written about what happened in Russia in the decade beginning with liberation. The inquests will be various and prolonged, and they will all be sad; but they will make vivid lessons we need to absorb, as we project the economic future of other nations to be sure, but also of our own.

The overarching lesson is that the elements of a good society oriented to the improvement of life aren't all disembodied, inanimate; weight scales at a free-market counter. There is the live component.

And it is not just formal self-rule. Democracy is a mantra, but it isn't an amulet. We can chant the benefits of democratic arrangements and cheer democratic practices; but these practices do not always lead to enlightened policies.

One third of the Duma in Moscow are Communists. The freedom the Russians had, for the first time, to vote, very nearly returned a Communist president in the election of two years ago. The popularity of the democratically elected president of Russia today is given as 1 percent. (He should try poking an intern.) A substantial number of Russians would exchange life as it is today for life as it was yesterday. Thirty million Russians have not been paid for weeks of work, in some cases for months of work. What is a Russian gravedigger supposed to do, if he is not paid? Dig his own grave?

At the other end of the world we have the dismaying spectacle of Japan, recently referred to as the Land of the Setting Sun. "It is quite amazing," Larry Kudlow recently opined: "They haven't managed to do anything right." Eight consecutive years of mismanagement by the second wealthiest country in the world. A democratic society whose people are demoralized, seemingly lost. The Reagan years accustomed us to a mood about life and about government. There were always the interruptions, the potholes of life.

But he had strategic visions. He told us that most of our civic problems were problems brought on or exacerbated by government, not problems that could be solved by government. That of course is enduringly true. Only government can cause inflation, preserve monopoly, and punish enterprise. On the other hand, it is only a government leader who can affect a national mood or summon up a historical period. One refers not to the period of Shakespeare but to the period of Elizabeth. Reagan's period was brief, but it put a stamp on the national mood. He did this in part because he was scornful of the claims of omnipotent government, in part because by nature and by the words he spoke, he felt, and expressed, the buoyancy of the American Republic.

We have now the paradoxical situation, a leader whom 75 percent of the American people don't wish to disturb, and whom 75 percent of the American people do not trust. It is comforting to tell ourselves that what this means is that we live in an age in which the long arm of government is so discredited, it can't really do us much damage.

To the library I'll convey in years ahead my own collection of letters from Ronald Reagan. The very last one written from the White House the day the Soviet Union announced that it would withdraw from Afghanistan was addressed, "Dear Mr. Ambassador:

"Congratulations! The Soviets are moving out of Afghanistan. I knew you could do it if I only left you there long enough, and you did it without leaving Kabul for a minute." He closed by saying, "Nancy sends her love to you and Pat."

That was eleven years ago, and we cherish it today, and through her, convey our own love and gratitude to the President, on his 88th birthday.

While we speak of the influences on Ronald Reagan and his policies we must discuss Arthur Laffer. an American economist who became influential during the Reagan administration as a member of Reagan's Economic Policy Advisory Board (1981–1989). Laffer is also known for the Laffer curve, an illustration of tax elasticity which asserts that, in certain situations, a decrease in tax rates could result in an increase in tax revenues.

Laffer was born in Youngstown, Ohio. Although he does not claim to have invented the Laffer curve concept (Laffer, 2004), it was popularized with policy-makers following an afternoon meeting with Nixon/Ford Administration officials Dick Cheney and Donald Rumsfeld in 1974 in which he reportedly sketched the curve on a napkin to illustrate his argument. The term "Laffer curve" was coined by Jude Wanniski, who was also present. The basic concept was not new.

A simplified view of the theory is that tax revenues would be zero if tax rates were either 0% or 100%, and somewhere in between 0% and 100% is a tax rate which maximizes total revenue. Laffer's postulate was that the tax rate that maximizes revenue was at a much lower level than previously believed: so low that current tax rates were above the level where revenue is maximized. At the time of the now famous napkin incident with Jude Waniski, Don Rumsfeld and Dick Cheney, Laffer was a tenured professor at the University of Chicago Graduate School of Business.

Later on, after leaving U of C and during his tenure at the University of Southern California, Marshall School of Business, Laffer played a key role in the writing of Proposition 13, the California property tax cap initiative that spawned a host of similar laws around the United States. Laffer is the author and co-author of many books and newspaper articles, including *Supply Side Economics: Financial Decision-Making for the 80s*.

Laffer received a BA degree in economics from Yale University in 1962. He graduated from Stanford University with an MBA in 1965 and a PhD degree in economics in 1971. He is Policy Co-Chairman (with Lawrence "Larry" Kudlow) of the Free Enterprise Fund. Laffer identifies himself as a staunch fiscal conservative and libertarian. Ronald Reagan was the last president that really owned the office instead of being owned by special interests or by their perception of what people wanted. He had a set of beliefs that guided him and it guided us as well to become that bright shining city on a hill.

CHAPTER FOURTEEN - And now where are we?

William Jefferson "Bill" Clinton was the 42nd President of the United States from 1993 to 2001. At 46 he was the third-youngest president. He became president at the end of the Cold War, and was the first baby boomer president. His wife, Hillary Rodham Clinton, is currently the United States Secretary of State. Each received a Juris Doctor (J.D.) from Yale Law School.

Clinton has been described as a New Democrat.- Some of his policies, such as the North American Free Trade Agreement and welfare reform, have been attributed to a centrist Third Way philosophy of governance, while on other issues his stance was left of center.- Clinton presided over the continuation of an economic expansion that would later become the longest period of peace-time economic expansion in American history. Clinton's centrist economics and his inheritance of the Reagan revolution deserve much credit for this economic expansion. The Congressional Budget Office reported a budget surplus in 2000, the last full year of Clinton's presidency.- After a failed attempt at health care reform, Republicans won control of the House of Representatives in 1994, for the first time in forty years.- Two years later, in 1996, Clinton was re-elected and became the first member of the Democratic Party since Franklin D. Roosevelt to win a second full term as president. Later he was impeached for perjury and obstruction of justice in connection with a scandal involving a White House intern, but was subsequently acquitted by the U.S. Senate.

Clinton left office with the highest end-of-office approval rating of any U.S. president since World War II. Since then, he has been involved in public speaking and humanitarian work. Clinton created the William J. Clinton Foundation to promote and address international causes such as treatment and prevention of HIV/AIDS and global warming.

In 2004, he released his autobiography *My Life*, and was involved in his wife Hillary's 2008 presidential campaign and subsequently in that of President Barrack Obama. In 2009, he was named United Nations Special Envoy to Haiti. In the aftermath of the 2010 Haiti earthquake, Clinton teamed with George W. Bush to form the Clinton Bush Haiti Fund.

Having been transformed into the consensus candidate, he secured the Democratic Party nomination, finishing with a victory in Jerry Brown's home state of California. Bill Clinton with Ross Perot, Independent, and President George H. W. Bush, Republican, in a national debate. Clinton won the 1992 presidential election (43.0% of the vote) against Republican incumbent George H. W. Bush (37.4% of the vote) and billionaire populist Ross Perot, who ran as an independent (18.9% of the vote) on a platform focusing on domestic issues; a significant part of Clinton's success was Bush's steep decline in public approval. Because Bush's approval ratings were in the 80% range during the Gulf War, he was described as unbeatable. However, when Bush compromised with Democrats in an attempt to lower Federal deficits, he reneged on his promise not to raise taxes, hurting his approval rating.

Clinton repeatedly condemned Bush for making a promise he failed to keep.- By election time, the economy was souring and Bush saw his approval rating plummet to just slightly over 40%.

Finally, conservatives were previously united by anti-communism, but with the end of the Cold War, the party lacked a uniting issue. When Pat Buchanan and Pat Robertson addressed Christian themes at the Republican National Convention with Bush criticizing Democrats for omitting God from their platform many moderates were alienated. Clinton then pointed to his moderate, "New Democrat" record as governor of Arkansas, though some on the more liberal side of the party remained suspicious. Many Democrats who had supported Ronald Reagan and Bush in previous elections switched their allegiance to Clinton.

However, during the campaign, questions of conflict of interest regarding state business and the politically powerful Rose Law Firm, at which Hillary Rodham Clinton was a partner, arose. Clinton maintained questions were moot because all transactions with the state were deducted prior to determining Hillary's firm pay.

The administration faced serious political opposition in 1994 when Republicans took control of both houses of Congress but Clinton was reelected in 1996, after a failed attempt at health care reform. The administration had a mixed record on taxes but produced the first federal budget surplus since 1969. Clinton supported the North American Free Trade Agreement, which he signed into law in 1994. His presidency saw the passage of welfare reform, which received support from both political parties.

The administration took office less than two years after the fall of the Soviet Union, and the administration's foreign policy addressed conflicts in Somalia, Rwanda, Bosnia and Herzegovina, Kosovo, and Haiti. Clinton made efforts to try to end conflicts in the former Yugoslavia, Northern Ireland, and the Middle East, with the Israeli Palestinian conflict in particular. The Clinton presidency also saw the passage and signing of the Iraq Liberation Act of 1998 which was a bipartisan measure expressing support for regime change in Iraq. On three separate occasions, in 1996, 1998, and 2000, the administration unsuccessfully attempted to capture or assassinate Osama Bin Laden.

Socially, the administration began with efforts by Clinton to allow gays and lesbians to serve openly in the military, which culminated in a compromise known as "Don't ask, don't tell", allowing gays and lesbians to serve in the military if they did not disclose their sexual orientation. Clinton considered himself a "New Democrat" and was a founding member of the Democratic Leadership Council, a centrist group of Democrats, who promoted moderate policies.

Clinton left office with the highest end of office approval rating of any president since World War II, but he was the first US president to be impeached since Andrew Johnson, and only the second in US history, as a result of the Lewinsky scandal, though like Johnson, he was acquitted by the Senate. President Clinton was the Democrats version of Nixon in that he was a chameleon who could become what he needed to become based on polls rather than beliefs. It was really more about getting power and amassing wealth than what was best for America.

One of the prominent items on Clinton's legislative agenda, however, was a health care reform plan, the result of a taskforce headed by Hillary Clinton, aimed at achieving universal coverage via a national healthcare plan. Though initially well-received in political circles, it was ultimately doomed by well-organized opposition from conservatives, the American Medical Association, and the health insurance industry. Despite his party holding a majority in the House and Senate, the effort to create a national healthcare system ultimately died under heavy public pressure. It was the first major legislative defeat of Clinton's administration.

Two months later, after two years of Democratic party control under Clinton's leadership, the mid-term elections in 1994 proved disastrous for the Democrats. This was the first time the democratic party had lost control of both houses of Congress in 40 years. One of Clinton's major policy initiatives in his first term was on the American economy. Clinton's economic plan included a major expansion of the existing Earned Income Tax Credit, aimed at working class families just above the poverty line, which helped ensure that it made sense for them to work rather than seek welfare. John F Harris, argues that "this would prove to be one of the most important and tangible progressive achievements of the Clinton years".

A major problem with the economy at the time was the issue of the massive deficit and the problem of government spending. In order to address these issues, in August 1993, Clinton signed the Omnibus Budget Reconciliation Act of 1993 which passed Congress without a single Republican vote.

It raised taxes on the wealthiest 1.2% of taxpayers, while cutting taxes on 15 million low-income families and making tax cuts available to 90 percent of small businesses. Additionally, it mandated that the budget be balanced over a number of years and the deficit be reduced. This was to be achieved through the implementation of spending restraints.

In the 1996 presidential election a few months later, Clinton was re-elected, receiving 49.2% of the popular vote over Republican Bob Dole 40.7% of the popular vote and Reform candidate Ross Perot 8.4% of the popular vote, becoming the first Democrat to win reelection to the presidency since Franklin Roosevelt. The Republicans lost a few seats in the House and gained a few in the Senate, but overall retained control of the Congress. In 1997 Clinton finally had a chance to sign a major health care bill into law. The State Children's Health Insurance Program, passed through the efforts of Hillary Rodham Clinton who wrote and chaired the task force on the unsuccessful universal plan in the first two years of the Clinton Administration, Senator Ted Kennedy, and Senator Orrin Hatch, expanded coverage to approximately six-million children. Also, through Mrs. Clinton's work, childhood immunizations reached over ninety percent and funding for research on Gulf War Syndrome, breast cancer, prostate cancer, and asthma was increased.

Throughout 1998, there was a controversy over Clinton's relationship with a young White House intern, Monica Lewinsky. Clinton initially denied the affair while testifying in the Paula Jones sexual harassment lawsuit. The opposing lawyers asked the president about it during his deposition.

He stated "I have never had sexual relations with Monica Lewinsky. I've never had an affair with her." Four days later he also said," There is not a sexual relationship, an improper sexual relationship, or any other kind of improper relationship." Clinton then appeared on national television on January 26 and stated: "Listen to me, I'm going to say this again. I did not have sexual relations with that woman, Miss Lewinsky." However, after it was revealed that investigators had obtained a semen-stained dress as well as testimony from Lewinsky, Clinton changed tactics and admitted that an improper relationship with Lewinsky had taken place: "Indeed I did have a relationship with Miss Lewinsky that was not appropriate. In fact, it was wrong. It constituted a critical lapse in judgment and a personal failure on my part for which I am solely and completely responsible."

Faced with overwhelming evidence, he apologized to the nation, agreed to pay a $25,000 court fine, settled his sexual harassment lawsuit with Paula Jones for $850,000 and was temporarily disbarred, for a period of five years, from practicing law in Arkansas and before the U.S. Supreme Court. He was not tried for perjury in a court. However, he did admit to "testifying falsely" in a carefully worded statement as part of a deal to avoid indictment for perjury.

In a lame duck session after the 1998 elections, the Republican controlled House voted to impeach Clinton. The next year, the Senate voted to acquit Clinton, and he remained in office. Clinton remained popular with the public throughout his two terms as President, ending his presidential career with a 65% approval rating, the highest end-of-term approval rating of any President since Dwight D. Eisenhower.

In addition to his political skills, Clinton also benefited from a boom of the US economy. Under Clinton, the United States had a projected federal budget surplus for the first time since 1969.

Capturing Osama bin Laden has been an objective of the United States government since the presidency of Bill Clinton. It has been asserted that on three separate occasions in 1996, 1998, and 2000, while the Clinton Administration had begun pursuit of the policy, the Sudanese government allegedly offered to arrest and extradite Bin Laden as well as to provide the United States detailed intelligence information about growing militant organizations in the region, including Hezbollah and Hamas, and that U.S. authorities allegedly rejected each offer, despite knowing of bin Laden's involvement in bombings on American embassies in Kenya and Tanzania.

However, the 9/11 Commission found that although "former Sudanese officials claim that Sudan offered to expel Bin Laden to the United States", "we have not found any reliable evidence to support the Sudanese claim."

Clinton issued 141 pardons and 36 commutations on his last day in office on January 20, 2001. Most of the controversy surrounded Marc Rich and allegations that Hillary Clinton's brother, Hugh Rodham, accepted payments in return for influencing the president's decision-making regarding the pardons. Some of Clinton's pardons remain a point of controversy.

The 1996 United States campaign finance controversy was an alleged effort by the People's Republic of China to influence the domestic policies of the United States, prior to and during the Clinton administration, and also involved the fundraising practices of the administration itself. I believe that this influence of China is chiefly responsible for the shift to China of business. Most favored nation status et all.

Bill Clinton was another Nixon, a chameleon; tell me what you want me to be and I'll be that for you. He watched polls and governed accordingly. The people did like Clinton and he was a great TV president.
The United States presidential election of 2000 was a contest between Republican candidate George W. Bush, then governor of Texas and son of former president George H. W. Bush and Democratic candidate Al Gore, then-Vice President. Bill Clinton, the incumbent President, was vacating the position after serving the maximum two terms allowed by the Twenty-second Amendment. Bush narrowly won the November 7 election, with 271 electoral votes to Gore's 266 with one elector abstaining in the official tally.

The election was noteworthy for a controversy over the awarding of Florida's 25 electoral votes, the subsequent recount process in that state, and the unusual event of the winning candidate having received fewer popular votes than the runner-up. It was the closest election since 1876 and only the fourth election in which the electoral vote did not reflect the popular vote.

As the incumbent Vice President, Al Gore of Tennessee was a consistent front-runner for the Democratic nomination, with his only serious challenge coming from former

Senator Bill Bradley of New Jersey. Other prominent Democrats mentioned as possible contenders included Nebraska Senator Bob Kerrey, Missouri Congressman Dick Gephardt, Minnesota Senator Paul Wellstone, and famous actor and director Warren Beatty, who declined to run.- Of these, only Wellstone formed an exploratory committee. Several Republican candidates appeared on the national scene to challenge Gore's candidacy.

George W. Bush became the early front-runner, acquiring unprecedented funding and a broad base of leadership support based on his governorship of Texas and the name recognition and connections of the Bush family. Several aspirants withdrew before the Iowa Caucus because they were unable to secure funding and endorsements sufficient to remain competitive with Bush. These included Elizabeth Dole, Dan Quayle, Lamar Alexander, and Robert C. Smith. Pat Buchanan dropped out to run for the Reform Party nomination. That left Bush, John McCain, Alan Keyes, Steve Forbes, Gary Bauer, and Orrin Hatch as the only candidates still in the race.

On January 24, Bush won the Iowa caucus with 41% of the vote. Forbes came in second with 30% of the vote. Keyes received 14%, Bauer 9%, McCain 5%, and Hatch 1%. Hatch dropped out. On the national stage, Bush was portrayed in the media as the establishment candidate. McCain, with the support of many moderate Republicans and Independents, portrayed himself as a crusading insurgent who focused on campaign reform.

On February 1, McCain won a 49%–30% victory over Bush in the New Hampshire primary. Gary Bauer dropped out. After coming in third in Delaware Forbes dropped out, leaving three candidates.

In the South Carolina primary, Bush soundly defeated McCain. Some credit Bush's win to the fact that it was the first major closed primary in 2000, which negated McCain's strong advantage among independents. Some McCain supporters blamed it on the Bush campaign, accusing them of mudslinging and dirty tricks, such as push polling that implied that McCain's adopted Bangladeshi-born daughter was an African-American child he fathered out of wedlock. While McCain's loss in South Carolina damaged his campaign, he won both Michigan and his home state of Arizona on February 22.

On February 24, McCain criticized Bush for accepting the endorsement of Bob Jones University despite its policy banning interracial dating.

On February 28, McCain also referred to Rev. Jerry Falwell and televangelist Pat Robertson as "agents of intolerance", a term he would later distance himself from during his 2008 bid for the party's nomination. He lost the state of Virginia to Bush on February 29. On Super Tuesday, March 7, Bush won New York, Ohio, Georgia, Missouri, California, Maryland, and Maine. McCain won Rhode Island, Vermont, Connecticut, and Massachusetts, but dropped out of the race. On March 10, Alan Keyes got 21% of the vote in Utah. Bush took the majority of the remaining contests and won the Republican nomination on March 14, winning his home state of Texas and his brother Jeb's home state of Florida among others.

At the Republican National Convention in Philadelphia George W. Bush accepted the Nomination of the Republican party.

Bush asked former Secretary of Defense Dick Cheney to head up a team to help select a running mate for him, but ultimately, Bush decided that Cheney should be the vice presidential nominee. While the U.S. Constitution does not specifically disallow a president and a vice president from the same state, it 'does' prohibit electors from casting both of his or her votes for persons from his or her own state. Accordingly, Cheney who had been a resident of Texas for nearly 10 years changed his voting registration back to Wyoming. Had Cheney not done this, either he or Bush would have forfeited their electoral votes from the Texas electors.

George W. Bush is the 43rd President of the United States. He was sworn into office on January 20, 2001, re-elected on November 2, 2004, and sworn in for a second term on January 20, 2005. Before his Presidency, he served for 6 years as Governor of the State of Texas. Since his election to the Presidency in 2000, President Bush has worked to extend freedom, opportunity, and security at home and abroad. His first initiative as President was the No Child Left Behind Act, a bipartisan measure that raised standards in schools, insisted on accountability in return for federal dollars, and led to measurable gains in achievement especially among minority students.

Faced with a recession when he took office, President Bush cut taxes for every federal income taxpayer, which helped set off an unprecedented 52 straight months of job creation. And President Bush modernized Medicare by adding a prescription drug benefit, a reform that provided access to needed medicine for 40 million seniors and other beneficiaries.

President Bush also implemented free trade agreements with more than a dozen nations; empowered America's armies of compassion by creating a new Faith-based and Community Initiative; promoted a culture of life; improved air quality and made America's energy supply more secure; set aside more ocean resources for environmental protection than any predecessor; transformed the military and nearly doubled government support for veterans; pioneered a new model of partnership in development that tied American foreign aid to reform and good governance; launched a global HIV/AIDS initiative that has spared millions of lives; expanded the NATO alliance; forged a historic new partnership with India; and appointed Chief Justice John Roberts and Justice Samuel Alito to the U.S. Supreme Court.

The most significant event of President Bush's tenure came on September 11, 2001, when terrorists killed nearly 3,000 people on American soil. President Bush responded with a comprehensive strategy to protect the American people. He led the most dramatic reorganization of the federal government since the beginning of the Cold War, reforming the intelligence community and establishing new institutions like the Department of Homeland Security. He built global coalitions to remove violent regimes in Afghanistan and Iraq that threatened America; liberating more than 50 million people from tyranny. He recognized that freedom and hope are the best alternative to the extremist ideology of the terrorists, so he provided unprecedented American support for young democracies and dissidents in the Middle East and beyond. In the more than seven years after September 11, 2001, the United States was not attacked again.

After September 11, Bush announced a global War on Terrorism. The Afghan Taliban regime was not forthcoming with Osama bin Laden, so Bush ordered the invasion of Afghanistan to overthrow the Taliban regime. In his January 29, 2002, State of the Union address, he asserted that an "axis of evil" consisting of North Korea, Iran, and Iraq was "arming to threaten the peace of the world" and "posed a grave and growing danger".- The Bush Administration proceeded to assert a right and intention to engage in preemptive war, also called preventive war, in response to perceived threats. This would form a basis for what became known as the Bush Doctrine. Another tip of the hat from Woodrow Wilson.

The broader "War on Terror", allegations of an "axis of evil", and, in particular, the doctrine of preemptive war, began to weaken the unprecedented levels of international and domestic support for Bush and United States action against al Qaeda following the September 11 attacks.

On October 7, 2001, U.S. and Australian forces initiated bombing campaigns that led to the arrival on November 13 of Northern Alliance troops in Kabul. The main goals of the war were to defeat the Taliban, drive al Qaeda out of Afghanistan, and capture key al Qaeda leaders. In December 2001, the Pentagon reported that the Taliban had been defeated but cautioned that the war would go on to continue weakening Taliban and al-Qaeda leaders Later that month the UN had installed the Afghan Interim Authority chaired by Hamid Karzai.

Efforts to kill or capture al Qaeda leader Osama bin Laden failed as he escaped a battle in December 2001 in the mountainous region of Tora Bora, which the Bush Administration later acknowledged to have resulted from a failure to commit enough U.S. ground troops.- Bin Laden and al Qaeda's number two leader, Ayman al-Zawahiri, as well as the leader of the Taliban, Mohammed Omar, remain at large.

Despite the initial success in driving the Taliban from power in Kabul, by early 2003 the Taliban was regrouping, amassing new funds and recruits.- In 2006, the Taliban insurgency appeared larger, fiercer and better organized than expected, with large-scale allied offensives such as Operation Mountain Thrust attaining limited success. As a result, Bush commissioned 3,500 additional troops to the country in March 2007.

Beginning with his January 29, 2002, State of the Union address, Bush began publicly focusing attention on Iraq, which he labeled as part of an "axis of evil" allied with terrorists and posing "a grave and growing danger" to U.S. interests through possession of weapons of mass destruction.

In the latter half of 2002, CIA reports contained assertions of Saddam Hussein's intent of reconstituting nuclear weapons programs, not properly accounting for Iraqi biological and chemical weapons, and that some Iraqi missiles had a range greater than allowed by the UN sanctions. Contentions that the Bush Administration manipulated or exaggerated the threat and evidence of Iraq's weapons of mass destruction capabilities would eventually become a major point of criticism for the president.

In late 2002 and early 2003, Bush urged the United Nations to enforce Iraqi disarmament mandates, precipitating a diplomatic crisis. In November 2002, Hans Blix and Mohamed ElBaradei led UN weapons inspectors in Iraq, but were forced to depart the country four days prior to the U.S. invasion, despite their requests for more time to complete their tasks.

The U.S. initially sought a UN Security Council resolution authorizing the use of military force but dropped the bid for UN approval due to vigorous opposition from several countries.

The war effort was joined by more than 20 other nations most notably the United Kingdom, designated the "coalition of the willing".- The invasion of Iraq commenced on March 20, 2003, and the Iraqi military was quickly defeated. The capital, Baghdad, fell on April 9, 2003.

Following Republican efforts to pass the Medicare Act of 2003, Bush signed the bill, which included major changes to the Medicare program by providing beneficiaries with some assistance in paying for prescription drugs, while relying on private insurance for the delivery of benefits.

The retired persons lobby group AARP worked with the Bush Administration on the program and gave their endorsement. Bush said the law, estimated to cost $400 billion over the first ten years, would give the elderly "better choices and more control over their health care".

One of the administration's early major initiatives was the No Child Left Behind Act, which aimed to measure and close the gap between rich and poor student perform-ance, provide options to parents with students in low-performing schools, and target more federal funding to low-income schools. This landmark education initiative passed with broad bipartisan support, including that of Senator Ted Kennedy of Massachusetts.

In 2004, Bush commanded broad support in the Republi-can Party and did not encounter a primary challenge. He appointed Kenneth Mehlman as campaign manager, with a political strategy devised by Karl Rove. Bush and the Republican platform included a strong commitment to the wars in Iraq and Afghanistan. support for the USA PA-TRIOT Act, a renewed shift in policy for constitutional amendments banning abortion and same-sex marriage, reforming Social Security to create private investment accounts, creation of an ownership society, and oppos-ing mandatory carbon emissions controls. Bush also called for the implementation of a guest worker program for immigrants, which was criticized by conservatives.

Bush's emerging opponent, Massachusetts Senator John Kerry. Kerry and other Democrats attacked Bush on the Iraq War, and accused him of failing to stimulate the economy and job growth. The Bush campaign portrayed Kerry as a staunch liberal who would raise taxes and in-crease the size of government. The Bush campaign con-tinuously criticized Kerry's seemingly contradictory state-ments on the war in Iraq, and argued that Kerry lacked the decisiveness and vision necessary for success in the war on terrorism.

In the election, Bush carried 31 of 50 states, receiving a total of 286 electoral votes. He won an outright majority of the popular vote 50.7% to his opponent's 48.3%.- The previous President to win an outright majority of the popular vote was Bush's father in the 1988 election. Additionally, it was the first time since Herbert Hoover's election in 1928 that a Republican president was elected alongside re-elected Republican majorities in both Houses of Congress. Bush's 2.5% margin of victory was the narrowest ever for a victorious incumbent President, breaking Woodrow Wilson's 3.1% margin of victory against Charles Evans Hughes in the election of 1916.

In his 2005 State of the Union Address, Bush discussed the potential impending bankruptcy of the program and outlined his new program, which included partial privatization of the system, personal Social Security accounts, and options to permit Americans to divert a portion of their Social Security tax (FICA) into secured investments. Democrats opposed the proposal to partially privatize the system.

Bush embarked on a 60-day national tour, campaigning vigorously for his initiative in media events, known as the "Conversations on Social Security", in an attempt to gain support from the general public.

Despite the energetic campaign, public support for the proposal declined and the House Republican leadership decided not to put Social Security reform on the priority list for the remainder of their 2005 legislative agenda. The proposal's legislative prospects were further diminished by the political fallout from the Hurricane Katrina in the fall of 2005.

After the Democrats gained control of both houses of the Congress as a result of the 2006 midterm elections, the prospects of any further congressional action on the Bush proposal were dead for the remainder of his term in office.

In January 2005, free, democratic elections were held in Iraq for the first time in 50 years. According to Iraqi National Security Advisor Mowaffak al-Rubaie, "This is the greatest day in the history of this country." A referendum to approve a constitution in Iraq was held in October 2005, supported by the majority Shiites and many Kurds. On January 10, 2007, Bush addressed the nation from the Oval Office regarding the situation in Iraq. In this speech, he announced a surge of 21,500 more troops for Iraq, as well as a job program for Iraqis, more reconstruction proposals, and $1.2 billion for these programs. On May 1, 2007, Bush used his veto for only the second time in his presidency, rejecting a congressional bill setting a deadline for the withdrawal of U.S. troops. Five years after the invasion, Bush called the debate over the conflict "understandable" but insisted that a continued U.S. presence there was crucial.

In December 2007, the United States entered the longest post-World War II recession, which included a housing market correction, a sub prime mortgage crisis, soaring oil prices, and a declining dollar value. In February, 63,000 jobs were lost, a five-year record. To aid with the situation, Bush signed a $170 billion economic stimulus package which was intended to improve the economic situation by sending tax rebate checks to many Americans and providing tax breaks for struggling businesses.

The Bush administration pushed for significantly increased regulation of Fannie Mae and Freddie Mac in 2003, and after two years, the regulations passed the House but died in the Senate. Many Republican senators, as well as influential members of the Bush Administration, feared that the agency created by these regulations would merely be mimicking the private sector's risky practices. In September 2008, the crisis became much more serious beginning with the government takeover of Fannie Mae and Freddie Mac followed by the collapse of Lehman Brothers and a federal bailout of American International Group for $85 billion.

Many economists and world governments determined that the situation became the worst financial crisis since the Great Depression. This corporate welfare makes Bush in the same league as the most of the other modern executives, more worried that he not be thought of as the newest Herbert Hoover than doing the right thing.

Additional regulation over the housing market would have been beneficial, according to former Federal Reserve Chairman Alan Greenspan. Bush, meanwhile, proposed a financial rescue plan to buy back a large portion of the U.S. mortgage market. Vince Reinhardt, a former Federal Reserve economist now at the American Enterprise Institute, said "it would have helped for the Bush administration to empower the folks at Treasury and the Federal Reserve and the comptroller of the currency and the FDIC to look at these issues more closely", and additionally, that it would have helped "for Congress to have held hearings".

In November 2008, over 500,000 jobs were lost, which marked the largest loss of jobs in the United States in 34 years. The Bureau of Labor Statistics reported that in the last four months of 2008, 1.9 million jobs were lost. By the end of 2008, the U.S. had lost a total of 2.6 million jobs.

In a crowded primary of several prominent Republicans eying the nomination, moderate New York City mayor Rudy Giuliani was the early front runner. However, Governor Mike Huckabee won the Iowa Caucuses as he gained momentum just two months prior to the primary. Moderate U.S. Senator and former presidential candidate John McCain won the New Hampshire primary, eventually leading to Giuliani's fall, as the mayor didn't win a single primary. McCain ended up winning the nomination after winning most of the primaries against Huckabee and Governor Mitt Romney on Super Tuesday. Both McCain and Romney addressed the Conservative Political Action Conference in Washington, DC on February 7, while Mike Huckabee spoke on February 9. Romney used his speech to announce the end of his campaign, saying, "Now if I fight on in my campaign, all the way to the convention. I want you to know I've given this a lot of thought. I'd forestall the launch of a national campaign and, frankly, I'd be making it easier for Senator Clinton or Obama to win. Frankly, in this time of war, I simply cannot let my campaign be a part of aiding a surrender to terror." McCain spoke about an hour later, again appealing to right-wing uncertainty about his ideology. He focused on his opposition to abortion and gun control, as well as his support for lower taxes and free-market health care solutions.

The 2008 Democratic presidential primaries were the selection process by which voters of the Democratic Party of the United States chose their candidate for the 2008 United States presidential election. The Democratic Party candidate for president was selected through a series of primary elections and caucuses culminating in the 2008 Democratic National Convention held from Monday, August 25, through Thursday, August 28, 2008, in Denver, Colorado.

To secure the nomination at the convention, a candidate needed to receive at least 2,117 votes from delegates a simple majority of the 4,233 delegate votes, including half votes from American Samoa, Guam, the United States Virgin Islands, and Democrats Abroad. However, this total included votes from so-called "super delegates" party leaders and elected officials, and the race was complicated by a controversy over the scheduling of the Michigan and Florida state primaries, which had been scheduled earlier than party rules permitted. Due to a close race between Senators Barrack Obama and Hillary Rodham Clinton, the contest remained competitive for longer than expected, and neither candidate received enough delegates from state primary races and caucuses to achieve a majority without super delegate votes.

Although Obama lead Clinton in delegates won through state contests, Clinton claimed the popular vote lead as she had more actual votes from the state contests. However, this total included Michigan and Florida, where Obama had been unable to campaign due to the Democratic National Committee's penalization of those states for violating primary rules.

Obama received enough super delegate endorsements on June 3 to claim that he had secured the simple majority of delegates necessary to win the nomination, and Clinton conceded the nomination four days later. Obama was officially recognized as the Democratic nominee at the August convention.

Democrat Barrack Obama, then junior United States Senator from Illinois, defeated Republican John McCain. Nine states changed allegiance from the 2004 election. Each had voted for the Republican nominee in 2004 and contributed to Obama's sizable Electoral College victory. The selected electors from each of the 50 states and the District of Columbia voted for President and Vice President of the United States on December 15, 2008. Those votes were tallied before a joint session of Congress on January 8, 2009. Obama received 365 electoral votes, and McCain 173.

There were several unique aspects of the 2008 election. The election was the first in which an African American was elected President, and the first time a Roman Catholic was elected Vice President Joe Biden, then U.S. Senator from Delaware. It was also the first time two sitting senators ran against each other.

The 2008 election was the first in 56 years in which neither an incumbent president nor a vice president ran Bush was constitutionally limited from seeking a third term by the Twenty second Amendment; Vice President Dick Cheney chose not to seek the presidency. It was also the first time the Republican Party nominated a woman for Vice President Sarah Palin, then Governor of Alaska.

Additionally, it was the first election in which both major parties nominated candidates who were born outside of the contiguous United States. Voter turnout for the 2008 election was the highest in at least 40 years.

Barrack Hussein Obama (born August 4, 1961) is the 44th and current President of the United States. He is the first African American to hold the office. Obama previously served as a United States Senator from Illinois, from January 2005 until he resigned after his election to the presidency in November 2008.

A native of Honolulu, Hawaii, Obama is a graduate of Columbia University and Harvard Law School, where he was the president of the *Harvard Law Review*. He was a community organizer in Chicago before earning his law degree. He worked as a civil rights attorney in Chicago and taught constitutional law at the University of Chicago Law School from 1992 to 2004.

Obama served three terms in the Illinois Senate from 1997 to 2004. Following an unsuccessful bid for a seat in the U.S. House of Representatives in 2000, he ran for United States Senate in 2004. Several events brought him to national attention during the campaign, including his victory in the March 2004 Democratic primary and his keynote address at the Democratic National Convention in July 2004. He won election to the U.S. Senate in November 2004.

As president, Obama signed economic stimulus legislation in the form of the American Recovery and Reinvestment Act in February 2009. On October 8, 2009, Obama was named the 2009 Nobel Peace Prize laureate.

In March 2010, he signed the Patient Protection and Affordable Care Act into law, a piece of health care reform legislation. In foreign policy, Obama began a gradual withdrawal of troops from Iraq, increased troop levels in Afghanistan, and signed an arms control treaty with Russia.

On February 17, 2009, Obama signed the American Recovery and Reinvestment Act of 2009, a $787 billion economic stimulus package aimed at helping the economy recover from the deepening worldwide recession. The act includes increased federal spending for health care, infrastructure, education, various tax breaks and incentives, and direct assistance to individuals, which is being distributed over the course of several years.

In March, Obama's Treasury Secretary, Timothy Geithner, took further steps to manage the financial crisis, including introducing the Public-Private Investment Program for Legacy Assets, which contains provisions for buying up to $2 trillion in depreciated real estate assets. On March 23, *The New York Times* noted that "investors reacted ecstatically, with all of the major stock indexes soaring as soon as the markets opened."

Obama intervened in the troubled automotive industry- in March, renewing loans for General Motors and Chrysler to continue operations while reorganizing. Over the following months the White House set terms for both firms' bankruptcies, including the sale of Chrysler to Italian automaker Fiat- and a reorganization of GM giving the U.S. government a temporary 60% equity stake in the company, with the Canadian government shouldering a 12% stake.

In June 2009, dissatisfied with the pace of economic stimulus, Obama called on his cabinet to accelerate the investment. He signed into law the successful Car Allowance Rebate System, known colloquially as "Cash for Clunkers", running from July to August 2009, which not only reduced inventories but set off increased production runs at GM, Ford and Toyota, resulting in the rehiring of laid-off workers.

In mid-November 2009, Obama acknowledged the concern that adding too much more debt could cause the economy to slide into a "double dip" recession. Although total spending and loan guarantees from the Federal Reserve and the Treasury Department authorized by the Bush and Obama administrations was about $11.5 trillion, only $3 trillion had actually been spent by the end of November 2009. Unemployment numbers rose briefly to as high as 10.1% in October 2009 the highest since 1983, and the "underemployment" rate to 17.5%, before decreasing and holding at 9.7% in early 2010. In the third quarter of 2009, the U.S. economy expanded at a 2.8% and in the fourth quarter it grew at its fastest rate in six years, 5.7%. Other possible signs of recovery included an upturn in exports and a rise in consumer spending.

The Congressional Budget Office and a broad range of economists credit Obama's stimulus plan for the economic growth. The CBO released a report stating that the stimulus bill increased employment by 1–2.1 million, while conceding that "It is impossible to determine how many of the reported jobs would have existed in the absence of the stimulus package."

Although an April 2010 survey of members of the National Association for Business Economics showed an increase in job creation over a similar January survey for the first time in two years, 73% of the 68 respondents believed that the stimulus bill has had no impact on employment.

Obama called for Congress to pass legislation reforming health care in the United States, a key campaign promise and a top legislative goal. He proposed an expansion of health insurance coverage to cover the uninsured, to cap premium increases, and to allow people to retain their coverage when they leave or change jobs. His proposal was to spend $900 billion over 10 years and include a government insurance plan, also known as the public option, to compete with the corporate insurance sector as a main component to lowering costs and improving quality of health care. It would also make it illegal for insurers to drop sick people or deny them coverage for pre-existing conditions, and require every American carry health coverage. The plan also includes medical spending cuts and taxes on insurance companies that offer expensive plans.

On November 7, 2009, a health care bill featuring the public option was passed in the House. On December 24, 2009, the Senate passed its own bill without a public option on a party-line vote of 60 -39.-On March 21, 2010, the health care bill passed by the Senate in December was passed in the House by a vote of 219 to 212. Obama signed the bill into law on March 23, 2010.

During his presidential transition, President-elect Obama announced that he would retain the incumbent Defense Secretary, Robert Gates, in his Cabinet.

On February 27, 2009, Obama declared that combat operations would end in Iraq within 18 months. His remarks were made to a group of Marines preparing for deployment to Afghanistan. Obama said, "Let me say this as plainly as I can: By August 31, 2010, our combat mission in Iraq will end."

Early in his presidency, Obama moved to bolster U.S. troop strength in Afghanistan. He announced an increase to U.S. troop levels of 17,000 in February 2009 to "stabilize a deteriorating situation in Afghanistan", an area he said had not received the "strategic attention, direction and resources it urgently requires." On December 1, 2009, Obama announced the deployment of an additional 30,000 military personnel to Afghanistan. He also proposed to begin troop withdrawals 18 months from that date. On June 23, 2010, interview comments by McChrystal and his staff led him to tender his resignation and Obama nominated General David Petraeus to directly command Afghanistan operations.

Barrack Obama is the most transforming liberal since Woodrow Wilson. He ran as a moderate and is governing as a liberal. No surprise to anyone who looked at his voting record. But like presidents since Nixon with the exception of Reagan, Obama will say whatever he needs to get elected.

CHAPTER FIFTEEN - Discovering the promise

How did it happen? After previous attempts to push the Federal Reserve Act through Congress, a group of bankers they were members of the Round Table Group, which changed its name in 1920 to: The Council On Foreign Relations funded and staffed Woodrow Wilson's campaign for President. He had committed to sign this act. In 1913, Nelson Aldrich, a Senator, and the maternal grandfather to the Rockefellers, pushed the Federal Reserve Act through Congress just before Christmas when much of Congress was on vacation. When elected, Wilson passed the Federal Reserve Act.

In 1913, before the Senate Banking and Currency Committee, Mr. Alexander stated: "But the whole scheme of a Federal Reserve Bank with its commercial-paper basis is an impractical, cumbersome machinery, is simply a cover, to find a way to secure the privilege of issuing money and to evade payment of as much tax upon circulation as possible, and then control the issue and maintain, instead of reduce, interest rates. It is a system that, if inaugurated, will prove to the advantage of the few and the detriment of the people of the United States. It will mean continued shortage of actual money and further extension of credits; for when there is a lack of real money people have to borrow credit to their cost."

The Federal Reserve was illegally established, in 1913, by corrupt legislators in sufficient numbers to sneak the legislation through just hours before Christmas when the honest legislators who would have blocked it were home for the holidays folks traveled by horse and buggy and trains back then. The details of that are not sufficiently important to this presentation to merit their lengthy disclosure here. Suffice it to say that it was a deliberate move designed to give the organization total control of the United States and its vast assets.

As the National Debt has risen, your money has lost its Purchasing Power. In fact since 1913, when the Federal Reserve was created by Congress, your money has lost 96% of its purchasing power due to inflation. The more money the Federal Reserve creates the less your money buys. It is the Federal Reserve who creates inflation when it issues US dollars backed by government debt.

From 1913 to 2001, the national debt grew to $6 trillion in 88 years. In the next three years it increased a trillion to $7 trillion dollars in 2004. In the following years it increased approximately a trillion per year. Now the national debt is over $12 trillion dollars! It has Doubled in only eight years!

And the government now projects to add Three trillion dollars to the national debt every year for the foreseeable future!! The acceleration of our national debt is very dangerous and warning you that your money will rapidly lose its purchasing power shortly.

The Tea Party movement is a United States movement that emerged in 2009 through a series of locally and nationally coordinated protests.

The protests are partially in response to several Federal laws: the Emergency Economic Stabilization Act of 2008 ("bailout"), the American Recovery and Reinvestment Act of 2009 ("stimulus package"), and the 2009–2010 health care reform bills.

The name "Tea Party" is a reference to the Boston Tea Party of 1773 a protest by American colonists against taxes imposed on them by the British government, and against the colonists' lack of direct representation in the British Parliament. Tea Party protests have invoked themes, images and slogans similar to those used during the pre-revolutionary period in American history. The 'tea' in Tea Party has been used as an acronym standing for Taxed Enough Already. The Libertarian theme of the "tea party" began with Republican Congressman Ron Paul supporters as a fundraising event during the 2008 presidential primaries to emphasize Paul's fiscal conservatism, which laid the groundwork for the modern-day Tea Party movement. On December 16, 2007, the anniversary of the Tea Party, Ron Paul supporters raised 6 Million dollars in 24 hours in individual donations.

The term "porkulus" was coined by radio talk-show host Rush Limbaugh on his January 27, 2009, broadcast in reference to both the 2009 stimulus bill, which was just introduced to the House of Representatives the day before, as well as to pork barrel spending and earmarks. This proved very popular with conservative politicians and commentators, who began to unify in opposition to the September 2008 bailout package.

On February 19, 2009, in a broadcast from the floor of the Chicago Mercantile Exchange, CNBC Business News editor Rick Santelli criticized the government plan to refinance mortgages, which had just been announced the day before.

He said that those plans were, "promoting bad behavior," by, "subsidizing losers' mortgages." He suggested holding a tea party for traders to gather and dump the derivatives in the Chicago river on July 1. A number of the derivative traders around him cheered on his proposal, to the apparent amusement of the hosts in the studio. Video of Santelli's 'rant' went viral after it received a red siren headline on the news aggregation website, Drudge Report.

In response to Santelli, websites such as ChicagoTeaParty.com registered in August 2008 by Chicago radio producer Zack Christenson were live within twelve hours. About 10 hours after Santelli's remarks, TeaParty.com was bought to coordinate Tea Parties scheduled for July 4 and, as of March 4, was reported to be receiving 11,000 visitors a day.

According to *The New Yorker* writer Ben McGrath and *New York Times* reporter Kate Zernike, this is where the movement was first inspired to coalesce under the collective banner of "Tea Party." By the next day, guests on Fox News had already begun to mention this new "Tea Party."

As reported by The Huffington Post, a Facebook page was developed on February 20 calling for Tea Party protests across the country.-Soon, the Nationwide Chicago Tea Party protest was coordinated across over 40 different cities for February 27, 2009, thus establishing the first national modern Tea Party protest.

The Contract from America was the idea of Houston based Tea Party Patriots national leader Ryan Hecker. Hecker states that he developed the concept of creating a grassroots call for reform prior to the April 15, 2009 Tax Day Tea Party rallies. To get his idea off the ground, he launched a website, ContractFromAmerica.com, which encouraged people to offer possible planks for the contract. Hecker told the New York Times, "Hundreds of thousands of people voted for their favorite principles online to create the Contract as an open-sourced platform for the Tea Party movement."

The agenda had the imprint of everyday citizens every step of the way (in the online voting process.)" Hecker said the Republicans' 1994 Contract with America represented the nation's last intellectual economic conservative movement, but the new list, he said, was "created from the bottom up. It was not crafted in Washington with the help of pollsters."

The Contract lists 10 agenda items that it encourages congressional candidates to follow:

Identify constitutionality of every new law: Require each bill to identify the specific provision of the Constitution that gives Congress the power to do what the bill does (82.03%).

Reject emissionns trading: Stop the "cap and trade" administrative approach used to control pollution by providing economic incentives for achieving reductions in the emissions of pollutants. (72.20%).
Demand a balanced federal budget: Begin the Constitutional amendment process to require a balanced budget with a two-thirds majority needed for any tax modification. (69.69%)

Simplify the tax system: Adopt a simple and fair single-rate tax system by scrapping the internal revenue code and replacing it with one that is no longer than 4,543 words -- the length of the original Constitution.(64.9%).
Audit federal government agencies for constitutionality: Create a Blue Ribbon taskforce that engages in an audit of federal agencies and programs, assessing their Constitutionality, and identifying duplication, waste, ineffectiveness, and agencies and programs better left for the states or local authorities. (63.37%)

Limit annual growth in federal spending: Impose a statutory cap limiting the annual growth in total federal spending to the sum of the inflation rate plus the percentage of population growth. (56.57%).

Repeal the health care legislation passed on March 23, 2010:
Defund, repeal and replace the Patient Protection and Affordable Care Act. (56.39%).

Pass an 'All-of-the-Above' Energy Policy: Authorize the exploration of additional energy reserves to reduce American dependence on foreign energy sources and reduce regulatory barriers to all other forms of energy creation. (55.5%).

Reduce Earmarks: Place a moratorium on all earmarks until the budget is balanced, and then require a 2/3 majority to pass any earmark. (55.47%).

Reduce Taxes: Permanently repeal all recent tax increases, and extend permanently the George W. Bush temporary reductions in income tax, capital gains tax and estate taxes, currently scheduled to end in 2011. (53.38%).

The Tea Party Patriots have asked both Democrats and Republicans to sign on to the Contract. No Democrats have signed on, and the contract has met resistance from some Republicans who have since created "Commitment to America." Brendan Buck, a spokesman for that agenda said, "We totally are on board with what they did." Buck explained that it the contract is too narrow in focus, and not exactly what the Republican party would include in its own top-10 list of priorities. "We just want to have as big and open process as we can," he said, while making sure to add, "The tea party people will have a seat at the table."

Candidates who have signed the Contract from America include Utah's Mike Lee, Nevada's Sharron Angle, U.S. Senator Tom Coburn of Oklahoma, Sen. Jim DeMint (R-S.C.). Other Republicans who have signed on include Newt Gingrich and Dick Armey.

Newt Gingrich or Ron Paul maybe Conservative hopes for the future. Both of these men are owned only by their beliefs and neither are indebted to anyone but the people and constitution of America.

Newt" Gingrich is an American politician who served as the Speaker of the United States House of Representatives from 1995 to 1999. In 1995, *Time* magazine selected him as the Person of the Year for his role in leading the Republican Revolution in the House, ending 40 years of the Democratic Party being in the majority. During his tenure as Speaker, he represented the public face of the Republican opposition to President Bill Clinton.

A college professor, historian, and author, Gingrich twice ran unsuccessfully for the House before winning a seat in the election of November 1978. He was re-elected ten times, and his activism as a member of the House's Republican minority eventually enabled him to succeed Dick Cheney as House Minority Whip in 1989. As a co-author of the 1994 *Contract with America*, Gingrich was in the forefront of the Republican Party's dramatic success in that year's Congressional elections and subsequently was elected Speaker of the House.

Gingrich's leadership in Congress was marked by opposition to many of the policies of the Clinton Administration. Shortly after the 1998 elections, when Republicans lost five seats in the House, Gingrich announced his resignation from his House seat and as Speaker.

Since resigning his seat, Gingrich has maintained a career as a political analyst and consultant. He continues to write works related to government and other subjects, such as historical fiction. Recently, he founded the nonpartisan 527 group American Solutions for Winning the Future. He is a critic of Barack Obama's presidency.

In the 1994 campaign season, in an effort to offer a concrete alternative to shifting Democratic policies and to unite distant wings of the Republican Party, Newt Gingrich with the help of other Republicans came up with a Contract with America, which had ten items in it.

The contract was signed by Gingrich and other Republican candidates for the House of Representatives. The contract ranged from issues with broad popular support, including welfare reform, term limits, tougher crime laws, and a balanced budget law, to more specialized legislation such as restrictions on American military participation in U.N. missions. In the November 1994 elections, Republicans gained 54 seats and took control of the House for the first time since 1954.

Long-time House Minority Leader Bob Michel of Illinois had not run for re-election in 1994, giving Gingrich, the highest-ranking Republican returning to Congress, the inside track to becoming Speaker. Legislation proposed by the 104th United States Congress included term limits for Congressional Representatives, tax cuts, welfare reform, and a balanced budget amendment, as well as independent auditing of the finances of the House of Representatives and elimination of non essential services such as the House barbershop and shoe shine concessions.

Congress fulfilled Gingrich's Contract promise to bring all ten of the Contract's issues to a vote within the first 100 days of the session, even though most legislation was held up in the Senate, vetoed by President Bill Clinton, or substantially altered in negotiations with Clinton.

Ronald Ernest "Ron" Paul is an American physician and Republican Congressman for the 14th congressional district of Texas. Paul is a member of the Liberty Caucus of Republican congressmen which aims to limit the size and scope of the federal government, and serves on the House Foreign Affairs Committee, the Joint Economic Committee, and the Committee on Financial Services, where he has been an outspoken critic of American foreign and monetary policy. He has gained notoriety for his right-libertarian positions on many political issues, often clashing with both Republican and Democratic Party leaders. Paul has run for President of the United States twice, first in 1988 as the nominee of the Libertarian Party and again in 2008 as a candidate for the Republican nomination.

He is the founder of the advocacy group Campaign for Liberty and his ideas have been expressed in numerous published articles and books, including End The Fed 2009, and *The Revolution: A Manifesto* 2008. By one measure, Paul has the most conservative voting record of any member of Congress since 1937.

The Federal Reserve is the chief culprit behind the economic crisis. Its unchecked power to create endless amounts of money out of thin air brought us the boom and bust cycle and causes one financial bubble after another.

For the past 30 years, Congressman Ron Paul has worked tirelessly to bring much needed transparency and accountability to the secretive bank.

And in 2009 his unfaltering dedication showed astonishing results: HR 1207, the bill to audit the Federal Reserve, swept the country and made the central bankers shudder at their desks. The bill passed as an amendment both in the House Financial Services Committee and in the House itself.

But the usurpers of America's future didn't take it lying down. They weren't about to allow their secrets to be exposed and their magic money machine to be put under close scrutiny. They worked frantically behind the scenes to quietly derail all efforts to open up the Federal Reserve to an independent audit.

A handful of Fed loving U.S. senators led by Chris Dodd rewrote the Senate version of the Financial Reform Bill to strip out Ron Paul's Audit the Fed amendment and actually expand the Fed's power over banks, lending and money. As Alan Grayson pointed out here, and Ron Paul commented on here, the Dodd bill completely eliminated legislation to audit the Federal Reserve, which already passed in the House.

Sen. Bernie Sanders (I-Vt.) introduced an amendment on the floor effectively adding the Grayson-Paul language to the Senate bill, but later changed his amendment under pressure by the Federal Reserve and the Obama administration. The altered Sanders amendment passed the Senate on May 11, 2010 by a unanimous 96-0 vote.
Sen. Vitter reintroduced an amendment with the original Audit the Fed language. The Senate rejected the amendment on May 11, 2010 by a 37-62 vote.

The House and Senate went to the conference committee which attempted to reconcile the differences between the two bills and their amendments. Unfortunately, Ron Paul's tough language ended up not being included in the final bill.

Patrick Buchanan has been a senior advisor to three Presidents, a two-time candidate for the Republican presidential nomination, and was the presidential nominee of the Reform Party in 2000. From 1966 through 1974, Mr. Buchanan was an assistant to Richard Nixon, and from 1985 to 1987, White House Director of Communications for Ronald Reagan. In 1992, Mr. Buchanan challenged George Bush for the Republican nomination and almost upset the President in the New Hampshire primary. In 1996, he won the New Hampshire primary and finished second to Sen. Dole with three million Republican votes.

Born in Washington, D.C., educated at Catholic and Jesuit schools, Pat Buchanan received his master's degree in journalism from Columbia in 1962. At 23, he became the youngest editorial writer on a major newspaper in America, the *St. Louis Globe-Democrat*.
In 1966, Mr. Buchanan became the first full-time staffer to Richard Nixon in his legendary comeback. He traveled with the future President in the campaigns of 1966 and 1968, and served as special assistant through the final days of Watergate.

On leaving the Ford White House in 1974, Mr. Buchanan became a syndicated columnist and founding member of three of the most enduring if not endearing talk shows in television history: NBC's *The McLaughlin Group*, and CNN's *Capital Gang* and *Crossfire*.

In his White House years, Mr. Buchanan wrote foreign policy speeches, and attended four summits, including Mr. Nixon's historic opening to China in 1972, and Ronald Reagan's Reykjavik summit in 1986 with Mikhail Gorbachev.

Mr. Buchanan has written ten books, including six straight New York Times best sellers *A Republic, Not an Empire*; *The Death of the West*; *Where the Right Went Wrong*; *State of Emergency*; *Day of Reckoning* and *Churchill, Hitler and The Unnecessary War*.

Mr. Buchanan is currently a columnist, political analyst for MSNBC, chairman of The American Cause foundation and an editor of *The American Conservative*. He is married to the former Shelley Ann Scarney, who was a member of the White House Staff from 1969 to 1975. Sarah Louise Palin; born February 11, 1964 is an American politician, author, speaker, and political news commentator who was the youngest person and the first woman elected Governor of Alaska. She served as governor from 2006 until she resigned in 2009. Chosen by Republican Party presidential candidate John McCain in August 2008 to be his running mate in that year's presidential election, she was the first Alaskan on the national ticket of a major party, as well as the first female vice-presidential nominee of the Republican Party.

On July 3, 2009, Palin announced she would not seek reelection as governor and that she was resigning effective July 26, 2009, eighteen months before the completion of her term.

She cited ethics complaints that had been filed following her selection as running mate to John McCain as one of the reasons for her resignation, saying the resulting investigations had affected her ability to govern the state. Speculation that she will run for the Republican Party presidential nomination in 2012 began prior to the defeat of the McCain – Palin ticket in 2008. In February 2010, she stated she would not close the door on the possibility.

Before she was elected governor, she was a member of the Wasilla, Alaska City Council from 1992 to 1996, and the city's mayor from 1996 to 2002. After an unsuccessful campaign for lieutenant governor of Alaska in 2002, she chaired the Alaska Oil and Gas Conservation Commission from 2003 until she resigned in 2004.

In November 2009, her autobiography *Going Rogue: An American Life* was released and it quickly became a best-seller, selling more than two million copies. In January 2010, Palin began providing political commentary to the Fox News Channel under a multi-year contract. It was announced in March 2010 that she was to host her own TV show, called *Sarah Palin's Alaska*. Palin is authoring a second book, *America By Heart*, which is expected to be on shelves by November 23, 2010.

On February 6, 2010, Palin appeared as the keynote speaker at the inaugural Tea Party convention in Nashville, Tennessee. Palin said the Tea Party movement is "the future of politics in America." She criticized Obama for rising deficits, and for apologizing for America in speeches in other countries.

Palin said Obama was weak on the war on terrorism for allowing the so-called Christmas bomber to board a plane headed for the United States. "To win that war, we need a commander in chief, not a professor of law," Palin said.

Palin's speaking fee was reported to be $100,000, which some in the Tea Party movement criticized as being too high for fiscal conservatives to pay. Judson Phillips, the founder of Tea Party Nation, the social networking site that sponsored the convention, did not confirm the amount paid to Palin saying he was contractually obligated not to speak about it. "I'll simply say this: when you get a speaker of the caliber of Governor Palin, it's not done on the basis of a handshake," he said. Palin said she made no apologies for the fee, which she plans to use to fund conservative causes.

The rich are getting richer and the poor are getting poorer at a staggering rate. Once upon a time, the United States had the largest and most prosperous middle class in the history of the world, but now that is changing at a blistering pace. So why are we seeing such fundamental changes? Well, the globalism and free trade that our politicians and business leaders insisted would be so good for us have had some rather nasty side effects. NAFTA, GAT and all the other initials our left leaning politicians have heaped on us particularly over the past forty years or so.

It turns out that they didn't tell us that the global economy would mean that middle class American workers would eventually have to directly compete for jobs with people on the other side of the world where there is no minimum wage and very few regulations.

The big global corporations have greatly benefited by exploiting third world labor pools over the last several decades, but middle class American workers have increasingly found things to be very tough.

85 percent of all U.S. stocks are in the hands of 1 percent of the people. 63 percent of Americans always or usually live paycheck to paycheck. 70 percent of the income growth between 2001 and 2009 went to the top 1% of all Americans. Over 1.4 million Americans filed for personal bankruptcy in 2009, which represented a 32 percent increase over 2008. Only the top 5 percent of U.S. households have earned enough additional income to match the rise in housing costs since 1975. For the first time in U.S. history, banks own a greater share of residential housing net worth in the United States than all individual Americans put together. In 1950, the ratio of the average executive's paycheck to the average worker's paycheck was about 30 to 1. Since the year 2000, that ratio has exploded to between 300 to one. Average Wall Street bonuses for 2009 were up 17 percent when compared with 2008. In the United States, the average federal worker now earns 60% MORE than the average worker in the private sector. The top 1 percent of U.S. households own nearly twice as much of America's corporate wealth as they did just 15 years ago. This is what American workers now must compete against: in China a garment worker makes approximately 86 cents an hour and in Cambodia a garment worker makes approximately 22 cents an hour.

The reality is that no matter how smart, how strong, how educated or how hard working American workers are, they just can't compete with people who are desperate to put in twelve hour days at less than a dollar an hour on the other side of the world. After all, what corporation in their right mind is going to pay an American worker 10 times more plus benefits to do the same job? The world is fundamentally changing. Wealth and power are rapidly becoming concentrated at the top and the big global corporations are making massive amounts of money. Meanwhile, the American middle class is being systematically wiped out of existence as U.S. workers are slowly being merged into the new "global" labor pool.

So corporations are moving operations out of the U.S. at breathtaking speed. Since the U.S. government does not penalize them for doing so, there really is no incentive for them to stay. What has developed is a situation where the people at the top are doing quite well, while most Americans are finding it increasingly difficult to make it. There are now about six unemployed Americans for every new job opening in the United States, and the number of chronically unemployed is absolutely soaring. Many of those who are able to get jobs are finding that they are making less money than they used to. In fact, an increasingly large percentage of Americans are working at low wage retail and service jobs. The truth is that the middle class in America is dying and once it is gone it will be gone.

To remake America we need to take several steps to begin to reverse our statist, socialist and globalist policies and return to the federalist conservative policies that made our country great.

For example we should as many Tea Party organizations of asked have a litmus test for the constitutionality of all of our government agencies. If something isn't constitutional it's not legal until we the people change the constitution.

In government it works well to have term limits for the president we should do likewise for Congress. No one should serve more than twelve years in elected office. All campaigns must be financed by the the government by providing all citizens with TV and each candidate to equally bring their case to the American people. No lobbyists, they would be illegal. No financing of any kind, just tell us what you are for and against we will watch and we will vote. A simple process that will assure honesty and transparency.

We can start the transparency by getting our currency off the fiat system and back to a system backed by gold or silver. This will give our money intrinsic value that will bolster it's strength and value. This will be a stabling force and by radically restructuring our central banking system we can replace the current federal reserve system with a new Bank of the United States.

All of the Above Energy is the stuff of life. With it, we can accomplish practically anything; we grow food, make necessities, provide warmth and shelter and comfort, education and entertainment. The Bureau of Land Management (BLM) estimates U.S. supplies at 117 billion barrels of oil and 651 trillion cubic feet of natural gas, on shore and off. This is enough oil to replace entirely our OPEC imports for more than 50 years, and enough natural gas to supply all U.S. needs for more than 30 years.

That's not counting our even more vast supplies of coal, counting in the centuries. We must no longer deny ourselves access to our most productive and affordable energy types.

The BLM found that 60 percent of the onshore federal lands with potentially significant domestic amounts of natural gas and crude are politically inaccessible. We as a nation are sitting on vast deposits of oil and natural gas that we could be using to reduce our imports. Increasingly, our coal reserves are subject to similar political constraints, even as we pour billions into clean coal technologies.

This should be done with regard to exploring and delivering energy efficient and cost effective products to the American people.

Government spending should be significantly reduced. It has grown far too quickly in recent years, and most of the new spending is for purposes other than homeland security and national defense. Combined with rising entitlement costs associated with the looming retirement of the baby-boom generation, America is heading in the wrong direction. To avoid becoming an uncompetitive European-style welfare state like France or Germany, the United States must adopt a responsible fiscal policy based on smaller government.

Budgetary restraint should be viewed as an opportunity to make an economic virtue out of fiscal necessity. Simply stated, most government spending has a negative economic impact.

To be sure, if government spends money in a productive way that generates a sufficiently high rate of return, the economy will benefit, but this is the exception rather than the rule. If the rate of return is below that of the private sector-as is much more common-then the growth rate will be slower than it otherwise would have been. There is overwhelming evidence that government spending is too high and that America's economy could grow much faster if the burden of government was reduced.

The deficit is not the critical variable. The key is the size of government, not how it is financed. Taxes and deficits are both harmful, but the real problem is that government is taking money from the private sector and spending it in ways that are often counterproductive. The need to reduce spending would still exist-and be just as compelling-if the federal government had a budget surplus. Fiscal policy should focus on reducing the level of government spending, with particular emphasis on those programs that yield the lowest benefits and/or impose the highest costs.

Controlling federal spending is particularly important because of globalization. Today, it is becoming increasingly easy for jobs and capital to migrate from one nation to another. This means that the reward for good policy is greater than ever before, but it also means that the penalty for bad policy is greater than ever before.

For most of America's history, the aggregate burden of government was below 10 percent of GDP. This level of government was consistent with the beliefs of the America's founders.

Classical economists and political philosophers generally advocated the minimal state-they saw the government's role as limited to national defense, police, and administration.

That's not counting our even more vast supplies of coal, counting in the centuries. We must no longer deny ourselves access to our most productive and affordable energy types.

The BLM found that 60 percent of the onshore federal lands with potentially significant domestic amounts of natural gas and crude are politically inaccessible. We as a nation are sitting on vast deposits of oil and natural gas that we could be using to reduce our imports. Increasingly, our coal reserves are subject to similar political constraints, even as we pour billions into clean coal technologies.

This should be done with regard to exploring and delivering energy efficient and cost effective products to the American people.Government spending should be significantly reduced. It has grown far too quickly in recent years, and most of the new spending is for purposes other than homeland security and national defense. Combined with rising entitlement costs associated with the looming retirement of the baby-boom generation, America is heading in the wrong direction.

To avoid becoming an uncompetitive European-style welfare state like France or Germany, the United States must adopt a responsible fiscal policy based on smaller government.

Budgetary restraint should be viewed as an opportunity to make an economic virtue out of fiscal necessity. Simply stated, most government spending has a negative economic impact. To be sure, if government spends money in a productive way that generates a sufficiently high rate of return, the economy will benefit, but this is the exception rather than the rule. If the rate of return is below that of the private sector-as is much more common-then the growth rate will be slower than it otherwise would have been. There is overwhelming evidence that government spending is too high and that America's economy could grow much faster if the burden of government was reduced.

The deficit is not the critical variable. The key is the size of government, not how it is financed. Taxes and deficits are both harmful, but the real problem is that government is taking money from the private sector and spending it in ways that are often counterproductive. The need to reduce spending would still exist-and be just as compelling-if the federal government had a budget surplus. Fiscal policy should focus on reducing the level of government spending, with particular emphasis on those programs that yield the lowest benefits and/or impose the highest costs.

Controlling federal spending is particularly important because of globalization. Today, it is becoming increasingly easy for jobs and capital to migrate from one nation to another. This means that the reward for good policy is greater than ever before, but it also means that the penalty for bad policy is greater than ever before.
For most of America's history, the aggregate burden of government was below 10 percent of GDP. This level of government was consistent with the beliefs of the Amer-

ica's founders. Classical economists and political philosophers generally advocated the minimal state-they saw the government's role as limited to national defense, police, and administration.

America's policy of limited government certainly was conducive to economic expansion. In the days before income tax and excessive government, America moved from agricultural poverty to middle-class prosperity. Reducing government to 10 percent of GDP might be a very optimistic target, but shrinking the size of government should be a major goal for policymakers. The economy certainly would perform better, and this would boost prosperity and make America more competitive. Earmarks must be eliminated from all legislation they amount only to payoffs for congressman and should be illegal and forbidden. All laws that are enacted by congress should apply to congress. We must eliminate the ruling class system in this country and get back to a citizenry that elects and serves the nation.

Congress must give the chief executive a line item veto for the budget and all federal budgets must be balanced by law, no exceptions no excuses. We don't spend money we don't have and we must get back to a government that is fit and trim.

We can simplify our tax system in two ways, first eliminate all income and estate taxes. Replace these with a national sales tax so that people will pay in direct proportion to what they consume. Tolls and tariffs should also be used to help pay for our infrastructure and ease the burden on citizens by taxing goods coming into America. Yes this may be somewhat inflationary but it will also bring jobs back to the US.

I believe that we can balance what we lose by gaining a new American industrial and technological revolution.

Transfer of government services or assets to the private sector. State-owned assets may be sold to private owners, or statutory restrictions on competition between privately and publicly owned enterprises may be lifted. Services formerly provided by government may be contracted out. The objective is often to increase government efficiency; implementation may affect government revenue either positively or negatively. Privatization is the opposite of nationalization, a policy resorted to by governments that want to keep the revenues from major industries, especially those that might otherwise be controlled by foreign interests.

Social Security will be phased out so that in twenty years it will become completely privatized. Each American will have their own accounts that will help to supplement their retirement. Welfare will be eliminated by guaranteed jobs for all. Eliminate Medicaid and Medicare to create a health care system that is private but operates like an exchange. If we have more say in our care and the cost of it will come down. Of course we must have a safety net for those that are incapable to care for themselves but first we should look to religious and other non profits for help, government must never be the answer it is always the problem.

One of the more difficult problems attached to all wars is that of relations between belligerents and neutrals. In land wars the question is not of such magnitude, although Switzerland is probably the only nation to have arrived at a satisfactory solution.

In naval wars, however, in situations where maritime commerce and other activities are involved, the question of the relationship between belligerents and neutrals, that is, of neutral rights, has long been debated, almost always with inconclusive results.

The question of neutral rights in wartime is almost always discussed, especially by neutrals, within the context of international law. It is usually claimed that such international law is supported by principles established either by earlier treaties or by practice or both, that it is an expression of some accepted view of maritime conduct in wartime, which should therefore govern relations between belligerents and neutrals.

The problem is that international law has no validity beyond that accorded it in particular situations by particular nations. It only exists either when nations agree that it does or when they can uphold their interpretation of it by whatever means are appropriate. In a narrower context, the problem with stating and attempting to uphold neutral rights at sea is that, in the end, neutrals have no rights except those that they can maintain by their own actions, in which case they often cease to be neutrals, as the Dutch discovered in the American Revolution. Again, the example of the Swiss is instructive. They have preserved their neutrality inviolate for hundreds of years by the simple but effective expedient of placing themselves in such a position that challenging their neutrality would not be worth the cost.

The introduction of principles to regulate relations between belligerents and neutrals has never been motivated by anything other than self-interest.

Since at least the seventeenth century, declarations, opinions, judgments, and conventions on neutral rights in seaborne commerce have been common. But if one strips away the philosophical disguises, legal circumlocutions, and endless casuistry, what remains is really very simple: neutrals have constantly been trying to trade with some or all of the belligerents in a given war while some or all of the same belligerents have been trying to stop neutral trade with their enemies. For example, the cause of most of the problems concerning the West Indies, particularly the French islands, during the American Revolution was the clear and avowed intent of the French to assist the Americans and the equally firm intent of the British to stop this. What mattered in this situation was not declarations of neutral rights or expressions of principle but the possession of the force required to carry out national policy.

There has, nevertheless, developed during the last three hundred years a great body of pronouncements on neutral rights as both neutrals and belligerents have sought to regulate their relations and to justify their self-interested conduct by appeals to principle and to precedent. No nation has been absolutely consistent in the principles and doctrines to which it has appealed and on which it has acted, and this has been as true of the United States as of any other nation.

All of our troops come home on a timetable of sorts. For example in Germany we can bring home all troops easier than we could in Afghanistan. However it should be our goal to bring all troops home within 10 years. We would proclaim ourselves a neutral trading partner ready to do business with the world, but we retire as policeman of the world.

We withdraw from NATO, the UN and all permanent alliances should end. As long as you trade with us and do no physical or economic harm there will be peace. However as one of our great presidents said " we will speak softly and carry a big stick".

A new doctrine that would proclaim America a free and neutral nation if we are harmed physically or economically we will have the right to terminate another nations existence. Just like the cold war kept the peace between the Soviets and the US, this concept of assured destruction will keep us at peace. No more can smaller countries rely on us to do their fighting. We mind our own business, but stand with a military strength that can destroy any potential enemy. No more foreign entanglements period, the only wars we will fight in the future will last as long as it takes to deliver nuclear annihilation to the enemy.

There are many faces of globalism and it comes with many names, but in all cases the goal of globalism is to erase national borders, eliminate national sovereignty, reduce national identities and move toward global governance through the United Nations.

 The European Union is the prime example of the results of globalism, where once-proud nations have surrendered famous currencies like the deutsche mark, the franc and the lira. It's where ancient cultures like Greece and Rome have erased their borders and buried their cultures to be led by a Union of Socialists with loyalty to nothing but the drive for more and more power.

Yet it's done in the name of equity, economic prosperity and ecological integrity. Globalism is sold to the unsuspecting public with words like free trade, open borders and environmental protection, but it's really about redistribution of wealth; your wealth. It's about erasing national borders and national sovereignty.

Globalism calls for a wrenching transformation of our society, away from representative government and independent nations to the establishment of a global village with global citizens. Smart Growth is the plan to herd us all into specific human habitat areas, out of the suburbs and our beautiful yards and into crowded cities and high rises. As one smart growth advocate gleefully put it: "It will be the humans in cages with the animals looking in." The goal of Sustainable Development is to transform the world into feudal-like governance by making NATURE the central organizing principle for our economy and society.

On immigration all illegals that are here and have been working for 3 or more consecutive years they and the companies that employ them will be exempted from prosecution. In fact most of these illegals will be granted citizenship after that if an illegal comes into this country they will be deported.

Any crime committed by an illegal alien we will try and convict, they will then be sent to their country of origin with a sentence to be carried out by their government. America is a land of immigrants and it will always be one, but it also will be a land of hard working legal immigrants who want to be Americans.

By harkening back to our roots as a nation of life, liberty and the pursuit of happiness we can rebuild the great Federalist conservative principles that our country was built on.

BIBILOGRAPHY

Miller, Alice P., *Edmund Burke: a biography,* New York: Allwyn Press, 1976.

The Writings and Speeches of Edmund Burke. 9 vols. Oxford and New York, 1981.

Russell Kirk, *The Conservative Mind: From Burke to Eliot* (7th ed. 1992).

Kirk, Russell. *Edmund Burke: A Genius Reconsidered* (1997) by a leader of American conservatism online edition

Adair, Douglass. *Fame and the Founding Fathers.* Indianapolis: Liberty Fund, 1974. A collection of essays; that used here is "The Disputed Federalist Papers."

Wills, Gary. *Explaining America: The Federalist*, Garden City, NJ: 1981.

Banning, Lance. *The Jeffersonian Persuasion: Evolution of a Party Ideology*(1978)

Jenkinson, Clay S. *Becoming Jefferson's People: Reinventing the American Republic in the Twenty-first Century*. Bismark, ND: Marmarth Press, 2004.

Donald, David Herbert. *We Are Lincoln Men: Abraham Lincoln and His Friends* Simon & Schuster, (2003).

Belz, Herman. *Abraham Lincoln, Constitutionalism, and Equal Rights in the Civil War Era* (1998)

Mayer, George H. *The Republican Party, 1854-1966.* 2d ed. (1967)

Gienpap, William E. *The Origins of the Republican Party, 1852-1856* (1987)

Holt, Michael F. (1999). *The Rise and Fall of the American Whig Party: Jacksonian Politics and the Onset of the Civil War.* Oxford University Press.

Schlesinger, Arthur Meier, Jr. ed. *History of American Presidential Elections, 1789–2000* .

Republican National Political Conventions 1856–2008

The Forgotten Man, and Other Essays, an 1876 collection of essays by William Graham Sumner

George, Henry (1879). *Progress and Poverty: An Inquiry into the Cause of Industrial Depressions and of Increase of Want with Increase of Wealth*.

Morgan, H. Wayne. *William McKinley and His America*. (1963).

Harbaugh, William Henry. *The Life and Times of Theodore Roosevelt*. (1963), full scholarly biography.

Rothbard, Murray *A History of Money and banking in the United States: The Colonial Era to world War II*(2002).

Cherny, Robert W. *American Politics in the Gilded Age, 1868-1900* (1997)

Charles R. Morris, *The Tycoons: How Andrew Carnegie, John D. Rockefeller, Jay Gould, and J. P. Morgan Invented the American Supereconomy* (2006)

MacKay *Little Boss: A life of Andrew Carnegie*

Robert Sobel. *The Big Board: A History of the New York Stock Market* (1965), reprinted Beard Books (May 2000)

Stiles, T.J., *The First Tycoon: The Epic Life of Cornelius Vanderbilt* (Knopf Publishing, 2009),

Nevins, Allan. *Grover Cleveland: A Study in Courage* (1932)

Lewis L. Gould, *Four Hats in the Ring: The 1912 Election and the Birth of Modern American Politics* (2008)

Wicker, Elmus (2005), *The Great Debate on Banking Reform: Nelson Aldrich and the Origins of the Fed*.

Chandler, Jr., Alfred D. *Scale and Scope: The Dynamics of Industrial Capitalism* (1990).

Irwin Unger, These United States (2007)

Hewes, James E. Jr. (August 20, 1970). "Henry Cabot Lodge and the League of Nations". *Proceedings of the American Philosophical Society*

Letters from Albert Jay Nock, 1924-1945, to Edmund C.

Evans, Mrs. Edmund C. Evans, and Ellen Winsor. The Caxton Printers, 1949.

Henry George: An Essay. William Morrow & Company, 1939.

Adams, Samuel Hopkins (1939). *Incredible Era: The Life and Times of Warren Gamaliel Harding*.

McCoy, Donald R. (1967). *Calvin Coolidge: The Quiet President*. Macmillan.

Brandes, Joseph (1962). *Herbert Hoover and Economic Diplomacy*

Hawley, Ellis. *Herbert Hoover and the Historians* (1989).

Smith, Richard Norton. *An Uncommon Man: The Triumph of Herbert Hoover*, (1987)

Patrick D. Reagan, *Designing a New America: The Origins of New Deal Planning, 1890–1943* (2000).

Allan M. Winkler, *Franklin D. Roosevelt and the Making of Modern America* (Pearson Education: New York, 2006)

Goodwin, Doris Kearns. *No Ordinary Time: Franklin and Eleanor Roosevelt: The Home Front in World War II* (1995).

Flynn, John T. *The Roosevelt Myth* (1948).

Smiley, Gene. *Rethinking the Great Depression* (1993) short essay by economist who blames both Hoover and FDR.

Wolfe, Alan. *The Future of Liberalism*. New York: Random House, Inc., 2009.

Harbaugh, William H. *Lawyer's Lawyer: The Life of John W. Davis*. New York: Oxford University Press, 1973.

George Wolfskill. *The Revolt of the Conservatives: A History of the American Liberty League, 1934-1940* (1962).

John Shelton Lawrence and Robert Jewett, *The Myth of the American Superhero*, (Wm B. Eerdmans Publishing, 2002).

Armstrong John P. "The Enigma of Senator Taft and

American Foreign Policy." *Review of Politics* 17:2 (1955).

Kirk, Russell, and James McClellan. *The Political Principles of Robert A. Taft* (1967).

Gaddis, John Lewis (1990). *Russia, the Soviet Union and the United States. An Interpretative History.* McGraw-Hill.

Dennis Merrill, "The Truman Doctrine: Containing Communism and Modernity," *Presidential Studies Quarterly*, March 2006.

Merrill, Dennis (1969). *Documentary History of the Truman Presidency.* Frederick, Md.: Univ. Publ. of America.

Reinhard, David W. *The Republican Right Since 1945* (1983).

Harris, Douglas B. "Dwight Eisenhower and the New Deal: The Politics of Preemption" *Presidential Studies Quarterly*, Vol. 27, 1997.

McDonald, W. Wesley, 1982. *The Conservative Mind of Russell Kirk: `The Permanent Things' in an Age of Ideology.*

A Dispassionate Assessment of Libertarians" in *The Politics of Prudence* (1993).

Bridges, Linda (2007). *Strictly Right: William F. Buckley Jr. and the American Conservative Movement.* New York: Wiley, John & Sons, Incorporated.

John B. Judis (1990). *William F. Buckley, Jr.: Patron Saint of the Conservatives.*

Campbell, Angus; et al. (1966). *Elections and the Political Order.*

Aitken, Jonathan (1996). *Nixon: A Life.* Regnery Publishing.

Ambrose, Steven E (1991). *Nixon: Ruin and Recovery 1973–1990.*

The Conservative Intellectual Movement in America George H. Nash

Goldberg, Robert Alan. *Barry Goldwater* (1995).

Goldwater, Barry. *The Conscience of a Conservative* (1963).

Freedman, Lawrence. *Kennedy's Wars: Berlin, Cuba, Laos and Vietnam* (2000).

Hellmann, John. *The Kennedy Obsession: The American Myth of JFK* (1997).

Lewis L. Gould (1993). *1968: The Election that Changed America.*

Jeffrey W. Helsing *Johnson's War/Johnson's Great Society: the guns and butter trap* Praeger Greenwood 2000

Turning Right in the Sixties: The Conservative Capture of the GOP by Mary C. Brennan (Mar 16, 2007).

Black, Conrad (2007). *Richard M. Nixon: A life in Full.* New York, NY: PublicAffairs Books.

Tucker, Spencer. ed. *Encyclopedia of the Vietnam War* (1998) 3 vol. reference set; also one-volume abridgment (2001).

Doyle, James (1977). *Not Above the Law: the battles of Watergate prosecutors Cox and Jaworski.* New York: William Morrow and Company.

Frum, David (2000). *How We Got Here: The '70s.* New York, New York: Basic Books.

Ribuffo, Leo P. (1997). "'Malaise' revisited: Jimmy Carter and the crisis of confidence". John Patrick Diggins (ed.). *The Liberal Persuasion: Arthur Schlesinger, Jr. and the Challenge of the American Past.* Princeton: Princeton University Press.

Cannon, Lou (2005). *Governor Reagan: His Rise to Power.* Public Affairs.

Hayward, Steven F. *The Age of Reagan: The Conservative Counterrevolution: 1980-1989* (2009).

Barilleaux, Ryan J.; Stuckey, Mary E. (1992). *Leadership and the Bush Presidency: Prudence or Drift in an Era of Change.*

Buckley, William F., Jr. *Happy Days Were Here Again:*

Reflections of a Libertarian Journalist, Random House.
David Maraniss *First in His Class: A Biography of Bill Clinton* (1996).
Brinkley, Douglas (2001). *36 Days: The Complete Chronicle of the 2000 Presidential Election Crisis*. Times Books.
Sabato, Larry J. ed. *The Sixth Year Itch: The Rise and Fall of the George W. Bush Presidency* (2007).
Congressman McFaddenon the Federal Reserve Corporation
Remarks in Congress, 1934.
 Wardner, James (1994) [1993]. *The Planned Destruction of America*. Longwood Communications.
Paul, Ron (2009). *End the Fed*. New York, NY: Grand Central Publishing.
Paul, Ron (2000). *A Republic, If You Can Keep It*. Lake Jackson, Texas.
Contract with America (co-editor). Newt Gingrich, Times Books, December 1994.
Winning The Future. Newt Gingrich, Regnery Publishing, January 2005.
Drill Here, Drill Now, Pay Less: A Handbook for Slashing Gas Prices and Solving Our Energy Crisis. Newt Gingrich With Vince Haley. Regnery Publishing, September 2008.
Ron Paul's New Book, The Revolution: A Manifesto".
Pat Buchanan Biography. Thomson Gale. Retrieved 2006-11-01.

www.ingramcontent.com/pod-product-compliance
Lightning Source LLC
Chambersburg PA
CBHW081343280526
45788CB00009B/2754